THE MAGIC OF MANIFESTING COLLECTION

45 Advanced Manifestation Techniques
to Shift to Your Dream Reality and
Attract Money, Love, and Abundance

RYUU SHINOHARA

Omen
Publishing

The Manifestor Masterlist
(It'll be near impossible without this...)

This Masterlist includes:

- ✓ Top 3 daily habits for manifesting.
- ✓ Simple layout to track your progress.
- ✓ Instructions to help you get started today!

The last thing I want is for you to read this book and forget everything you read...

Let's make manifestation a daily habit!

>> Scan the QR Code above with your smartphone to receive your free Manifestor Masterlist. <<

TABLE OF CONTENTS

THE MAGIC OF MANIFESTING
(BOOK 1)

THE MAGIC OF MANIFESTING MONEY
(B O O K   2)

THE MAGIC OF MANIFESTING LOVE
(B O O K   3)

THE **MAGIC** OF **MANIFESTING**

15 Advanced Techniques to Attract Your Best Life, Even If You Think It's Impossible Now

INTRODUCTION

How does one live their best life? Is it by taking risks or is it by simply doing the things they've always wanted to do? Well, if that is the case, should you just give up when things become tough or distasteful for you? Such questions often lead us down paths of confusion which pose more questions than answers.

This much is simple: The universe works through a set of basic laws whose existence is undeniable. Ancient spiritual teachers, through the practice of meditation, hinted at what science has only recently discovered. That nothing in this universe is constant and that everything is vibration.

Furthermore, this vibration produces an energy field; these energy fields attract and repel other fields and vibrations, which are either similar or dissimilar to them. Thus, living the life you want is simple. Simply vibrate at the energetic frequency of what you want and you will attract it into your life.

What does that sentence really mean though? Is it really that simple? If you could just think of what you want, will it really manifest into your life? Well, not quite. While the law of attraction definitely exists, it has been misinterpreted in many ways which has led to even more frustration for those who have practiced it, or to be more accurate, those who thought they were practicing it.

Like everything else, it begins with the basics.

To master anything, you need first to establish a good foundation upon which you can build. Unfortunately, a lot of the material out there about manifestation and creation miss the mark with this regard. By skipping some fundamental information, what people end up doing is running before they can crawl. Is it any wonder then, that they fail to manifest what they truly want?

The entire process of utilizing your subconscious to manifest desires is thoroughly misunderstood, and it is precisely this misunderstanding you will gain clarity on once you read this book. A vital component of the entire process of manifestation is faith. I'm not talking about faith in a religion or anything of that sort, but faith in the process.

If you don't understand the scientific and spiritual basis for manifestation techniques, you will likely not believe in them and thus, there is no way you can manifest the life you want to live, at least with ease and alignment. Faith is what moves mountains and in this case, faith is born out of "an opening of the mind to the truth . . . a plunge into the unknown," as Alan Watts famously said.

The great thing about the advanced manifestation techniques you will learn in this book is that as you read along, you will gain a bedrock of information and knowledge within you. Once this is achieved, the miraculous power of your subconscious will be apparent to you because you've already experienced it.

That's right! You've already experienced the power of creation. It's just that you don't know it yet or haven't attuned yourself to it. Much like a baby who sees water for the first time and doesn't know what it is but drinks it anyway, you are constantly co-creating things but don't know the depth or the extent of power you're utilizing.

The laws of the universe are very simple. Thus, it is crucial for you to understand the way in which all things are connected before you proceed to use them. This is where this book can help you.

WHO AM I?

It all started when I was down in the dumps myself. I read a few inspirational books and started practicing spiritual techniques because of the anxiety and depression that consumed me in my early adulthood. I needed something to be able to free me from it. Decoding the process of manifestation was certainly not my primary intention!

As I progressed further into freeing my mind from egoistic thinking, I began noticing changes in my life and how they correlated back to the way my thoughts flowed. At first, I didn't really understand what was going on but soon, I began experiencing and witnessing its effects around me. Clearly, I was doing something, but what exactly was I doing?

I decided to investigate further and as I learned, I began to become consciously aware of the universal connections all around us. The law of attraction is a very real thing; it is but a small cog in the overall machinery of how the universe works. I began understanding what I was doing and in the process, found my life's passion.

For close to a decade now, I have guided people to solve deep emotional problems in their lives and helped them realize how they can achieve their goals, no matter their current life situation. All you need to do is open your eyes and the answers will find you themselves. It really is that simple — you'll soon find out!

It is possible to attract the life of your dreams. Your past is exactly that: the past. It has gone and it will never return. Now is the moment for you to begin living your real-life and attracting all that you want for it.

MANIFESTATION IN THE TRUE REALITY

Time is something that has a massive grip on all of us. We live our lives by the clock and have developed Pavlovian responses to it. The minute it strikes one in the afternoon, our stomachs rumble. The minute the clock goes past eleven at night on a weekday, we feel sleepy and so on.

Here's the thing: Time is no longer an asset, but a psychological need for the ego. It's just a construct we have created to organize ourselves better. Somewhere along the way, we forgot this and began treating time as the endgame to everything. We get caught up in our future and our past, and end up ignoring the only real component of time: the present.

Since time is a mental construct, we do not need to build our lives around it. What we need to do is choose the reality we wish to pull into the present moment. This may sound way out in left field, but it is simply the truth about how the true reality works. Your goals, aspirations and desires do not come with time but only when you change your inner perspective do you realize the true concept of shifting your reality.

Love, prosperity, and happiness are all available now. You need to realize the true reality that we are living in order to begin attracting what you want out of life. When you acknowledge this and take action, the universe responds in kind ways and sends you opportunities to lead yourself to fulfillment and happiness.

The universe is one generous machine and it gives you what you want, all the time. You are a creator and you are meant to create consciously instead of unconsciously as you've been doing thus far. You need to start recognizing the immense power you have to shift your life in the direction you want.

MY PROMISE

True happiness is your right and is fully available to you, I guarantee it. You don't need to live in the situation you've created for yourself by living life on autopilot all the time. The information available in this book can shift your perspective on how to propel your life to greater heights.

This universal knowledge has helped people who lost everything or haven't achieved anything, realize the power they possess to manifest their best life. This book will open the eyes of those who feel they are eternally doomed to be stuck in their life situations and help them realize that they are powerful co-creators — both of the reality they currently have and the lifestyle they desire.

It is 100% possible for you to go from unhappy and broken to living a life of security and love. In return, all I ask is for you to have an open mind and trust the power that you have. Trust the universe. Trust that it is kind and benevolent, waiting to give you everything you want out of life. It doesn't want you to unconsciously stroll through life with no sense of purpose or direction.

Open your eyes to the miracles of the universe and watch how it rewards you with its gifts. Take control of your life by realizing your creative powers right now! After all, it is the only moment in time you have.

CHAPTER 1

THE MULTIFACETED REALITY

Reality is at once definite and temporary. It is both absolute and relative. Depending on one's viewpoints, reality can be hell or heaven or both at the same time. Understanding reality is the first step to knowing how you can manifest anything into your life. After all, if you cannot properly understand the state of things you live in, no amount of work will help you.

People who blindly apply spiritual techniques and methods of self-improvement are a lot like those who would use a rowboat to cross a desert. They're completely ignorant of what their environment is — how it affects them or not — and end up choosing the wrong tools.

So without further adieu, let's jump in and breakdown the reality of 'reality.'

THE NATURE OF REALITY

To truly understand what reality is, we need to deconstruct the very process of creation. After all, reality is full of things we create. For example, someone afraid of dogs will be afraid of all dogs, whether they're playful or vicious. The mental creations living in their mind creates their absolute reality. So how does creation occur in the first place?

The easiest way to understand this process is to simply look around you. What do you see? A book, a computer, a phone and so on. But what are you really seeing? Well, light of course! The things you see are visible to you because they reflect waves of light back to your eyes and thus, give themselves a form.

Sunlight in and as of itself is thought of as white light. In other words, we don't associate a color to it. However, when passed through a filter, like a prism, we clearly observe a rainbow of colors emerge. Applying a filter is simply the process of separating what we want from infinite choices.

What I mean is, if you wish to drown your room in red light, you apply a red filter to the lightbulbs and instantly, you've got yourself a red room. Similarly, you apply filters to create any other color you'd like. In other words, what you're doing is, you're removing every color except red from your light source and creating a situation where everything is red.

Our lives play out in much the same way. We receive a stream of infinite possibilities from the universe and we filter it to create a reality for ourselves. The large majority of us do this unconsciously. Think of it as you applying a green filter to your light source and then wondering why nothing you see is red? Well, change the filter!

This stream of infinite possibilities we receive is called the quantum field. This field contains information at the atomic and subatomic level about the movement of matter. Thus, it is the record of infinite parallel realities that exist based on the filters you apply to this stream. The quantum field is a complex energy structure and as such, can only be described in a theoretical manner by current physics.

Physical reality is what we interact with on a daily basis, but there is no denying that there are things we know of but cannot explain or experience. This is the metaphysical component of reality and this is where we, understandably, experience the most debate and resistance within us.

Our minds are receptors of infinite consciousness, but are not fully equipped to handle the metaphysical realities of our existence. We are always requiring proof in the form of physical reality and end up choosing only that which we can comprehend. Thus, we end up creating whatever it is we understand possible for us, whatever we believe in.

When viewed in this light, Henry Ford's quote, "Whether you believe it or don't, you're right," opens up a whole new world of possibilities, doesn't it? The infinite stream is really just a huge tree with numerous branches, all of them interconnected with one another. The filter you apply determines which reality or branch you choose.

BALANCE

Another aspect of the infinite stream is balance. Our lives are filled with obstacles and walls that are thrown up by other people and the constructs of our physical world. This is simply the truth of our existence. There is no reality where obstacles do not exist. Wishing them away is merely trying to go against truth and is a futile exercise.

Obstacles are major drains of energy and by giving them undue importance, we end up prioritizing them within our lives. One of the reasons unhealthy obsessions with obstacles leads to poor results is that it puts you squarely up against another fundamental truth of life. That everything is balanced.

To realize the good, you need evil. To understand the masculine, you need the feminine. Polarity is nature's way of letting us know that balance exists and reminds us of the need to stick to the middle. Buddhism refers to this as the middle path, avoiding the extremes.

The forces that are in charge of maintaining balance usually end up being destructive because they are completely opposed to your current way of being. When you build up an excess of emotion towards a particular thing in your life, nature acts swiftly to remove that excess.

A key concept to understand here is that the negative is not repulsed by the positive. Instead, the negative excess is removed by the realization of those negative thoughts. For example, the imbalance caused by discontent with a particular situation doesn't get removed by creating content. Instead, it is removed by becoming aware of your negative thought patterns.

If you overvalue something, the exact opposite happens in order to restore you to objective reality. Thus, if you really want that job and exaggerate its importance beyond its reality, you'll end up pushing it further away from you because you're out of balance.

In order to create anything in your life, a balanced intention towards that goal is required. If you're excessively critical and harsh towards yourself, the balancing forces of the universe will give you more opportunities to stop these negative thinking patterns. But it is precisely these negative thoughts that prevent us from seeing these opportunities.

This is why it is so easy to down a negative spiral. You think of a shortcoming and remove yourself from balance by overvaluing something negative and this leads to its fulfillment. This further throws you out of balance and soon, you're in a personal hell.

The importance you give something, whether excessively positive or negative, acts as a filter and propels you down your chosen branch in the infinite reality. So what is the solution here? Well, quite simply, stop being so serious all the time. The very awareness and realization that there are infinite realities for you to choose from should reduce your belief that this current reality is the only one which you're committed to.

Stop giving the barriers in your life so much importance and recognize the reality of the situation: Obstacles have to exist to maintain the existential balance in the universe. Instead of seeking to remove them, seek to move past them by focusing on what it is you wish to birth into existence. If you pay obstacles all the importance in the world, you'll only push yourself into a reality where only obstacles exist and your life is a slave to it.

Does this mean you should become comatose to life's issues and simply not care about anything? No, this is adopting the other extreme and you'll expose yourself to the harmful effect of the forces that maintain equilibrium. Instead, you need to adopt a balanced approach which really means coming to accept things as they are.

Obstacles exist and you need to find a way past them. By focusing on the solution more than the obstacle, you consciously choose the reality where it exists and soon, the obstacle exists no more. "Choose" is the operative word here. You can either choose to be miserable by exaggerating the importance of things in your life or you can choose to view reality as it is — objectively — and remain in balance with everything.

EVERYTHING IS CONNECTED

While we do have the power of choice, choice by itself distorts our reality. We are capable of losing ourselves within our world of choices and exaggerating their importance. This puts us out of equilibrium as well since in such a reality, we fail to recognize the truth that everything is one and everything is interconnected.

The infinite stream that is the quantum field is filtered from our consciousness when we only focus on which choice we need to make. It prevents us from being overwhelmed by the realization of the full stream of consciousness. In our everyday lives, we rarely scratch the surface and realize this full stream thanks to our fixations on the choice we apply. We slip into dualistic thinking, which implies "either/or" and not 'both.' In other words, we think that if we choose positive, we reject the negative.

The truth is that despite this rejection, the negative still exists in a parallel reality and which means on an absolute scale, everything exists as one. Dualistic thinking leads to the imposition of a lot of negative filters since it creates scarcity within our minds. We put ourselves against one another, thinking that we need to grab what we can while it lasts.

On an absolute level, oneness exists, and this cannot be quantified but only experienced. In order to describe it, it needs to be compared to something, and this implies duality. Absolute reality and pure consciousness are non-dual. Love is the ultimate expression of oneness. It implies the fusion of souls — when you love everything around you, it is impossible to cause harm, much less create negativity.

When we connect with the power of love, we no longer communicate with our minds, instead we communicate with souls. The soul is merely an expression of and a part of oneness.

THE POWER OF THE SOUL

The soul has awareness of everything that is and will be. It has access to all our parallel realities and the implications of our choices. In other words, it knows which branch we're currently on, which ones we avoided, and where certain filters will take us. It knows the consequences of these choices and will warn us of negative ones.

This communication doesn't occur through our thoughts, rather it occurs through our emotions — our gut instinct, that nudge in our heart, that spidey sense we feel instinctually — which is the language of oneness. Happiness and a feeling of comfort after making a choice is an indication of your soul commending you on a choice that will benefit you. Constant discomfort and feelings of stress, negativity, and resistance are indicators that your soul has seen the consequences of this decision and does not recommend it.

Intuition or a "sixth sense" is inherent within each of us. It helps us tune into our soul while recognizing and interpreting these messages from our soul. Thus, open your mind and really listen to what your soul is telling you. Invariably, you'll find yourself along the right path. This will lead to you swimming the river of life the right way.

People usually treat the act of living with an imbalanced view. They either drift along aimlessly and go where life takes them or they swim ferociously against the current, trying to teach life a lesson — challenging the natural balance of life. Both of these ways will result in negative realities because the former removes all elements of choice and the latter simply results in removing the connection of the mind and the soul from their existence.

Accepting reality is misunderstood as simply going with the flow, but this isn't the truth. The true way to live is to simply go towards what you want, consciously, while accepting the reality of what is around you. It is expressing your intention to bring something into your life and communicating this to your soul, recognizing that all obstacles exist.

You also recognize that by traveling towards this intention, you're simply choosing a particular branch in your tree of life and since this is infinite, your intended destination exists in some form or another. Your soul knows what is best for you and is constantly communicating with you, thus your job is to simply move in the direction it points you toward, without resistance and in constant communication.

Thus, be on the lookout for signs of your soul communicating with you and be wary of complicated solutions. Often, by simply aligning yourself with the world, you'll find that the solutions to your obstacles are pretty simple and they keep you balanced instead of feeling obligated to expend great effort or make sacrifices for them.

UNDERSTANDING CHOICE

Choices govern every aspect of our life, and there is simply no avoiding it. What you choose is up to you, and your choices are what create your reality. Your choices are what propel you along a path through your tree of life. The emotions you experience while choosing a certain outcome are what helps you birth more of these choices into your reality. It is what impacts and influences your future choices. You can choose to ignore your soul — how it is interconnected to everything — and thereby expose yourself to the equilibrium forces which will push you along a path that is hellish for you. Alternatively, you could listen to your soul and create positive emotions and changes in your life, thus maintaining balance.

Emotions transmit energy into the quantum field, hence manifesting your meta-realities into realities around you.

It's one thing to say that you should listen to your soul and pay attention to positive emotion, but how do you actually go about doing this? Well, it all begins in the present moment by declaring your intention to create what it is you want the most in your life and taking ownership of creating that reality.

The purpose of declaring this intention is to recognize that the only one in command is you. It is simply bringing together everything that you've learned thus far into one conscious act of declaration. Whether the goal is achievable or not is beside the point. Your intention and your soul are not concerned with any of that. All that matters is that you've decided to go somewhere — create a different reality, choose a different lifestyle for yourself — and now you need to act.

As you move along your path, remember to always activate positive emotions from your soul by letting it guide you along the way. Let your choices along your path be guided by the emotions you feel and let them keep you balanced — away from the destructive forces of equilibrium. Your choices are the same as the filters you apply to the light color of your choice, as we saw previously.

Apply positive filters full of images that feel good to you, deep down. Do not adopt someone else's filters or filters which you think society will accept. This gives undue importance to your obstacles and will throw you off balance. Focus inward and prioritize yourself — your desires, your vision of the life you want to live — to determine what sort of filters make you feel good.

Some examples of filters are visual pictures and affirmations. Affirmations are positive statements that help you reinforce the idea that you are in control and you are making a conscious choice to engage with your tree of life, instead of floating around passively waiting for things to happen to you.

Visualization is a powerful tool you can use to manifest your reality. You can use visualization to manifest every single stage of your life — your desire may not arrive in the exact fashion in which you visualize them, but know that they will manifest in some form. Visualization need not only be used for what you desire in the future, but also at your current stage. Every goal can be broken down into steps and stages, and while it's great to visualize your end destination, your attention should primarily be focused on achieving what you need to achieve right now.

Thus, make this primary goal the subject of your mental images and you'll find it coming to fruition in no time. This is how you achieve your goals. Goals are based on what you consider important, and the things you consider important are the source of your joy. The thoughts and opinions of others have a right to exist, as everything does, but there's no hard and fast rule that says you need to engage with them. Stay true to your intention and proceed along your chosen path to living the life you've always wanted.

Remember, your path is yours alone; nobody else can take that journey for you. What may work for you or seem right for you can be harmful to someone else and vice versa. Always check with your soul to determine what is right for you and start acting. The only time you have is now — the present — and this is the only place where happiness exists.

By aligning your goal to your current existence, aided by the knowledge you've gained in this chapter, you'll realize true happiness in the current moment is the only place you can realize it, after all.

CHAPTER 2

UNLOCKING THE NOW

Happiness exists right now, but what is 'now' defined as? This poses larger and more complicated questions: What is time? Does it even exist? How real is it? All of us have had experiences where time slows down or speeds up depending on our perception of it. When working at a boring, soul-sucking job, time comes to a standstill; the clock ticks ever so slowly, each moment feels as though an eternity is passing us by.

When having a lot of fun, time literally flies. The problem is that our world is built around the concept of time and this causes a ton of conflict because time in and of itself is deluded and is against the nature of reality. This illusion will affect how we approach the idea of manifestation.

THE ONLY REALITY

Science has created wonders within our world, however we take a lot of it for granted such as the medium through which you are consuming this information: iPads, smart phones, eBook readers. None of these would have come to fruition without scientific advances. Science suffers from a peculiar condition: Despite the numerous strengths it possesses, there is one particular weakness which far outweighs all its strengths.

As a result, whenever this problem rears its head, scientific principles breakdown completely and what we're left with is simply inexplicable. This weakness is time and science's definition and treatment of it. For any real-world problem to be understood better and solved effectively, it is necessary to develop what is called a model.

A model is an idealized situation that ignores certain real-world technicalities in order to arrive at a passable solution. This approach works wonders almost always. When adapting the model solution to the real world, the solution is tweaked to account for the practicalities that were ignored and hence helping us organize our lives.

However, a huge problem occurs as this approach gains maturity. Quite simply, we forget that the model has weaknesses and start assuming that the model is an accurate reflection of reality. Scientific treatment of time has suffered from this exact problem, which has resulted in us now living in a world where things are built to an imperfect understanding of it. There is no accountability built in for non-scientific, intangible outcomes.

The scientific model of time presumes it to be a straight line that always moves forward. The current moment, or the present, is simply a dot along this line. This works brilliantly as a model, but our practical experience with time shows that this is simply not true. The weaknesses of this model is proved by the fact that traditional physics breaks down when talking of quantum level phenomena, where time does not exist.

Traditional physics also breaks down when time becomes warped and Albert Einstein's musings on this confirm the fact that he clearly recognized the limitations of modeling time as a straight line. The reality is that time simply does not exist. It is a made-up construct that was created to bring order into our lives.

The current time is always 'now' and now is the only moment we have to manifest. We cannot change our past, but our lives from here on out are directly affected by what we do in this very moment to get to where we want to be. If we reject the present moment, we are rejecting reality, and rejecting reality is rejecting the possibilities of manifesting anything you desire.

Our brains work in a relative manner. This is to say that we learn better when comparing things to one another. Thus, it becomes easier to understand time by creating contrasts. That happened, this is happening, and this will happen — the past, present, and future. While contrast was originally used to bring order into our lives, we have lost sight of this. Instead, we have adopted it in a manner that causes us to be stuck, fixated, and feel chaotic at all times.

You see, time is not something that can be felt or touched. It is experienced and is thus a metaphysical reality. Time is not linear; it is constant. It never changes. It is always here and now. Science has begun realizing this and highlights the importance of the present moment in the writings of eminent physicists such as Stephen Hawking, Einstein, and David Bohm.

Dr. Bohm even went so far as to suggest that physics was wrong to assume time was a straight line; his opinions line up with much of what is taught in Zen Buddhism. One of the more insidious creations of this time as a line model is the creation of the ego. So let's take a deeper look at this.

THE EGO

In order to understand the nature of manifestation it is imperative to know that time is fertile ground for the ego to grow rooted into. You see, the ego depends on this poor understanding because it needs the construct of time. Using the events of the past, it either props itself up to reject reality, or it exaggerates the importance of such events to create a hellish present. In other words, the ego can influence the direction of our lives, if we allow it to.

The ego peeks into the future and projects similar positive or negative images, all of them wildly exaggerated in order to build itself up. It is not the positivity or negativity that feeds it. Instead, it sustains itself through drama and pure emotional turmoil.

The present moment that is simply focusing on the right here/right now, lacks any drama whatsoever. This is because when you simply align yourself with presence, there is no room for drama or emotional turmoil. You simply execute what needs to be done in order to achieve your goals. It is the ego that needs to hop back and forth in time in order to build constructs.

The present moment doesn't need past and future events to propagate itself. It simply exists continuously and always, no matter what you do. Thus, when challenged in this manner, you can bet that the ego will throw all sorts of obstacles in your path which will snap you out of the present moment and plunge you into an unreal dimension of time.

Examining the nature of the ego is the first step to overcoming it because you cannot dissolve something you don't understand. Aside from an emotional attachment to time, the ego loves judging and labeling all sorts of things. This sort of judgment usually results in the ego placing itself as inferior or superior to the object being judged. Whenever you find yourself in this frame of mind, remember that it is the ego asserting itself and you need to snap out of it. Otherwise, this will perpetuate you into a life where your ego takes control.

Another marker of the ego is its insistence on identifying with and attaching itself to objects and events. Remember that the ego loves drama. The way it uses these events is to paint itself an identity that is superior or inferior. An example of this is when the ego paints itself as the victim of unfortunate circumstances and complains about how nothing ever goes right. Victim behavior is food for the ego since by focusing on the so-called wrongdoing, it gets you to direct your energy toward it and thus, you end up having a perception of the obstacle being bigger than it actually is. You bring into play the disruptive equilibrium forces which will only intensify the strength of the obstacle, and the ego manages to prolong its control.

As you can imagine, when someone tries to come along and tell you that whatever you want is possible, thanks to the complex structure of human psychology, the ego is massively challenged. It will react in the only way it knows: by creating drama.

Focusing on the now and continuing to be incomplete presence is the best way to defeat the ego's attempts to divert you from your goals. You don't need time since time doesn't exist. It is a collection of nows. Even if you extend the field of view, every year is but a collection of todays. The present moment is the only moment that exists fully, so devote yourself to it wholeheartedly and let the ego keep making noise in the background.

The key to overcoming the ego is the same as you would any obstacle. Simply don't focus on its existence; no, this doesn't mean to pretend it doesn't exist. Instead, observe its existence with passive acceptance. Then, focus on how to get past it by focusing on the present. Do this, and you'll find the ego dissolving itself.

PSYCHOLOGICAL TIME

One of the key concepts that prop up the ego is the notion of psychological time, as Eckhart Tolle calls it. In fact, he goes as far as saying that the only thing preventing us from seeing the light is time and anything that is attached to time. Thus, putting time limits on relationships or any aspect of our lives ultimately dooms it.

Psychological time is contrasted with clock time. Clock time is exactly what it means. It is a mechanical thing that we use to divide our day into manageable pieces and use to be productive. However, psychological time is a fully different beast. It is fluid and is non-linear. It jumps back and forth from the past and into the future and is never in the present. It is the ego's greatest fuel source.

Psychological time aims to transport us to the past or the future and keeps us stuck there. I mention this because it is perfectly fine to decide to finish something by say four o'clock. This is the usage of clock time. However, to travel there and always be there instead of getting the job done is to use psychological time. It almost certainly ensures we'll be unhappy.

By projecting into the future or traveling to the past, we affirm to ourselves that the present moment isn't good enough for us. In short, we're rejecting reality. By doing this, we continue to build certain structures and beliefs in our minds — which we think will comfort us and reassure us — but instead, they are merely creating obstacles on our journey to achieving our best lives.

Hence, you end up trapping yourself in your own mind and strengthening the stronghold your problems have over you. Combating the grip of psychological time can be tough since it is easy to be misled. Much like how not focusing on your obstacles can be misinterpreted to mean that you "don't care about them," not paying heed to psychological time can be construed as though you are in denial and choosing to ignore your problems.

Of course, this is not the right way to go about it. Instead, focus on the existence of solutions and give your emotions the space they need to coexist with each other comfortably. A lot of time traveling occurs because we reject the validity of our emotions, especially negative ones, instead of fully feeling each emotion. Remember that everything has a reason to exist, whether you understand it or not. Feelings of sadness and anxiety exist for a reason. Problems only occur when our emotions are imbalanced, where the negative outweighs the positive and vice versa.

If you are currently in a tough situation and if the present moment is extremely painful, allow yourself to express the negative emotions that are surfacing within you. Do not think that it is wrong to feel such emotions or that they are invalid, since doing so will cause you to travel back into the past or future to seek solace. Focus on what you can do to make the situation better, right in this moment.

If there isn't anything you can do to remedy the situation in the moment, that's okay, simply acknowledge its existence. Know that since there is nothing to be done right now, except wait for the right moment. At first, this will be quite a struggle, but over time, you'll find yourself getting better at it.

There are some techniques you can use to loosen the grip of psychological time and the ego over your life and live fully in the present moment. Remember it will be tough at first if you're used to time-traveling quite a lot. Your ego will vehemently reject these, but with persistence, you'll find yourself living more and more in the 'now.'

TECHNIQUE #1: STICKY THOUGHTS TECHNIQUE

The first practice you can implement takes advantage of the fact that your thoughts have a sticky quality to it. What I mean is that once a thought snowballs, it perpetuates itself, and once it gets rolling, it can be extremely difficult to snap out of. Those who have experience with anxious thoughts and fear know what I'm referring to. Once those thoughts start spinning rampantly in your mind, no matter what you do, it seems as if they keep pulling you back under their spell.

Well, the objective is to use this stickiness to your advantage. If your thoughts have to be sticky, why not make them positive? Why not adopt thought patterns that make you feel good and self-perpetuate on those instead? Well, this is easier said than done. The negative spiral will eventually draw you back in, even if it needs to take long detours.

One way to combat this is advance preparation. When you're feeling calm and at peace or simply not negative, take the time to visualize a mental frame of what you want to manifest. This frame should be four to ten seconds long. Fill it with all the things you want and things that bring you peace. Draw from memory or from fantasy, it doesn't matter. Through more practice, it will become more vivid and detailed. Make this frame as real as possible to pull it into the present moment.

Whenever you find your negative thoughts becoming excessively sticky, recall your happy place within your memory and use the momentum that has been built to perpetuate the positive thought. You'll find yourself feeling lighter and your mind calming down. Your level of awareness determines how early you can nip the negative thought process in the bud. The more aware you are, the quicker you can deploy your happy place thoughts and make them stick.

TECHNIQUE #2:
OBSERVING THE EGO

Developing your awareness is the objective of the second practice. Call it mindfulness or meditation or whatever you want, learning to simply observe and not interact with your thoughts emotionally will help you detach yourself from the ministrations of the ego. Allowing you to make the decisions necessary to guide you towards your desires. The best way to carry this out is to build up your strength.

Start by setting aside a few minutes daily to observe your breath. You'll find that your mind will wander and it is impossible to maintain focus, even for a few seconds. This is fine and is completely normal. The objective here isn't to achieve divinity or some absurd notion but to simply observe and not judge. Every time your mind wanders off, bring it back gently and focus on your breath. Think of it as a child who doesn't know what they are doing.

As you go about your day, put as much focus as possible onto what you're experiencing and thinking, without judgment. For example, if you're washing your dishes, feel the water on your fingers, the dish soap, etc. Notice what is running through your mind and do not judge or label anything.

If you find yourself in an egoistic frame of mind, then accept it and simply move on, continuing to observe what you're experiencing. Pay special heed to what your senses are communicating to you and feel them. Paying attention to what you're feeling in the moment via your senses is the best way of getting your mind to live in the present moment.

This is a powerful act, which, when done repeatedly, deactivates the ego and brings about a sense of peace and calm. As you've already learned, one of the key supporters of the ego is the notion of psychological time. The best way to undermine your reliance on psychological time is to use clock time and to stay present while you use it.

TECHNIQUE #3:
USING CLOCK TIME

For example, set long term goals and visualize them when you're free. However, when the time comes to work on them, focus solely on the present. Use clock time to enforce this focus by setting work and rest periods according to your mind's needs. This builds discipline and also helps you gain mental clarity on its next action steps. Clock time has immense power in helping us become productive. A loss or lack of productivity usually results from a lack of goals or a lack of purpose. Defining a goal that is true to you will be discussed in a later chapter.

So for now, use clock time to your advantage by building a work structure that will help you achieve your goals. This is the originally intended use of time after all, so use it and see what wonders it will work for you.

Ultimately, remember that everything exists in the present moment, and no other moment exists outside of this one. Reinforce this idea into your mind and simply observe the ego doing what it does without judgment. Soon, you'll find your mind naturally focusing on the present and letting go of the need for the ego.

CHAPTER 3

ALIGN WITH YOUR MANIFESTATION

Change is the only constant in this universe. It just so happens that our conscious minds are singularly ill-equipped to deal with and process change. This is due to the numerous constraints placed upon it as we grow older and by the time we reach the stage of adulthood, it's almost as if our minds don't belong to us anymore.

Let's take a deeper look at this.

SOCIAL CONDITIONING

One of the eternal questions that surround our behaviors and beliefs is whether they're influenced and caused by nature or nurture. In other words, what is the single biggest factor that determines why we behave and act the way we do? This is exactly the subject of determinism versus free will debate.

Determinism adopts the view that our behaviors often have a root cause. Furthermore, it states these causes are always external. As such, the notion of free will is rejected since exercising free will implies that human behavior can be controlled internally. Thus, all our behaviors are predictableand can be controlled and influenced by the environment around us and the incentives it offers.

Please note that the word external here is used in the context of the mind's ability to make decisions. There are a number of behaviors that are influenced by internal physical processes such as mental health, hormones, and so on. These are always the underlying causes of human behavior, and as such, the mind is powerless to reject them and acts appropriately. Such behavior is said to be influenced by internal determinism.

External determinism is when your behaviors are influenced by factors outside your physical body. It must be noted that determinism is but a model and should not be taken as a gospel truth. Indeed, the fact that psychologists cannot accurately predict a person's behavior has led to two levels of determinism forming, called hard and soft.

Hard determinism refers to those points of view where humans are viewed as nothing but biological machines and seek to impose rationality over behavior. Soft determinism is where instead of treating people as machines, some fraction of free-will is recognized. Conditions are viewed as 'likely' causing certain behaviors instead of outright saying they 'definitely' cause them.

Determinism also runs up against common social mores such as responsibility and morality. For example, if someone is on trial for murder and isn't insane and hasn't done it out of self-defense or unconsciously, it is pretty hard to justify the hard determinist approach of saying that this person had no choice in the matter.

Free will theory is an approach that is completely against the Determinism and its approach toward human behavior. Free will rejects the notion that all behavior can be predicted and that humans have no choice in determining their reactions to triggers. Free will is, in fact, seen as an important difference between human beings and other animals in our world.

Our ability to exercise our free will is what allows us to have control over our destiny. No other living being on the planet has this capability. In fact, the degree to which a species rejects deterministic triggers is an indicator of their average intelligence. This effect can be seen in human beings as well. Those considered free thinkers and major influencers of human society are often seen as being apart from the masses, accepting widely held beliefs.

Beliefs thus are formed thanks to deterministic forces during our upbringing and we unquestioningly adopt them. However, as our consciousness grows, so does our ability to select and adopt beliefs that help us grow. Yet, we remain slaves to our old beliefs and our needs to follow the deterministic way of living.

The key for you to realize is that you are subject to both forces — determinism and free will. One seeks to place you under the control of a mass mind and adopt its beliefs, whether they are right for you or not. The other, free will, is your expression of who you truly are. It comes not from a place of fear or resistance, but via communication from the soul itself.

In order to break your shackles and rid yourself of the diseases of the mass mind, you need to recognize your ability to exercise your will and quite simply, your right to do so. Far too many of us go around wearing the right masks and saying the right things to just fit in.

Instead, you need to connect with who you truly are and using your free will, express yourself fully as nature intended you to.

EMOTIONAL ADAPTATION

When you exercise your choice to recognize true reality and express yourself as nature intended you to, you'll find that your mind doesn't quite follow your lead willingly at first. Instead, it will remain stuck in its old patterns for a while and seek to placate the ego by time traveling.

As it travels and as you begin redirecting it patiently back to the present, you'll find that the negative emotions which the ego seeks to create by time travelling will be brought into the present moment. This is a particularly problematic thing because our first instinct is to run away from the negative instead of letting it surface and tune into the learning lessons it is trying to offer us.

We often face negativity by covering it up with something else or substituting it with positive emotion. The thing to do instead is to simply allow it to exist and not give it energy by prioritizing it. Let it simply exist. It has a right to exist, so acknowledge that by doing so, you're bringing into play an extremely powerful human ability: adaptability.

Adapting to our circumstances is an ingrained quality in every single one of us. It is what has enabled us to survive for this long. Adaptation helps us figure out the best way out of a negative situation and adjust to it in a manner that helps us overcome it. Resisting negative emotion, thus, only delays the adaptation process and will only make things worse.

Feelings of anxiety and depression are not combated by running away from them but by allowing them to bloom in you when they arise and letting yourself deal with it. By letting these feelings exist and receiving them, you are recruiting forces far greater than your rational mind can comprehend.

Resistance to your emotions is a lot like fighting fire with fire, and this only makes things worse. It is crucial that you do not pass any judgment on the negativity that crops up. Recognize that it exists and return to the present moment, as best as you can.

When you first start doing this, your mind will resist vehemently, but with continuous practice, it will get used to it and soon, you'll find yourself observing negative emotion passing you by like a temporary rainstorm. You'll have adapted to the situation and will no longer fear the onset of anxiety, no matter how bad your condition.

So, open yourself up and allow yourself to receive whatever emotion crops up within you.

ALLOWING YOURSELF TO HAVE

Our existence in this world is dependent on energy flow. Energy cuts to the very essence of who we are. When describing ourselves, we may state our name, our occupation, what we do in our lives, but does any of this truly describe "I"? The truth is that there is no "I' and that we are simply a subset of energy that flows around all of creation.

There are different types of energy that work together to maintain balance and keep our existence in equilibrium. These are active energy, receptive energy, and balanced energy. The first two can be thought of as the yin and the yang of our existence while the third is simply balancing the two counter energies.

Active energy is what is valued and highly desired in our current culture. We seek people who put themselves out there and attack things with gusto. Such people are often described as 'go-getters' and so on. All of these energies have a positive and a negative side to them. While the positive side of active energy results in success and achievement, when it turns negative, it can result in aggression and a lack of restraint.

Receptive energy manifests itself as having an open mind and the willingness to adopt different points of view. This energy is more soothing in nature and often manifests itself as waiting for the right moment to act and being alert, in a state of readiness.

The achievement of a balance between these energies results in an ability to adapt to any environment and the willingness to change. When imbalanced, it often results in rigid thinking and a general fundamentalist view towards a particular viewpoint, which is really just the adoption of a particular energy.

Of all the three, the receptive energy is the most important since this is what determines the health of the other two types of energy. A major reason for this is that receptivity is what determines our level of acceptance.

Without accepting things as they are, there can be no steps taken to either change or adapt to situations, which leads to rigidity.

When fully functional, receptive energy manifests as grounded-ness, awareness, and acceptance. It puts us fully in touch with who we are and the realities of our situation. With the help of active energy, we can take steps to rectify it if need be. Without the input of receptive energy, active energy becomes default, and this leads to imbalanced states where we simply won't know when to stop, so to speak.

However, the real power behind receptive energy is that it is crucial in determining our ability to give and receive love. Love is what ultimately moves the world and is the emotion that connects us directly to our soul and the infinite knowledge, as we've seen in the previous chapter.

Awareness is crucial for love to exist since love demands an attitude of leaving oneself behind and putting something else ahead of us, in a non-conditional way. Awareness is but an expression of receptive energy, as is acceptance. Both are crucial if we are to maintain the highest levels of honesty with ourselves.

Thus, to fully experience the fruits of joy, you need to allow yourself to receive. You need to open yourself to what is around you and become vulnerable to it. This doesn't mean you become a slave to it but merely open yourself up to it and know that whatever happens, you're finding your way back to your soul and that love will show you the way.

UNCONDITIONAL LOVE

When we're born, the large majority of us receive unconditional love. Babies of any life form elicit all forms of unconditional love and happiness in all of us, and this speaks to a fundamental human need: the need to receive unconditional love. Unfortunately, the memories we have as babies fade out and we grow up not knowing what unconditional love is.

The sad truth is that there are a lot of people who have no idea of what this is and the level of imbalance it causes in our lives. We end up thinking that love is a conditional thing, to only be given when we receive something else. Conditional love is simply an example of a societal construct that gets imposed on us as we move through the world. Like most societal constructs, it is merely an illusion and is far removed from the truth.

How does one begin shedding these constructs surrounding love? Well, the first step is recognizing that unconditional love exists and is something that you fully deserve. Next, in order to receive unconditional love, you need to start giving it.

TECHNIQUE #4: BECOMING PRESENT WITH YOUR EMOTIONS

Whatever it is that you put out into the world, is exactly what you will receive. If you choose the branch that leads to more love in your tree of life, then that is what will manifest in your physical reality. Thus, in order to receive something, you first need to give.

Now unconditional love doesn't mean you need to start confessing your love to random people around you. Far from it. Instead, understand that love is an energy form, and you need to engage with everything around you without judgment and with compassion. This is, after all, what love truly is. We're familiar, to varying degrees, on how we can express love, but how does one exude love as energy?

Well, this is simply conveying an energy of acceptance towards a particular subject. Is your coworker bothering you incessantly? Well, close your eyes and accept them for who they are and wish them the best in their lives. Wish for them to achieve everything that they want and that they receive unconditional happiness. You'll often find that by doing so, the quality of your life improves dramatically. Perhaps they no longer seem to irritate you (even if those qualities and habits still exist within them), because you have learned to accept them for who they are, flaws and all.

Release all expectations you have and simply give. Constraining your expression of love is simply trying to achieve a purpose that counteracts what you're trying to do. This really doesn't need any explanation. Initially, this might feel wrong if you're not accustomed to this, but with regular practice every day, it'll become second nature to you.

Start small by practicing during the more mundane moments of your day and build your way up toward more annoying moments. Soon, you'll find yourself in a blissful world, and the best part is that this is all your own creation!

Emotions are your key to happiness, even the negative ones. Remember that every emotion exists for a reason and indicates an imbalance or function as a warning sign. Thus, you need to give your emotions the space to play out and express themselves, instead of denying them and seeking to compensate in some other manner.

Awareness via meditation or mindfulness will help you accept your emotions. Remember that they are the connection to your soul and that your soul knows what is good for you since it has access to infinite information. Thus, any action you choose to pursue seeks confirmation from your soul prior to moving forward. Mindfulness will give you the markers you need to determine this.

TECHNIQUE #5: RECEPTIVITY

Open yourself up to the world and become more receptive to the energy that surrounds you. We're surrounded by miracles, but we often fail to take any note of them. Think of all the things around you right now. There's probably electricity, the internet, a computer, a smartphone. Consider how fantastic all of this would have been to someone who was born in the previous century. A lot of these miracles would have seemed like Star Trek to you when you were a kid!

Take the time to observe them. Pick one each day and truly observe it. Marvel at how ingenious its design is, even if it doesn't work properly. Consider how miraculous it is, that even a flawed computer is a miracle, requiring so many different components to be engineered precisely in order to form something. The words on your screen, the color of the things you create are all stored as energy on a disk which is then transmitted using another form of energy. As I said, we're surrounded by miracles!

Practicing minimalism is a great way to stop and recognize the miracle that is present in every individual thing. The fewer things that compete for your attention, the more time and energy you will devote to it, and the more you will appreciate it. If there was just one item in front of you, you're more likely to engage with it in a deeper, more meaningful way.

Increasing your level of receptivity has an added benefit in that you'll learn to ask better questions. Be engaging with the world in a more compassionate way; your questions will naturally end up being more open-ended. This will cause you to question a lot of your own assumptions and that of society too.

TECHNIQUE #6:
DETACHING FROM CONDITIONING

In order to detach from our conditioning, it is important for us to recognize that the stereotypical model that we live by is untrue. The roles we play in our everyday lives are a matter of convention, they are abstract. Thus, our conditioned character is tangible. Learning to be mindful and observing the conditions "pop up" within our everyday thoughts, emotions, and actions is a sure way to start the process of change.

Never hesitate to ask questions when confronted with a set of norms that you are forced to follow. Focus on questions that are open-ended and elicit a wide variety of responses. Questions that force you to consider all alternate viewpoints are a great example of this. One of the best ways to reinforce the oneness of everything in this world is to simply sit down and have a discussion with someone who has the diametrically opposite viewpoint as yours.

CHAPTER 4

HEART-MIND SYNCHRONICITY

Your body has two major nerve centers. While one of these centers receives a lot of attention, the brain, the other, which is your heart, tends to get ignored in favor of rationality and other modern constructs. Ancient mystics have written that our minds are not just our brains but really, are a combination of our brain and heart.

The mind to brain connection is something that you need to pay attention to and nurture in order to live your best life. Let's look at how to do this but first off, let's look at what the connection even is.

THE CONNECTION

The heart has always been considered in scientific circles to be nothing more than a muscle. It is the size of your fist and pumps out blood non-stop, day by day, and when it stops, you die. Simple, really. You're advised to exercise it by performing exercises that help the cardiovascular system and eating healthy. That's all there is to it, according to science anyway.

However, recent research shows that those ancient monks were onto something. You see, the heart is much more than a blood-pumping machine. It is one of your centers of communication. As much as your brain controls your ability to communicate and make decisions, your heart controls this, to a greater extent.

In fact, your heart creates an electromagnetic field that is sixty times greater than the one your brain creates. The heart is actually an advanced processing center and has functions that enable it to remember, make decisions, and learn. The electromagnetic field that the heart produces can be detected up to several feet away from a person's body.

Even more significant is that this electromagnetic field can be used to communicate between people. When two people are in close proximity or are in physical contact with one another, communication occurs. Now, this communication is of a very different nature from the type that occurs between brains.

While the brain uses words to encode its thoughts, the primary communication device for the heart is emotion and intuition. Communication occurs between individuals who are in different emotional states. Thus, a person who is in a negative state of mind and emotion can be influenced by someone who is in a positive state or communicating love to the former.

To conclude, a person's behavior and thought patterns could absolutely be changed by the regular encouragement of positive emotions. Thus, stressful thought patterns and behaviors can be replaced over time by consciously choosing to foster positive emotions, which originate from the heart.

The keyword here is emotion. Positive thoughts don't carry a lot of weight without the emotional heft to back them up. The heart plays an important role in communicating positive emotions to the brain as it formulates thoughts. Emotions can, of course, be transferred as well from what we've seen. A lot of people have practical experience with this. Hang around someone who is extremely negative, and you will feel worse about yourself. Hang around someone positive and optimistic, and you will soon feel that nothing is out of your reach, you can achieve everything.

Studies conducted with a mother holding her baby indicate that often, the mother's brain waves synchronize with her baby's heartbeat which makes her far more sensitive to her baby's needs.

Thus, synchronizing your heart and mind is crucial for a happy existence. Modern culture has marginalized and excluded the human heart from a holistic conversation in favor of rationality and pragmatism. However, all this has done is weaken your ability to deal with the world. In fact, a vast majority of communication is nonverbal (think body language and facial expressions), and by marginalizing your heart, you're depriving yourself of a powerful means of communicating with the world.

Let go of your brain's need for rationality and judgment of anything that seems irrational or doesn't make sense traditionally. The brain loves constructing abstract models and pondering over things. The heart by contrast simply accepts without judgment. It doesn't complicate things and communicates a lot faster than the brain does.

Nurture it, and you will notice that your life improves dramatically.

THE HEART SPEAKS

While your brain has the ability to perform gymnastics, convince you to avoid certain situations, and justify your actions — whether they're right or wrong — your heart has no such ability. Instead, the heart only knows truth and love — that is its superpower. Whenever it speaks, it only knows to speak the truth, and it does so out of a deep love for you.

The truth can sometimes hurt, especially if one is lost. This causes a lot of us to simply turn a deaf ear to the voice of our hearts. You must understand that one of the reasons we don't like hearing things that are unpleasant to us is due to judgment. Our brain specializes in judgment and when we hear negative things about ourselves, what we are really comprehending is that we are less than, we are not enough — good enough, successful enough, ambitious enough, and so on — we believe the judgment being passed onto us.

The heart has no business judging things. It accepts everything the way it is and only seeks to improve things out of deep love. The heart doesn't need or want anything; it is happy only when you are living your best life and fulfilling your purpose. The heart also knows things that you're not aware of.

You see, the heart is simply the body's connection to the soul and as such, is its primary communication device. Remember that the soul has access to infinite knowledge which is communicated to the heart. Your heart realizes that everything around you is simply a manifestation of the things you deeply believe in.

Thus, the conditions around you are not someone else's fault, but indicators of things within you that need to be addressed. It will always communicate this truth to you, but whether you choose to listen or not is up to you. A lot of people don't. They rationalize away their feelings and resist them, thereby hindering their ability to adapt and evolve, as we saw in the previous chapter.

Some of you might think that I'm advocating that one must only listen to their hearts and ignore their brain, but this is not the case. Instead, you need to take your brain and heart side by side and listen to both of them. The heart can be impetuous at times and needs the brain's help to slow it down. The brain, on the other hand, lacks the ability to decide quickly and doesn't have access to full knowledge. This is where the heart excels.

Always listen to the voice of your heart, even if you don't like what is being said. Never be afraid to open your heart to someone else for fear of being hurt. Remember that an open heart is far more powerful than anything else in this world. If you feel hurt or some negative emotion, this is simply a reminder to love yourself more and to stop running away from things, confront them instead and start taking ownership for all your emotions — they all have something to teach you.

Your heart speaks in whispers. These whispers speak and manifest as inexplicable feelings and intuition. This communication is beyond logic and reason since these are constructs of the brain. It will not make sense, and that is precisely the point. Sometimes, people struggle to differentiate between intuition and fear. The way to separate them will seem complicated at first.

Fear usually manifests itself as a physical response such as sweaty palms, racing heartbeat, etc. The only response that fear generates, when you retreat, is a relief. Intuition, on the other hand, will result in you feeling comfortable, whether you fully know what is going on or not.

So really, the key is to get familiar with the differences between the feelings of relief versus comfort. At first, these will seem the same but relief is felt to a far higher degree than comfort is. It is almost always in reaction to some negative experience, as opposed to comfort, which is felt as being at peace with things.

The key is to open up and listen to your heart. Be aware of your feelings and reactions. Also, recognize that your heart cannot speak to you when you're using your brain in a deep manner. If you attempt to access your intuition in such times, you'll end up activating your ego instead and end up being dictated by its norms and needs, which is exactly the thing to avoid.

CHOOSING YOUR GOAL

When you start listening to your heart, questions about your purpose and goals become a lot clearer. Our lives are profoundly impacted by this single most pivotal question (even if we choose to ignore it): What is our true purpose in this world? Think about it for a moment; why do you get out of bed in the morning? What is your reason? What is your 'why?'

Studies conducted on lifespans reveal that the places on earth where people tend to live the longest all have one thing in common: a blue zone. Every such place has a philosophy much like the Japanese goal-setting system of Ikigai. Okinawa in Japan happens to be one of these blue zones, and this is where the concept of Ikigai originates from.

Ikigai helps clarify your life's purpose. While there haven't been any studies proving that this particularly contributes to a longer and happier life, there have been numerous studies proving that a loss of purpose does lead to shorter life spans. Your personal Ikigai lies at the intersection of these four elements.

The first element is what you love doing or your passion. The second is whether the world needs this or not. The third is whether you're good at it vocationally and finally, whether you can get paid for it and thereby make a living doing it. As you can see, these are not easy questions to answer, and at first glance, a lot of us will not have these four elements intersect with one another.

We'll explore goal setting the Ikigai way in detail in the next section, but the key to figuring it out is to listen to your heart. It has a way of pushing your thoughts in a particular direction and getting you curious about things. Follow its lead and indulge your curiosity. You never know where they will lead you.

A classic example of this is when Steve Jobs decided to attend a calligraphy class in college, purely out of curiosity. Later, the lessons he learned in this class were applied to the font on Apple's computers, and this soon became one of the major selling points for their products.

Curiosity and our sense of wonder are just a couple of things we lose as we grow older and become indoctrinated with societal conditioning. Indulge your inner child and always be curious. Never stop exploring or take the world for granted.

TECHNIQUE #7: LISTENING TO YOUR INTUITION

The first practice which will enhance your brain and heart connection is to simply listen to your intuition. This is something which is difficult to describe since intuition is a metaphysical experience and is better felt than explained. A way of increasing your ability to be intuitive is to practice meditation or mindfulness.

Mindfulness helps you focus on the present moment and thereby eliminates distractions that cloud your judgment. Paying attention to your gut, literally, is a good way of enhancing your ability to be intuitive. Your gut is one of the places that reacts to intuitive impulses and biologically speaking, your gut health is an important marker of your overall health. As such, it is a major energy point in the body, so pay close attention to it.

Make every effort to listen to your dreams and record them as soon as you wake up. Memories of our dreams fade soon after waking, so it is crucial you do this as close to waking up as possible. Dreams are just a manifestation of our brains processing information throughout the day. A good way to make your dreams work for you is to consciously think about the possibility of success and abundance before going to sleep. As you sleep, your subconscious mind, which has an open connection to your heart, will go to work, and upon waking up, you'll find yourself with new insight.

When your intuition strikes, make sure you listen to it. Remember, in order to listen to your heart, you need to actually open yourself up to it. If you receive a message, don't simply ignore it or dismiss it. This will simply result in you becoming deaf to your intuition and missing any messages it's trying to send you. How do you know when your heart is speaking to you?

Well, your feelings are your best guide. If a decision you've taken doesn't make logical sense, but you feel happy or light in your heart or gut, then your heart is communicating to you that this was the right course of action, even if your brain hasn't quite understood this as of yet. Increasingly lucid dreams are another indicator of your heart talking to you.

Sometimes, events in your life will set themselves up in strange ways. For example, you will find that a particular series of events constantly occur, pushing you to take a particular course of action. This is your heart asking you to do something, and the more the pattern occurs, the more you've been ignoring it. Your thoughts will also wander over to a particular pattern repeatedly.

Your heart is in constant communication with your brain, and if you don't understand what you're feeling, it then uses your brain to influence your thoughts and push you toward a particular direction. If you find this happening to you, take the time to investigate and understand what is being communicated.

If you keep ignoring the signs, eventually you might even fall sick. Ignoring what your heart is telling you and ignoring your emotions will only add stress to your life and you will succumb to it. Other physical signs include creeping anxiety or nervousness. This sickness is simply your heart communicating with you in an extreme manner so you can awaken and do what it truly wants you to do.

TECHNIQUE #8: GOAL-SETTING WITH IKIGAI

Once you begin relying on your intuition to a greater degree, you'll find that setting your goals becomes a lot easier. The Ikigai process can become complicated by worrying too much about what the world needs. Instead, simply focus on what moves you and worry about the world later. What is it that you're curious about? Focus on this instead and move toward it.

A helpful tip to find your Ikigai is to stay active and engage your brain. This could be done by simply learning new things as much as possible. The brain loves to exercise and is capable of learning, understanding, and storing so much more than we give it credit for. Doing so will keep your mind fresh and alert while also strengthening the heart and mind connection. Stop trying to hurry things and really take the time to be present when completing any task.

Being present and grounded in your task will not only enable you to complete your work to a higher quality but will also keep you open to receiving intuitive flashes. Adopting a slow and steady pace of work is frowned upon by our societies where everything needs to be accomplished at a hurried pace and delivered "right now." This alone should convince you that adopting the opposite of this is the right way of doing things.

Ensure a good quality of life for yourself and be kind to yourself. A lot of people seem to think that goals require sacrifice and that struggle is necessary. This is simply adopting the attitude of fighting against the current, as we saw in the first chapter. You gain nothing by this and will only exhaust yourself. You've chosen to walk along a particular path, so embrace it fully and take in everything that it has to offer.

Surround yourself with people whose company you enjoy and connect with nature. Adopt simpler means of living and practice minimalism. Keep yourself active and physically fit, and be present in everything that you do. These nuggets of wisdom might not make sense from a goal-setting perspective but really, what you're doing here is simply reconnecting with the way life ought to be lived — in harmony with oneself — body, soul, and mind.

By living in a way that feels authentic to your body, mind, and heart, you are opening the connection your heart has to infinite knowledge, and you'll receive what you need to know when the time is right. Remember that finding your Ikigai is an emotional process and there isn't a step by step rational plan to follow here. You need to feel your way to it, and once you receive it, then comes the time to implement those insights and nudges from your heart by structuring it into rational plans using your brain.

CHAPTER 5

GETTING OUT
OF YOUR OWN WAY

The biggest obstacle to your success and happiness usually stares right back at you when you look into a mirror. We already know that by giving obstacles our attention, we only end up strengthening them. By giving our worst qualities our attention, we end up fortifying ourselves against what we really want, unintentionally.

Detachment and allowing nature to flow are crucial concepts you need to learn, and in this chapter, we're going to dive into these important concepts.

DETACHMENT AND OBSERVING

You've made your choices and are moving along with positive emotion. You're waiting for the thing you want to manifest, but really, nothing happens. Life carries on as usual and you keep waiting. Soon, you get sick of waiting and then begin feeling anxious, which is followed by anger at your helplessness. All in all, within a short time of making your choice, you're ready to call it quits and try something else.

Sadly, this is the experience a vast majority of people go through when they choose to assume control of their lives. The prospect of assuming control, when improperly understood, leads one to believe that you can perfectly coordinate everything about your life. Well, this is true and untrue. While you can manifest every single thing you want into your life, the key to successfully manifesting things in the manner you want and everything working out exactly how you envision it is by aligning yourself with the larger reality.

Larger reality involves understanding that all things are one. It is about learning how you can and need to remain in balance and about how your parallel realities coexist. Most of all, you need to understand that you cannot always control everything, in the traditional sense. Control is something that is defined by the ego and is governed by it. When I say you need to seize control of your life back from your ego, I'm not talking about initiating a power struggle and then seeking to impose yourself on nature.

This would be much like your arm deciding to declare independence from your body and then trying to punch you. No one will be happy with that chain of events. Controlling your life is really all about giving into nature and trusting in higher intelligence. It is about trusting your heart and its connection to infinite intelligence — having faith that it knows what is good for you and will always look out for you. The idea of imposition as control is an ego-driven construct and is completely wrong.

The very idea that you can control natural processes itself reeks of self-importance, and this is a hallmark of the ego. Once you make your choice and then apply this flawed understanding to it, what you're really doing is letting your ego convince you to hand over control via a clever argument.

While the ego is in control, all that will really happen is a drama-filled existence, and you'll get this in spades since you'll be convinced that you have no 'control' whatsoever. The key to snap out of this vicious circle is understanding what control means and then practicing it through detachment.

Detachment is a state of mind where you make your choice and then stop infusing it with negative energy by worrying about it coming true. You sit back and trust the universe to give you whatever it wants. Detachment takes you out of the cycle of giving your obstacles energy, which everyone does inadvertently. By genuinely not caring about outcomes and whether or not your wish will manifest, you encourage it to appear in your life.

This seems contradictory advice. After all, by making a choice you're displaying that you care about something. So are you supposed to care or not care? Well, you certainly should care about which direction you wish to take your life in. What you should not care about is whether or not this actually happens. By caring about the outcome, what you end up doing is resisting what life gives you back.

The truth is that when we make a choice, we don't fully know what is good for us. It could be that by aiming for one choice and being fixated on it, what is really happening on a grand scale is that we're opting for something much better than the actual choice presented to us at a surface level. Think back to the example of Steve Jobs and the calligraphy class. If he stubbornly insisted on becoming an ace calligrapher, the world would have been deprived of so much wonder, and Apple — it's technology, brand, devices — as we know it would not have existed.

We don't know the repercussions of our choices; only our hearts know this. Hence it is ideal to remain open to its suggestions at all times and look out for the many signs and ways it communicates with you. By doing so, you melt away any resistance. After all, if you're actively listening to your heart and are fully present, where is the space for any resistance to exist?

Leave your fate up to nature and detach yourself from the outcomes of what you think you need the most. Be comfortable with the knowledge that whatever happens, you're being looked after and that you'll be just fine, no matter what comes your way. What will end up happening is that you will expose yourself to working and thinking in a flow state, which is really just the universe's way of guiding you to your ultimate destination.

THE OPEN WINDOW

What if you could live in a place where time doesn't exist and the present is the only real thing? In this place, there is no such thing as effort, merely execution. Everything that you do is effortless and always results in a level of performance that you find awe-inspiring. Well, that place most certainly exists, and it is called the flow state, or as I like to think of it, the open window into the quantum field.

The quantum field contains all the information that exists, be it past, present, or future. It is the ultimate record of everything that has happened and all that has yet to take place. Your heart and soul have a direct connection to this information and channel this to you when you open your connection to them and are receptive. However, the large majority of us are simply not equipped within our environment to remain in a state of mind and heart that nurture this connection.

Instead, we're consumed by our daily woes and obstacles. We're fretting about this or that thing which ultimately is of no consequence, but at the moment seems like a big deal. This kind of worry is sometimes mistaken as being present, but that is certainly not the case. The very concept of worry is created by the ego since worry implies fear of something bad happening and some future state being worse than where we are right now.

This creation of contrast between the future and the present is just another way of believing in time and imposing its restrictions upon ourselves. True presence is being in the flow state and staring directly into the unlimited quantum field. This, contrary to what you might think, is not an overwhelming experience but actually the highest state of peace you can achieve.

The flow state is all about executing perfectly, and when we're carrying out an endeavor, we often stumble into this. It is the highest state of creation we can access. You often hear of athletes or musicians talking about how they don't know where the stuff they created came from, that it simply materialized in their heads. Well, this is the flow state.

Such states can occur individually or in groups. In groups, it occurs when there is a collective investment towards a goal, and everyone is fully focused on what is happening right now, in that moment. Think of an entire stadium watching and experiencing a close game in any sport. That particular moment is not something that is special individually, but if you recall, you almost always develop some sort of a connection with those who experienced it with you. This is merely the result of everyone involved being immersed into the flow state at once, as a group.

The flow state is also characterized by complete silence. As in, inner silence. The annoying voice inside your head that questions and debates your decision and causes anxiety vanishes, and you begin to fully invest in the present moment. The ultimate aim of a lot of practice, such as mindfulness or meditation, is to simply achieve this flow state.

Flow state occurs when your subconscious has been trained to such an extent that the action you wish to carry out is automatic. Your conscious brain simply shuts off and you're free to let your subconscious mind take over. Thus, the crazy thing about the flow state is that you do more by simply using less of your brain. If there was ever an explanation of how you are your own worst enemy, this is it. I mean to say that the best way to get things done and achieve peace is actually to shut down a part of your own brain.

This state is named as such because there are no obstacles in your path. You simply flow right over them as water would over rocks. You automatically know which path to take and do so without question or hesitation.

THE PATH OF LEAST RESISTANCE

If you observe anything in nature, such as a river or any living creature, you'll see how everything takes the path of least resistance. A river doesn't insist on cutting a straight line across a valley at all costs. It simply goes wherever there are lesser obstacles and maneuvers itself around the problematic areas in front of it. It doesn't stop to fight an obstacle or engage in a battle of egos.

Egos are something that are reserved for the human realm. These are erect barriers of our own making and they prevent us from taking the path of least resistance. This path is simply the shortest way to our goal, and almost always, we can't see it for what it is. We instead see it as a series of digressions and distractions, much like when we see a river snaking its way through and wonder how much faster it would be if it just took a straight line.

The path of least resistance unveils itself when we switch off our conscious mind, which contains the ego, and rely entirely on the subconscious mind which is always on but has its voice drowned out by the conscious critic. The subconscious mind is simply your true mind —the sum of your beliefs learned from consciousness and your heart's communication with the infinite. It contains everything you need to know and has a way, via the heart, to supply you with information with regards to things that you don't know yet.

The key to switching into subconscious mode is to stay present and to fully experience the present moment, without judgment, listening with an open mind and heart. Although this sounds simple enough, it is an extremely difficult thing to practice in reality, as all of us can attest. The subconscious will speak to you in many ways. Most of the time, it doesn't communicate via language, but through emotion, just like the heart.

Intuition, emotion, and feelings are how you will be given information and when you are immersed in the flow state, you'll simply know what to do. The key is to get yourself acquainted with your subconscious mind and the way to do this is by monitoring your emotional states. Understand that whenever you are under stress or are caught in a negative cycle, there is some element of time involved and that the ego is breaking your connection with the subconscious.

One of the best ways to short circuit the ego is by reducing your own importance. This is not to say that you should treat yourself poorly. Instead, notice how you are a part of the world, of nature, and not somehow above it or below it. Notice how nature nurtures everything within it and how you are a part of this circle. People who tend to struggle in their lives with unhappiness suffer from problems of the ego.

They refuse to see how, by prioritizing their ego's needs, they actually strengthen their obstacles and set a course headed right for those hurdles. Think of it like this. When walking, largely speaking, you'll go wherever you look. In the metaphysical realm, looking is done by allocating energy. Thus, whatever it is you're focusing the most energy on, that's what you're looking at and that's what you'll crash into.

Instead, finding the path of least resistance is simply looking where you're told to look. This is the exact opposite scenario of what the ego wants since the ego has to believe it is superior to everything around it. The thing guiding you on your path is your heart and your subconscious mind. Thus, by monitoring your feelings, listening to your intuition, and respecting your hunches, you figure out which path you need to take.

The flow state always directs you to the simplest solution for every problem, and the path of least resistance always lies in this direction. The flow state knows which solution to pick in advance, so don't worry about any temporary obstacles that you can foresee. If you start worrying about these, you end up engaging the ego and sure enough, your ego will lead you right into it, in direct opposition to the path of least resistance.

Instead, practice detachment. Make your choice and then relax and know that forces greater than you or I can comprehend are in motion. You're being taken toward your destination, whether you know it or not. Thus, become an observer instead of being a passenger to your ego. Trust that the universe is taking care of everything and that you will also be taken care of.

TECHNIQUE #9:
DETACHING & OBSERVING

Detachment is the first step to tapping into your subconscious mind and activating the flow state. Meditation remains the best way of practicing detachment, especially those practices which are dedicated to practicing equanimity, as opposed to focus. Take the time to observe your breath, without judgment, and whenever your mind wanders, simply bring it back to focus on your breath. This technique has been described before.

Take it a step further by observing the sensations occurring throughout your body and then practice observing them. Don't try to fix the condition or change it in any manner, simply observe. For example, you might be experiencing pain or numbness in your feet; your back might be stiff from sitting unsupported. Simply observe and note the sensation.

Notice how your conscious mind will react as if you're on fire and your existence is being threatened. This is simply the ego realizing it is under threat and being reactive, causing all sorts of drama. You will soon notice that the sensations ebb and flow and are not constant. Once you move past this stage, your ego will finally trick you into thinking that you're feeling tired and you'll be lured to fall asleep, in the name of relaxation. This is why it's important for you to have your back unsupported and not lie down when meditating.

TECHNIQUE #10:
ENTERING FLOW STATE

Stimulating your mind to enter the flow state is something that is an excellent exercise to carry out. Do note that you should not seek to control the state of your mind. Instead, the flow state is one of allowing, as you learned in a previous chapter when we spoke of energies. Seeking to force something is just an egotistical way of exerting control. The flow state is a channel of communication and you need to let go of your hold on the obstacles to allow it to come to you.

Setting goals that are challenging and inspiring is a great step to stimulate this. Inspiring goals that are just beyond your current comfort level in life switch your brain into creative thinking mode since you need to create a solution in order to achieve what you want. Use your conscious mind to map out a specific plan of action but don't be a stickler for it. Understand that your plans will change depending on the feedback you receive from your subconscious. After all, you can't see the path of least resistance, so make your plans but always look for feedback from your heart. Above all else, pick simple and obvious plans to execute and resist the temptation to complicate things.

TECHNIQUE #11: YIELDING TO SIMPLICITY

Our conscious mind loves to complicate things since it gets an opportunity to prove how smart it is. Instead, choose the simpler option since this is likely where the path of least resistance lies and watch out for feedback. Mind you, I said simpler, not necessarily easier. The simplest option may call for hard work and spending time. In the grand scheme of things, this will cost you less than seeking alternatives, seemingly 'easier' or 'faster' options.

Yielding to simplicity may come in the form of an opportunity that will help you expand and grow. Although growth may come with stepping outside of your comfort zone, it is a necessary part of the process in order for you to manifest that which you desire. Expanding and growing as a person is yielding to simplicity, and thus allowing the universe to gift you for the person you are becoming.

CHAPTER 6

SETTING INTENTIONS

Getting into a flow state requires you first to know where you wish to go. While it is easy enough to make a choice by listening to your heart, taking that first step requires another degree of awareness. Too many people seem to think that all it takes is making a choice and then life starts guiding you in the direction you need to go.

After making a choice, you need to start taking action by implementing the steps you need to take. Without this, there is no achieving your goal of choice. Doing is the most crucial step of the entire process.

TAKING ACTION

Have you ever noticed a key quality in people who seem to keep spinning their wheels in life? These people always seem to have the qualities necessary to succeed — they have brilliant ideas and the energy to carry things out, but for one reason or another, they always remain in place, perpetually devising new ideas to move forward.

Such people often have it worse than those who fail outright because they have the illusion of success. Their ego convinces them that they're doing the right thing. They're masters of retrofitting events to justify how the world is against them, and all that takes place is coated with a veneer of positivity.

Well, the common characteristic these people share is the quality of being able to come up with brilliant ideas. They're always full of them. They have the ability to debate an idea's merits and faults to the ends of the earth and know seemingly everything about everything. Anything that you say will be met with a response that makes perfect, logical sense.

Except for the small fact that these people have no idea what it is they're talking about. They have not actually done anything and are simply talking out of theoretical knowledge and are more concerned with placating their ego's need to be seen as someone superior. Their intention is to satisfy their ego, and that's it. They end up carrying this out with due purpose.

Intention is what focuses your mind like an arrow towards its target. It is your reason for doing something. While this sounds a lot like what a goal is, in reality, intentions are like the impetus while goals are the destination. Intention is what pushes you forward, relentlessly.

As such, they are extremely powerful and make no mistake, you will carry out and do whatever your intention is. This is why it is extremely important to set it up for action and not for thinking. If you were to observe the most successful people in our world, be it in terms of financial wealth or happiness, you'll notice that their intention is completely focused on doing, not talking.

While they may spend time talking about what they do, the majority of their time is spent carrying out what they preach. Thinking about doing something ultimately costs you more energy than actually doing the thing. There are many reasons as to why people refuse to do and are content with sitting there dreaming up different ideas and to do lists.

A big reason is the ego. Your ego needs constant external validation and unfortunately, the nature of our society provides more exposure to people who talk about doing than those who actually do. The internet is full of self-proclaimed gurus who know nothing about what they're saying and only know how to manipulate their viewers' egos.

By using the promise of an idea to improve one's life, people are lured into thinking about them incessantly while providing the ego the short term boost it requires through validation of its intelligence, further driving people to seek this. Here's the thing: Thinking is easy. Doing is the tough bit. It requires you to face problems and figure out solutions.

It requires you to make yourself vulnerable and be brave by opening yourself to feedback. People who never figure out their purpose in life tend to cower behind their egos, afraid of what sort of feedback they will receive. The way past this fear is to simply define your intention.

What is your intention in life? Is it to placate your ego, or is it actually to live the best life you can? Define your intention, and you'll automatically find yourself propelled into action.

POSITIVE INTENTIONS IN EVERYDAY LIFE

At its core, setting intentions is all about recruiting energy to help propel us towards our goals. While you'd figure that your purpose alone should provide this, as we discussed before, the reality is that your purpose and goals are destinations to shoot for. In the day to day grind of things, your focus will be entirely on executing the tasks on hand to reach that goal.

Actions carried out with positive intentions have far greater power than those simply carried out for the sake of it. Intention will propel you to full awareness because this is your 'why.' When fully aware of why you're doing something, the results you produce will reflect this awareness and will move you that much closer to where you want to be.

Given their power to inform your actions, your intentions are ultimately what determines your reality. It is your intentions that determine how focused your thoughts are and how well you carry out your actions. If your intentions come from a place of positivity and in line with the nature of reality, then you will find your life turns harmonious. If it comes from a negative place, such as pleasing the ego, then you'll find your life full of unnecessary drama.

By setting your intentions in a positive manner, all sorts of hurdles disappear, and you can focus your energy much better. This is because your decision making becomes far more streamlined. For example, if you know that you intend to go west in order to achieve your goals, why would you even consider going east or north?

Without that intention to set the tone, as you begin your journey, you will need to spend time trying to figure out which direction it is you need to go. Without the framework that intention-setting provides for your thoughts, you might even go in the wrong direction for a while before realizing your mistake and then double back, which is frustrating to say the least.

Intentions help you take responsibility for your happiness and help place control right in your hands, and with this, you can live a life by design, instead of one created by habit and conditioning. It's not just in your personal life where you will see the effects of positive intentions. Look around the workplace or in any professional setting — the best leaders are those who provide their teams with a clearly defined goal.

However, beyond just setting the goal, they also make it very clear that the goal is an objective and that it must be met within certain boundaries. This is nothing but providing the team an intention to meet their day to day tasks in pursuit of that goal. This ensures everyone is pointed in the same direction and that no energy is wasted going after things that are not in line with what needs to be achieved.

Positive intention also will work wonders for your interpersonal relationships. This much is true. We tend to see the world as a reflection of ourselves. By assuming a positive viewpoint of things in your life, you'll project the same attitude onto someone else. By simply assuming positive intent from your team member, your spouse or partner, your family, and so on, you'll eliminate a lot of conflicts.

None of us are mind readers, and misinterpreting intent is one of the primary causes of conflict. We get defensive and retreat into a shell when we hear things we don't like. Well, we don't like them in the first place because we frame these things as being against our goals. By assuming that the person you're speaking to intends their comments in a positive, helpful manner, you'll be surprised at how much more open and receptive you become to feedback from life.

This has the added benefit of opening yourself up to your heart and receiving negative feedback from the infinite knowledge. Always assume positive intent from everyone you interact with, including your heart. Assume everything is set up so as to help you improve and live life with greater joy and peace. You'll find that this turns into a reality.

SET INTENTIONS TOO, NOT JUST GOALS

Goal setting is just one half of achieving your objectives. The other half is all about setting your intentions. One of the things you must understand about intentions is that they are more of an energy than a particular statement. For example, you can define in words your intention to live your day in a particular manner.

You could wake up every day and tell yourself, "I will live today in a state of happiness and spread as much positivity to those I come in contact with." When setting goals though, your intention is usually implicit in the goal itself. If you need to inject your career with a flush of energy, defining where you wish to be is a good starting point.

A statement such as "I am a senior xxx for company xxx" or "I own and run my business xxx which is in such and such field," will help you keep your intent focused and purposeful. These statements are goal statements but have the energy of intention within them. By reminding yourself and visualizing these as a reality, you'll inject yourself with the purpose to go out and achieve them.

By repeating such statements or statements of intentions to yourself what you're doing is activating energies within you. These energies place you in the current moment and increase your focus. Thus, a side effect of these statements is that your ego is deactivated and sidelined. When the energy level of these statements is high enough, it opens up your channel to your heart fully and gives you full access to the infinite knowledge that awaits you as you carry out your tasks.

Setting your intention is one thing, but carrying them out is another. At first, just like with meditation, your mind will wander and you will need to bring it back to the present moment and focus on your intention. This becomes easier with repeated practice, so it is a good idea to take some time every day to write down and repeat your intention statements.

Visualizing these statements as reality will charge them positively and will bring great changes into your life. Remember, your intentions have the ability to greatly influence those around you. In fact, scientific research has proven that positive human intention has the ability to influence water, which happens to be what we're mostly made up of, physically speaking.

Your intentions and the energy they transmit will interact with other people's electromagnetic fields and you will find yourself getting out of your own head more and more. Daily positive intentions have the power to get you to focus on things greater than yourself and completely minimize the ego's contribution in your life.

The more you travel outside of yourself, the more present you will be and the greater your connection to your heart will be.

TECHNIQUE #12: SETTING INTENTIONS TO WATER

The power of intention can be used to improve your daily life through some very simple practices. The first of these practices may cause a lot of controversies, but it has its share of believers. This is the practice of setting positive intention to water. The method was conceived by Masaru Emoto, who is referred to as either a scientist or a pseudoscientist depending on which point of view you adopt.

Through experiments he conducted on setting positive intentions to water, Emoto claimed to find that the crystals of water which were formed by imparting positive emotion were of a more beautiful structure than those that were imparted with a negative energy.

Thus, he postulated that the energy transmitted through our intentions has a real impact on the molecular structure of water. Given that our bodies are almost entirely made of water, this is quite significant. There are multiple ways of transferring positive energy into the water we drink. The first is to hold a glass of water in our hands and to repeat our intention either out loud or in our minds. Our intention could be either a short term focused, daily one or something connected to our long term goals, it doesn't matter. As long as the emotion is positive and loving, you're on the right track.

A good way to further energize the water is to visualize yourself carrying out your intention and doing things in the manner you wish to. By doing this, you'll be recruiting the power of both your intention as well as visualization. Intention statements are not the only thing you can visualize and repeat.

If nothing particular strikes your mind, simply affirming a message of love and gratitude is enough to energize the water. Other things that offer you positive vibes, whether it is prayer or music, can also be used to energize the water. Consume this water intermittently throughout the day and repeat this practice before you go to bed at night.

For added effect, you could also use crystals to capture the positive energy and add this to your water prior to drinking it. In this manner, you'll build the positive energy within the water and also change the molecular structure of the water within you.

TECHNIQUE #13: SETTING INTENTIONS TO STATEMENTS

A far more palatable exercise for some might be the process of writing intention statements. These statements are affirmations that you can use to govern how you intend on living your life and what it is you would like to change. There are a couple of characteristics of these statements you should incorporate at all times, such as writing them in first person, using present tense.

In other words, the subject of these statements should always be you and not someone else. This would simply be you trying to control someone else's actions, and that isn't in line with the way nature works. Instead, focus on controlling your own actions and reactions to triggers.

The present tense is used to reinforce the fact that what you want in your life is real and that you have full faith that the universe will provide it for you. This is a step where quite a few people stumble. You see, you'll have faith in the realization of things that you believe possible. However, the point of setting goals and intentions is to push your limits and to achieve something that is outside your comfort zone.

Some people have confidence in themselves, but others struggle with this. For such people, writing statements they don't believe in will only reinforce their inadequacy. Thus, if you feel a negative push or have thoughts that seem to tell you that this is impossible, modify the statement.

Adding phrases such as "I am willing" or "My intention is" makes the sentence more believable and affirms to yourself that while the goal is outside your comfort zone, you're still willing to work for it and you will achieve it. This is a point of view that your brain and self-image will accept easily. So use these in place of strong statements such as "I am rich" or "I am surrounded by people who love me" and so on.

One thing to avoid is the use of words such as: try, but, and or. Your statements need to be as specific as possible. Specificity can be in the form of a quantifiable thing or in terms of emotion. What I'm saying is that you need to know if the goal or intention is met. So you can define reaching a goal in terms of feeling an emotion or in terms of something quantifiable.

A quantifiable goal is "I am a billionaire." A goal based on feeling is "I am in a loving and mutually healthy relationship." In both cases, you'll know when you get there. If you add doubt into the mix or indecision, you're scrambling your energy and conveying that this intention isn't really all that important to you and that it's okay not to follow it.

Monitor your self-talk constantly since this is just another form of stating your intention. If you detect negative talk, reframe it to positive by using the phrases mentioned previously. Always reframe negative talk and don't let it pass by without questioning and challenging it. Do this, and over time you'll find that your brain will get the message automatically correct itself.

CHAPTER 7

ENERGY OF ALL THINGS

We already know that everything is connected. Nothing exists in isolation, and cause and effect is simply the proof of this fact. However, the focus of this chapter is not to dissect this phenomenon or karma or whatever you wish to call it.

Instead, we're more concerned with how things exist, in what form, and how we can better align ourselves by using this knowledge. To do this, we need to dive back into quantum physics and understand certain principles.

THE CONNECTION BETWEEN ALL THINGS

The story of quantum mechanics all begins with Neils Bohr. Bohr was the first scientist to discover that everything is made up of atoms and that surrounding these atoms, in concentric circles were electrons. These electrons vibrated at specific frequencies and thus transferred energy to the atom and the overall object. Therefore, every object had a certain energy associated with it. All this was perfectly in line with classical physics which existed since the days of Newton.

What came next was mind-boggling. Bohr expected to see the electrons behaving in the manner that classical physics would suggest. That is, much like how planets revolve around the sun, he expected to see electrons exhibiting a similar relationship to the atom they surround. Instead, he saw nothing of the sort. What he actually saw was that the electrons did not even have a physical form.

This was because the frequency at which they vibrated was so high that it was impossible to observe any physical form. Think of a rubber band that vibrates back and forth when snapped. To the naked eye, it looks as if the rubber band is in multiple places at once. This is precisely what was going on with the electrons, except at ludicrously high frequencies.

Hence, Bohr and his proteges had proved that classical physics was all wrong. That form and matter don't really exist, as Einstein commented on their findings. What we perceive as matter or form is really just a bunch of microscopic particles vibrating a low frequency so that we can perceive a form. In other words, when the rubber band stops vibrating at high speeds, we can see that it is a band. The stuff we cannot see is simply vibrating at a much higher frequency — for example, light. We know light exists thanks to it reflecting off other objects, but we can't really see light as a form.

Thus, everything in this world is just a collection of energy. After all, that's what vibration is. It is simply a representation of energy existing within something. The higher the frequency, the higher the level of energy and vibration. While the scientific community was understandably shocked by these findings, quite a few of them could not help but notice that these statements were not new. If anything, they were decidedly archaic.

They had been first uttered by the Buddha and other ancient monks whose words have been preserved over the years. These people did not have any special equipment, but the fact that they were able to deduce the same conclusions proves that energy and the universe are the same thing. Communication is not restricted to just the forms of energy on this planet, but there also exists a link between pure energy and us.

All energy is converted and transferred, and according to scientific principles, it cannot be created — although there must have been some point where all the energy in this universe was created. Call it the big bang or God or whatever, it follows that all forms of energy originate from the exact same source and thus, everything is connected to one another. There is a universal mind to which we are all connected.

The problem is that as we've gone about our lives, we've dampened this connection by wrapping ourselves in the trappings of our own worlds. We value our possessions and believe that they define us. We have forgotten that things like intention are what really matters since this is what determines our energy levels and our experience in this world.

The ego is the biggest obstacle to realizing this connection. It convinces us that these physical forms are real and these are what matter. However, this is the wrong view and this throws us off balance with the way the world really is.

Think of it this way: Have you ever met a person and immediately got a feeling about them? It could be a positive or negative one, but there's no doubt we do sense something about the people we meet. We sometimes take an instant dislike to them or on the flip side, we instantly hit it off with them, forming lifetime friendships and more, and sometimes we even fall in love with each other at just a glance. The power of energy is undeniable.

The best public speakers often talk about feeling a room. The changes in energy within a group of people are very apparent and the ability to change energy, either increase or decrease it, is a hallmark of being able to wield influence in our world. Thus, while the law of attraction is a universal law, the reality is that there is another law that sits beneath it and governs every aspect of our existence. This is the law of vibrational frequency.

VIBRATIONAL FREQUENCY

There is a property in physics called resonance. The way it works is this: Everything in this world has a natural frequency at which it vibrates. Vibration can be visualized as a wave that emits a certain frequency and amplitude. Amplitude here refers to the size of the waves or the energy emitted. Thus, louder sounds are simply sound waves of a higher amplitude as are brighter lights.

When you bring another object which is vibrating at the same frequency as the natural frequency of another object, guess what happens? The second object begins to vibrate as well. This is why, when armies crossed bridges, they were told to break march since the synchronized steps produced a certain vibration that might inadvertently match the natural vibration of the bridge and cause it to twist and break apart.

When designing bridges that cross vast distances, designers have to take into account the effects of wind producing natural frequencies and inducing vibrations within the structure. Thus, the conclusion from the law of resonance is quite simple. In order to activate something in our world, you need to vibrate at its frequency. This applies equally to manifesting anything in your life.

In order to attract anything into your life, a goal or anything else, you need to vibrate at the frequency that it vibrates at. You need to match that state and resonate with it to induce it into your life. Have you ever walked into a group of people who are extremely animated and energetic? Have you been instantly energized by them?

What has happened here is that you have absorbed their energy. The old saying that you are the sum of the company you keep is very true. This simply validates the way the law of vibration works. We tend to vibrate at whatever frequency we surround ourselves with.

This is also why music resonates with us. Play your favorite music and you'll find your mood uplifted and play tracks which don't really appeal to you and you might as well draw fingernails on a chalkboard. Use this to your advantage by only focusing on music that makes you feel better and increases your vibrational state.

Aside from the people you surround yourself with, your environment also plays an important role in determining your current vibration. If you maintain an unclean and dirty environment, chances are that you will feel lazy and lethargic. Stay in a dirty locality or home and you'll start letting your own standards fall to the wayside. Vibrations induce themselves in us and it is very important to induce the correct frequencies within yourself.

Things that you see and expose yourself too also affect your frequency. If you constantly expose yourself to images of grief and struggle or images that are intended to lower yourself worth (hello social media!), you will end up feeling miserable as well. Energy flows into us in a variety of ways and in the next section, I'll be giving you a couple of exercises to clear your channels. However, it all starts with filtering in the correct energy sources and choosing the right vibrations in your life.

This is precisely why gratitude is so important. Gratitude opens your eyes to how wonderful things are and puts you on a positive vibrational plane. By doing so, you will attract things that make you more grateful. Speaking positively and holding positive beliefs work in the same fashion.

Your vibrational level is also determined by the degree to which you allow the flow of energy from the universe into you. While the food you eat gets transformed into energy within you and ensures your biological functions work as planned, the free energy from the universe flows into you in the form of intuition, gut feelings, etc.

Given that this energy comes from infinite knowledge, naturally, the frequency of this energy is on a far more evolved level. Things such as stress, the ego, and giving energy to the obstacles in your life cause you to vibrate further away from this energy and you end up attracting less of it into your life.

The more universal energy you have, the more proactive you will be toward your life since you will fully assume your position as a creator and as someone who can choose the life they wish to lead. Always monitor the level of your relaxation since this is a good indicator of how much you're currently allowing universal energy within you.

By relaxation, I don't mean to say you ought to sleep all the time. What I mean is your mental and physical state. Are you constantly on edge expecting something to go wrong? Constantly worried about negativity? This only causes stress and pushes you further away from true wisdom.

Of course, all of this is just another way of saying that your thoughts ultimately matter the most. Your thoughts are just energy within you and these are what determine, more than anything else, your vibrational frequency. Thus, fix your thoughts, and you fix your life.

THOUGHTS INFORM YOUR ENERGY

Your thoughts are instantaneous bursts of energy that travel within your brain. Think about something, and you're instantly doing it without any hesitation. Our thoughts exist on both the conscious and the subconscious plane with the latter accounting for the majority of them. By an estimate, over seventy thousand thoughts occur in the human brain throughout the day with ninety percent of that occurring in the subconscious.

There is a famous quote by Einstein, where he says that the definition of insanity is doing the same thing over and over again and expecting different results. In order to change your outer reality, you first need to change the reality that is within you. This is just a way of saying that you need to vibrate at the level of the energy you want within you, in order for it to manifest around you, through the law of resonance.

The challenge with changing your thoughts is that there is a lot of junk embedded in them — limiting beliefs, childhood conditioning, biases, judgments — all of which is just downright unhelpful. A lot of what we think is actually determined by what was installed within us when we were growing up, prior to the age of five.

At that age, our brains are not conscious, and we simply absorb whatever is around us. These thoughts are stored deep within for future use. When the time comes, some of these thoughts are discarded and the ones that remain form the basis for our actions for the rest of our lives. Unless we decide to change them, that is.

Given that your thoughts are just energy and your actions are expressions of this energy, by not giving certain energies the outlet to expend themselves, you can conceivably transform them into something else. What I mean to say is that you don't need to be a slave to every single thought that arises in your head; you have the choice to simply not act upon it. If you choose not to act on it, that energy remains within you, ready to be transformed into something else.

Transforming that latent energy is all about carrying out the actions that reflect the belief you wish to install. While thoughts inform actions, actions also inform thoughts and beliefs. Thus, if you behave in a certain manner, and visualize yourself behaving in the manner you wish to be, your brain will adopt beliefs that are in line with these actions.

In addition to visualization, we've already seen how affirmation statements can focus your intentions and get you to carry out actions that will result in massive changes in your life. A key concept to installing new beliefs that you must grasp is this: Change will not happen overnight. Those goals will not be achieved overnight. You will not live a life by design overnight. These are all built one action at a time. You need to keep repeating these new actions over and over until they get installed within you. There is no Matrix-like plug and play learning process.

There are further exercises that you can carry out, and I've listed them in the section that follows. These will help clear any blocks to universal energy you might have within you. Allowing this energy into your mind will do wonders for your understanding of what the correct beliefs are in order to live well.

You see, life is best lived when you go with the flow and don't oppose the current. You choose your stated goal and take action to progress towards it. You will meet obstacles along the way, but the universe will inform you as to which way to flow. Think of it as swimming in the ocean towards a rock which is at a distance away from shore.

When you first begin swimming, the waves will crash into you with great force, but as you go further in, you can either ride the momentum of the waves as they push you back and drag you in or you can simply swim under them. You will encounter various currents but by swimming sideways from them or with them, you navigate your way to your goal. This is how you navigate life as well in order to achieve your goals.

TECHNIQUE #14:
THE ASSEMBLAGE POINT EXERCISE

The first exercise which will enable you to allow the flow of energy within you is the Assemblage Point exercise. This exercise utilizes the power of visualization to manifest reality. It enables a full flow of universal energy within you and clears all the blocks to the universe.

To begin, stand in a relaxed manner with your feet comfortably apart. Take a few deep breaths to relax. Now, visualize a golden stream of energy entering you from below, from your feet. This energy is relaxing and moves through your body upwards. As it does so, you find that that particular portion of your body relaxes even more as you inhale. As you finish your inhalation, this golden energy exits into the universe from the top of your head.

As you begin your exhalation, visualize this golden energy now entering the top of your head and making its way down your body, through your spine and into your feet. Notice how relaxed you feel as this energy makes its way down and exits back into the universe through your feet, taking all the limiting blocks and impurities within you with it.

As you develop your ability in this exercise, you will yourself becoming more sensitive to the energy that enters you. At first, simply visualize this energy — it is more than enough to relax you and allow the energy to flow through you.

Once you have managed to relax properly with these two steps, it is now time to take things up a notch. Perform the first two steps again and after this is done, visualize both balls of energy entering you, one from the top and one from the bottom. These two pass one another as they travel through your body but they don't intersect with one another since one passes in front of your spine and the other behind it.

Try to synchronize your breath with the entry and exit of these energies from your feet and head. You can make the energy balls bigger in your imagination, but it's best to start small. The idea isn't to change the size of the energy just yet. Next, imagine that above your head is a fountain of this golden energy that is constantly pouring into you, and similarly, there is an upside-down fountain below your feet, energizing you from the bottom.

Gradually, imagine that these fountains are reaching out for one another, and eventually, they unite to form a golden sphere of pure energy around you. Feel your skin expanding with every intake of your breath as this energy continues to envelop you and protect you. Keep working on this for as long as you can.

It will be tough going at first, and you will feel tired. However, this is a muscle like everything else and the more you work at it, the better you'll be. Keep increasing the strength of the energy flowing into you gradually. Do not try to accumulate too much energy as this will throw you out of balance. Simply stick to what feels right.

CHAPTER 8

WEALTH AND ABUNDANCE

While this step is named wealth and abundance, what we're discussing in this chapter is happiness. How to figure out what it is and how to have more of it. Money and wealth are both tools as well as obstacles to this.

A lot of us have terrible beliefs about money — I simply mean imbalanced. Therefore, in order to restore a sense of balance, the universe's forces do their work to balance the equation, leaving us more miserable than ever. When this happens, instead of recognizing our faulty thinking, we blame the subject of our thoughts, which in this case is money.

Abundance, wealth, money, whatever you want to call it, is simply a manifestation of what you think and how you think about it. So let's take a deeper look at this.

MONEY WILL NOT MAKE YOU HAPPY

Well, we might as well get the bad news out of the way first. In case it isn't apparent to you, money will not make you happy. This has never been the case and never will be. However, a lot of people take this to mean that money will never make you happy under any circumstances. This is false and reflects an imbalanced view of things.

Consider this scenario. It's hot outside, and you really want an ice cream to cool off. The problem is that there's no ice-cream seller or truck in sight. You're sweating profusely, and the sun is now burning a hole, seemingly, in the back of your neck as you trudge through what seems to be a hot and humid day.

You're keenly on the lookout for an ice cream vendor, and just then, you spot a truck! You run toward it and ask for your favorite flavor of ice cream and the biggest possible serving. Let's assume the size of this serving is six scoops. So as the ice cream man scoops it out one by one, into your cup, you eye it hungrily and before they can take your money, you've begun devouring the ice cream.

The first few mouthfuls are about as close to heaven as you can get. The first scoop is wonderful. The second scoop is pretty good but not as good as the first one. By the time you reach the sixth scoop, you're actively sick of ice cream because you've already had so much of it that your craving has disappeared. Whereas just a few minutes ago, you were craving ice cream and would have done anything for six scoops of ice cream, you would now gladly give away that last scoop for free.

What's going on here is known as the law of diminishing returns which affects every single one of our desires. Once we get what we want, we simply value it less. This is not to say we seek to get rid of it. Instead, it no longer occupies our minds as much. As you continue to eat the ice cream, the amount of pleasure you receive increases to a certain point, beyond which, it simply stops rising. No amount of additional ice cream can increase that.

This law applies to money as well. Beyond a certain income level, which is usually pegged at 70,000-80,000 USD per year, additional income simply doesn't give you happiness. It does give you pleasure though. This is the first obstacle you need to sort out. A lot of people mistake pleasure for happiness, but they are two completely different things.

Pleasure is the feeling of eating that first scoop of ice cream on a hot day after craving it for so long. It is mercurial and memorable. It also lasts for a very short time. It can hit high peaks but by its very nature, doesn't have a long shelf life. Happiness, on the other hand, is more like your base level of existence. It depends on some very simple things being in place, namely love and security. Shelter, food, and so on fall under the security blanket, but you could place them in separate categories as well.

Money is crucial for these things. It doesn't buy love, but you cannot exhibit your best self without the protection that money provides you with. If you're constantly worrying about how you're going to pay your next bill, always anxious about making ends meet, you're not going to attract too many potential partners to yourself. Thus, money is necessary to a certain point. It is necessary for our basic needs of security, nourishment, and of course, survival. It isn't evil or bad. It is what it is, much like what ice cream is.

How you interpret it depends on your level of balance. The more balanced you are, the truer your interpretation of things. By confusing pleasure with happiness, once people experience the comfort that money provides, and the release from the anxiety that occurs, they start chasing more money thinking that it will bring them more happiness. However, such individuals are merely chasing pleasure. Is it a surprise that these people never find happiness?

Happiness depends on some very simple things, namely, your thoughts. What is it that you think about most of the time? That is the level of your happiness. More specifically, your mindset is what determines your base level of happiness. A scarcity-based mindset, where you think everything is fleeting and that the universe takes more than it gives, will result in you creating this reality for yourself and affirming your beliefs. You will create your own truth.

Happiness depends on you adopting an abundant mindset and thus creating it for yourself. Once your basic needs are met, happiness revolves around how you choose to spend your time. In other words, what is your true purpose, and how closely aligned to it are you? Pursuing that path and realizing your progress along it is what constitutes one of the pillars of true wealth.

Much like pleasure and happiness, money and wealth have the same relationship. Money can be quantified and when you receive it after a long barren spell, it takes you to heights you will relish. However, it will never bring those same heights again once you've ascended them.

Wealth has both qualitative and quantitative aspects to it. Pleasure, happiness, and any positive emotions you experience when living your life are all indicators of wealth — these are things that cannot be quantified, but they can only be felt. Money is the quantitative aspect of wealth such as the experiences we partake in — vacations, nutrition and supplements, wellness products and fitness memberships, books and movies, events we attend, the education we seek, etc., — are all tangible aspects of having wealth. Money is what helps us attain a basic level of comfort and seek newer, expansive experiences, while the feelings we get, the results we achieve (physically, emotionally, mentally) when engaged in those experiences is what constitutes and accounts for our level of happiness and other positive emotions.

Both are necessary and complement each other. By seeing them for what they are, you will be able to adopt a balanced mindset about them. When we confuse wealth and money to be the same thing, we create major imbalances in our life which only lead to us getting rid of our money, given that we turn it into our primary source of unhappiness. Thus, we will also rid ourselves of the security provided by money and become even more miserable.

It all starts with eliminating scarcity.

HOW TO CHANGE YOUR SCARCITY MINDSET

Let's say you and I are eating pieces of a delicious apple pie. Both of us love the pie so we're not experiencing any diminishing returns just yet and before we know it, there's just one piece left. Now, both of us want this piece dearly and all of a sudden, it's you versus me and we've turned adversaries temporarily. All over a piece of pie.

This is exactly how people live their lives, largely speaking. They believe that the world is one large pie and there isn't enough for everyone to go around. If someone takes a larger piece, it means that the rest of us have to be content with smaller pieces. Thus, everyone is an adversary and win-win situations simply don't exist. In order for you to win, someone must lose. Pretty soon, instead of focusing on how you can win, you focus on defeating someone else. Success that is achieved in this manner, if it ever does come, is a slog and grind. There is no purpose to it and it doesn't get you out of bed in the morning.

Once that initial thrill of having bested someone subsides, there's nothing left to drive you forward and life just becomes a series of uninteresting and stressful jousts after another.

Contrast this with an abundant mindset that sees the world as it truly is. In an abundant mindset, the metaphor of the world being one large pie is a fallacy in itself. The rationale behind this is that if we are co-creators of our world and can design our life to be whatever we envision it to be, then how can there ever be a limited supply of anything? Only those who believe that resources are finite will ever believe in such nonsense. In order to live larger lives, you need to simply create it. Believing in your ability to create this is the basis of the abundant mindset.

We grow up around scarcity when we're kids. If you're like most people, you were taught that "money doesn't grow on trees," that in order to come first in your class, someone else needs to come second, and so on. While competition is a good thing and can be healthy to an extent, our school systems turn them into something they were never intended to be: a rat race where we are pitted against each other. The beauty of abundance is that by adopting this mindset, you will create more of it for yourself, since you will manifest what you focus on the most. Focus on scarcity, and you will continue living in that vicious cycle of not having enough. Focus on abundance and how you can create your own opportunities, and you will be presented with more as a result. A crucial step in cultivating an abundant mindset and manifesting your desires is recognizing your power and ability to create and manifest your desires while understanding how energy works. Simply put, you get what you focus on and direct your energy toward.

Go back and read the part about resonance if you're still unsure about how this works and why this is true. Next, commit to improving yourself in small steps every single day. It doesn't matter how small the step is, simply take one to improve yourself and commit to it, every single day. Improving yourself can mean learning a new skill or reinforcing an old one. Keep your mind fresh by giving it a workout and providing it with novelty.

Novelty is a highly underrated tool when it comes to mental development. Exposing your mind to new things will help it navigate change better and will also expand your world considerably. By doing this, you're squarely attacking the idea that the world is a limited place. After all, if there are so many things in the world to learn, how can it ever be limited? Thus, explore ideas and concepts every day that expand your understanding of the world. This is what true self-development is.

Next, study and learn from others' mistakes and successes. The whole world is at your disposal and it functions as a sounding board for your ideas. If you wish to do something, explore whether others have done it and see how it worked out for them. Once our ancestors discovered fire and invented the wheel, there was no need for us to do the same every single time. We simply applied and refined their processes.

Similarly, there have been generations of brilliant women and men who have come before you who have experienced life in much the same manner as you. Seek to learn from them and absorb their learning from the mistakes they made. This way, you can dramatically improve your life since you will be tapping into a higher level of consciousness than just your own when it comes to learning.

One of the mistakes people make is when they realize how truly wonderful the abundant mindset is, they become hard on themselves and admonish themselves for having adopted a scarcity mindset for so long. Don't be too hard on yourself. After all, you're just as entitled to make mistakes as the next person. Learn from this and move on.

Being mindful of your thoughts and actions is a great practice for you to carry out. Practicing mindfulness will keep you rooted in the present, which will help you realize just how abundant the world is. Think about the present moment for a second. It is always there and it has no end. Anything can happen within this.

The past, in contrast, as well as the future is always fixed. It doesn't flow but it ends at a certain point once your projection and imagination runs out. Thus, it is limited. There is no sense of possibility with them since you can only come up with so many scenarios. However, the present moment depends on forces much larger than you and I. The possibilities are endless. If this is not abundance, what is?

Lastly, the most powerful way to develop an abundant mindset is to practice gratitude and altruism, or giving. More than anything else, these two things will guarantee an abundant mindset and true happiness, because of the simple principle: What you give is what you will receive. Let's take a look at this fantastic phenomenon.

GENEROSITY

Buddhist practice always emphasizes the importance of giving. Look around society and you'll often find that the happiest people are those who give back to the community. There is however, a danger of giving for the wrong reasons. Too many people look at charity as a means of inflating their egos and don't give with the right intentions.

The act of giving opens up your mind to abundance more than anything else because it teaches you that you can literally afford to give things away.

In other words, you are prosperous. No matter what problems you think you're dealing with, you can still afford to improve someone else's life.

According to Buddhist thought, the act of giving is far more powerful when it is carried out in favor of someone who is worthy as opposed to someone who doesn't deserve it. Now, this could be misinterpreted to mean that the poorest in society do not deserve charity, which is certainly not the case.

The truth is that determining who deserves charity and who doesn't is a purely personal choice and the motive behind charity should be to feel gratitude and thankfulness — for what you have and how grateful you feel to be able to be a blessing to others and help them better their lives. Your aim should not be something material in this regard.

Gratitude is an important practice for you to follow and quite simply, it is the most positive state of mind you can adopt. By being thankful for your blessings and looking at what you have, as opposed to what you don't have yet, you are further reinforcing the abundance of this world.

The fact of the matter is that human civilization is currently at its peak. In the west, we've never lived longer, had more comfortable lives or technology to aid us. However, we're more miserable than ever. This is solely due to a lack of focus on gratitude. We have it better than large parts of the world, but all we ever focus on is the lack of things or settling political scores.

Ultimately, it all boils down to what you want in your life. Put out positive energy and gratitude, you will receive it back tenfold thanks to the principle of resonance. Always take the time to relax and count your blessings. By blessings, I mean focusing on the positive things in your life despite the multitude of things that may not always be on point.

You'll find that all your problems will soon have solutions and that your life will move forward positively. Give whatever you can, without any need for reciprocation or don't give at all. Focus on feeling good when you give and make this your objective. Remember to differentiate between the fleeting feeling of pleasure and true happiness when you set your objective to give.

The practices for this chapter have already been talked about and explained, but I will sum it up for you here. Simply focus on being *grateful* for what you have and *give more* of what you want to develop *abundance*. With these simple practices you can reprogram your mind to believe that you already have what you want. With this, comes a paradigm shift that changes your external reality to correlate with your internal reality. Stop thinking of what you don't have and begin thinking of all the possibilities that exist for something wonderful to happen in your life.

CHAPTER 9

HOW TO CREATE YOUR BEST LIFE

One of the most powerful techniques you can use to improve your life is to utilize the power of imagination. Too often, those who have powerful imaginations get castigated as daydreamers or as those who aren't realistic. Well, imagination is the key to creation because if you can't see it in your head, you're unlikely to see it in real life.

Think of how popular movie directors go about their work or how artists approach their craft. They first begin by visualizing exactly how whatever it is they wish to produce will look like and how it will feel. Much like a movie or a beautiful picture, you too have the ability to direct your life in this manner.

In this chapter, we will show you exactly how you can do this.

THE POWER OF IMAGINATION

Do you know that your brain has no way to tell what is real and what is imagined? As far as it is concerned, if the visualized picture feels real enough, it adopts it as if it really happened. You see, consciousness and reality can be manipulated by strong visuals and emotions. Think back to some old memories of yours and you will find that while you feel things happened one way, the reality is that things were slightly different.

We tend to believe that whatever we get to experience is reality. However, with enough sensory information about an event added to our mental picture, we will end up experiencing the imagined picture as real as well.

In a nutshell, this is the power of visualization. Your ability to build pictures, which you know are not real but are nonetheless being created with the intention to improve your life is a direct testimony to your ability to be a creator.

Never underestimate the power of your imagination to create worlds for you. Using this tool, you get to experience an entire universe of possibilities, therefore truly freeing yourself since there is nothing and nobody else constraining you, but yourself, inside your head. One of the key indicators of a powerful mental image is its ability to transport you using your other senses.

We all have moments in our lives that have impacted us and shaped us profoundly. These moments create particular imprints on our senses — visual, sensory (taste, smell, sound, touch) or a feeling of some kind. This is one way to imagine and visualize your desired life. Thus far, you're probably just using your ability to imagine as idle daydreaming.

Visualizing pictures without consciously working to attain them is daydreaming. However, once you begin infusing them with the power of your intentions and goals, and practice visualization with discipline and faith, you will see these pictures manifest themselves in the real world. Will they be exactly as what you visualized? Maybe or maybe not. However, there's no denying that the essence of your visualization will come true in your life.

Imagination is integral to the entire process, and it is crucial that you let it roam freely. Use your imagination in a positive manner and watch how your life changes. Most of us are actually experts at imagination, but we simply don't realize it. Think back to when you felt anxious or sad about anything.

Your mind was producing pictures and imagining outcomes that hadn't yet occurred, which resulted in causing you to feel anxious and sad. Thus, instead of using the power of imagination to feel bad, simply turn this around and use it to feel good instead. Construct a life that you want and fill it with images and feelings that you desire.

Imagination also taps into the powerful placebo effect of healing. Simply put, our minds are easily influenced by whatever reality is imposed upon them. Numerous studies have shown that a powerful imagination can speed up recovery after an accident or illness. Imagine both the bird's and the worm's eye view of details in your visualization. This way, you'll fill in the details on all levels and will actively engage with your vision, thereby directing more of your focus towards it.

One of the best ways to utilize your imagination powerfully is by pairing it with a meditation technique.

MEDITATION WITH VISUALIZATION

The benefits of meditation have already been touched upon previously. There are a number of techniques you can use in your meditation practice — pairing meditation with visualization is just one of them. As a matter of fact, there are different ways in which you can use visualization to increase the potency of your meditation practice.

The first technique is to meditate with a focus on liberating the mind from every day worries. All you need to do is practice meditating using your usual technique every day in a disciplined manner. After a period of time, you will find that you will have access to your inner mind and its thoughts.

This inner mind is nothing but the subconscious mind, which is a sum of all of your beliefs as well as knowledge from the heart. When you first gain access to this inner layer, you will start seeing images and visuals in your head, which will guide you in a certain direction in your life. These images can be used as pointers for your next course of action.

Using meditation to clear your mind before your visualization practice is typically a great idea. This way, your mind will be calmer and more focused on the images you wish to create. The way to do this is by meditating as usual but ending your meditation with a visualization. Before meditation, pick a general topic you wish to visualize and create in your life. Fill it with an appropriate level of detail, as you feel. There's no right or wrong level of detail.

Once you've finished meditating, visualize the images in your mind and add as many details as you wish. Focus on making these pictures as real as possible by adding sensory information to these pictures and emotional impact as well. If you're not able to come up with visual imagery, simply use visualization to heal yourself.

Visualize yourself in nature, either a forest or on a hilltop or any natural surroundings which you prefer. Interact with this environment in your mind and note all the sensory information. This way, you will calm yourself and place yourself in a good spot in order to spread the gift of your love.

Your heart is the center of love and joy in your body — visualize it as beaming with golden energy, which is pure love. Imagine this power coursing through your body and then visualize sending this energy to your loved ones or to a destination of your choice via your palms. You can use your imagination to alter the future outcomes of past actions as well.

Once you've finished meditating, run the pictures of the past event in your mind once again. Remember to use as much information as possible and add as much sensory data as possible. Think about what you felt, what sort of touch you experienced, what emotions you felt as the event unfolded, what did other people or things in the picture experience, and so on. Detail is the key to making things as realistic and lifelike as possible.

Now, as you run the pictures in your mind, alter the elements you wish to change. For example, perhaps you reacted in a negative manner to something so now visualize yourself as reacting in the manner you wish you had reacted. Again, feel this new picture as deeply as possible in order to install it completely into your brain.

At first, your brain will likely reject this new picture, but continue doing this and over time you will find that your memory of this event changes completely. Build your pictures in layers and don't be in a rush to fill out your scenes all at once. So don't expect to have fully formed visions in your head after just one session of doing this.

Most of us are accustomed to using this power in a sparing and unconscious manner so it will take time to do so consciously. Fill in the main details and then add some atmosphere or color to the scenery. Next, infuse emotion and finally add the tiny details such as particular actions or the sensory information of certain inanimate elements in the picture.

Meditation will make the entire process easier since you will have a greater ability to focus your mind's energies and create exactly what you want.

MULTI-SENSORY VISUALIZATION

The process of using your senses to make your mental pictures more real might be confusing at first, so it's worth to go into this in a bit more detail. While most people are visually dominant, for some, the other senses might be more impactful. Then, there are certain scenarios that provoke an equal sensory response, other than just that of sight.

For example, if I ask you to visualize a beach, the first thing you probably hear is the sound of waves. Similarly, if I were to ask you to visualize a waterfall, it is the sound of the waterfall, which will likely come to mind at first thought. When visualizing rainfall, it is the touch of the water on your skin or the smell of the earth when the rain first hits that come to your mind.

As you visualize, play around with the various senses you can detect. Paint the original picture visually if necessary, but don't restrict yourself to just the visual image. Sticking with the beach example, your first step might be to paint a picture visually. Imagine the sun on the horizon casting an orange glow over everything as the waves crash onto the sparkling white sand.

You might choose to add people to this scene or leave the beach empty. How about the palm trees lining the beach? Add some hammocks or other accessories as you please. As you're doing this, become aware of the sounds that the waves make. Keep this in your awareness as you visualize this scene.

Next, add the sounds of the birds on the shoreline to your awareness. See them visually and add their chirping to the soundtrack, along with the sounds of the ocean. As you walk along the sand, notice how the sun feels on your skin. Does it feel searingly hot or pleasant and comfortable? Experience how this feels and assimilate this into your overall picture.

Next, become aware of how the sand feels between your toes. The sand probably feels dry and irritating. There might be some stones in there as well. As you get closer to the water, the sand firms up and the feeling of wetness can be detected by your toes. Furthermore, you're closer to the waves now, so the sound of the ocean is much louder and drowns out everything else.

Can you hear the sound of the spray as it washes ashore? It sounds like a hiss as the water recedes back into the ocean. Whether you choose to enter the water or remain ashore and walk along the water's edge, continue adding more sensory input into the picture.

As your ability to handle sensory input grows, start adding other living things into the picture such as other people or animals, and so on. Imagine their behaviors and reactions as your senses record them. Whatever it is you choose to add, remember to focus on how good the picture feels and the swell of positive emotion that is growing within you. This positive emotion should underline everything in your scene at all times.

To some, everything I've just written will seem like common sense, but for those who really struggle with visualization and can't seem to build any power into their pictures, this example will help flesh out a lot of things.

In such cases, I recommend starting small with an equally small intention. Simply visualize walking on the beach and feeling good. That's it.

Don't add anything extra like the sound of the waves or the specifics of your location. Simply feel the sand, hear the sea, and look a few steps ahead as you feel good. Building your picture slowly will get your brain accustomed, and soon, you will be building complex pictures using your mind and even better, having these manifest into reality.

TECHNIQUE #15: MEDITATION AND VISUALIZATION WITH EMOTION

As mentioned before, meditation is a practice that will take your visualization practice to the next level, thanks to its ability to help you minimize mental distractions. There are many meditation practices you can choose to follow. The most common starting point for most people is simply becoming aware of their breath.

While that exercise increases your overall awareness, you can develop your focus by tweaking it a little bit. Start off by relaxing your body and becoming aware of your breath. Once your mind quiets down a bit, count your breaths up to twenty. When reaching twenty, count backwards to one.

The trick is, as you're counting, if you find yourself getting distracted by other thoughts or images that pop into your mind, you need to reset the count. The first time you do this, you'll struggle to get past three, so remember that getting a high count isn't all that important.

What is important is that you simply notice how unfocused your mind can be. Keep persisting and resetting the count. If you manage to get a high number and you've never meditated before, you're probably not aware enough of your mind to begin with so I suggest going back to the breathing exercise to build it up first. Any picture that flashes in your mind's eye or any thought that pops up counts as a distraction where you need to reset the count.

Remain patient with this exercise and don't do this for more than five minutes in the beginning. You will find yourself becoming tired when doing this in the beginning, but keep persisting with it and you'll find that your ability to focus your mind increases exponentially.

The other exercise you can do is simply setting aside some time every day to visualize your future. This is the future that you choose and deeply want and are willing to work toward making it happen. Remember, just like your intention, this picture needs to be measurable in some form so you can identify and know when you're there. This could either be in some material way or as an emotion.

Beware of the dangers of chasing pleasure if you decide to define your goal in terms of material terms. It is far better to set an emotion to your picture and then, just as in the example in the previous section, begin building your picture step by step. The truly powerful visualizations are one where the heart and the brain come together.

Thus, aligning your visualized pictures to your purpose, your intention, and your goals is what will bring it into reality. This is the best way of signaling your intent to the universe and getting yourself vibrating at a more positive frequency in order to attract what it is you desire.

Always feel the positive emotion from the scene since this is what causes you to vibrate on a better plane. The emotion you feel is the most important and when it becomes deep enough and the pictures are real enough, you'll actually see them with your eyes open, either when they manifest around you or when you go about your daily tasks, you'll be able to access that feeling without any problems.

CHAPTER 10

BECOMING FULLY ALIVE

What is the nature of this universe we live in? How do we surrender to its current yet chart our own course? This book thus far has dealt with these questions in detail and now, it is time to take things one step further. You see, to fully commit yourself to the way things ought to be and to extract everything that life has to offer, we need to delve into a few more fundamentals.

Things such as belief and faith, feedback loops from the universe, the power of patience, and lastly dispelling your fear of yourself will be discussed in this chapter.

FAITH AND BELIEF

Anyone who has ever undertaken a trip to the other side of the world, usually places like Indonesia, Thailand, India, etc., has encountered all forms of spiritual awareness. Some of these actually work and are not some elaborate hoax. Spirituality has a religious angle to it, and indeed, every religion seems to start off as a bunch of spiritual beliefs which then get warped into something else entirely, and call for faith.

The call for faith is an interesting phenomenon since in reality, what a lot of religions and people who cling onto dogma demand is belief, not faith. Beliefs are statements that are held as truth and are not allowed to be questioned. Think of how strongly you hold onto your own beliefs about the world and feel uncomfortable every time they are challenged or questioned.

Belief requires you to adopt a narrow mindset of things and stick to a narrow path — a path that hinders growth and expansion. Anything outside this path is simply deemed irrational and wrong. Ironically, a person who believes the most claims to have the highest degree of faith. This is categorically untrue. Faith is the exact opposite of belief. Faith requires you to open your mind and consider a variety of options and to be comfortable with ambiguity, with not knowing which one is right.

While belief demands that you hold onto something — an outcome, a fundamental system, an answer — and never let go, faith demands no such thing. Instead, faith merely asks that you keep an open mind and evaluate things based on your understanding of the truth — an objective truth. An analysis of any religious text will result in this sort of philosophy. However, this doesn't serve the needs of narrow-minded spiritual leaders, and hence, belief and faith are often switched around. Faith is needed at the start of any spiritual practice but should never morph into belief.

This would simply be adopting a position of imbalance in the universe, which, to your own detriment, would soon be corrected and brought to equilibrium thanks to the natural forces of energetic balance. The conflict between science and religion often reflects the misunderstanding that occurs when you have two sides clinging to their own beliefs. No one really wins in such cases since beliefs are self-affirming and are immune to attack, unless the individual who holds these beliefs wishes to change them.

Given that these people have adopted an extremist view, it is unlikely they wish for change, and thus the cycle continues. The truth is that everything is one, and everything exists in one large feedback loop. To say that science is against spirituality is to argue that your leg is against your arm.

The rate of change that is currently occurring in our society on a global level requires us to adopt an attitude of faith. Faith is the willingness to accept whatever comes, no matter what the truth will be. Faith is believing in an abundant universe and in the justification for everything to exist. This is what enables us to live life to the fullest and interact with our environments successfully.

Both our environment and us exist in a feedback loop that impacts us on a daily basis. Given the rate at which our environments are changing, it is natural that we should feel a sense of imbalance, which is only made worse by trying to cling onto beliefs. Let us examine this feedback loop a bit more.

ONTOLOGICAL DESIGNERS

Ontological design is a fancy way of saying that the way our world is designed affects us and that we, in turn, affect the way our world is designed. It goes beyond saying that our environments affect us or that our socio-cultural values, beliefs, and norms affect us. Ontological design takes into account that the feedback loop exists, whereas these latter statements don't.

Taking the example of language, we are born into a particular language and use it to think and to express ourselves. Our ability to enunciate our thoughts depends directly on the language and our beliefs are formed by it as well. In turn, we also modify the language and thus reinforce the feedback loop. A good example of this is how new words come into being to describe phenomena that have sprung into the environment recently.

Prime examples of this are "fake news" and "alternative facts." Both these phrases warp the original meaning of the terms they describe but do a very good job of describing the current information cycle. There are simply too many sources of news to monitor, and there's no way of knowing immediately which one is right and which one is wrong.

Thus, every single fact has now been opened up for questioning, and by doing this, there is a growing movement of irrationality. The flat earth movement is such an example. By simply covering the existence of such people, the movement gains more followers.

Please note that I'm toning down a lot of the heavy philosophy on this topic. If you're interested in this, you can refer to the academic paper written by Anne-Marie Willis. The really interesting bit is to figure out what all of this means. Well, in short, it means that the process of effecting change has transformed.

While change previously was a bottom-up phenomenon, perhaps moving forward, the best way to induce change is to start from within. This form of change starts with a trigger from our environment. In turn, the change, when it manifests, affects our environment and thus the feedback loop perpetuates.

This has significant implications for the design of technology, which has transformed human behavior to an extent never seen before. However, from a more personal standpoint, it means that to manifest a change in your future, you need to interact with your environment and start things in motion. Once this motion begins, your environment will act back upon you, and thus, you will end up realizing your vision.

This is in contrast to the typical advice about manifesting, which proposes that visualization and positivity are all you need and that the universe will bring it to you. Nothing is farther from the truth. You need to go out and engage with your environment and gain feedback in order to move forward.

Thus, when designing your vision for the future, don't start with what sort of an environment you want. Instead, begin with what sort of a person you wish to be and work from there. What sort of qualities do you wish to develop in yourself? How do you wish to interact with the world? By designing your future self, you will end up designing your environment.

In turn, this environment will give you feedback, and as both of you interact with one another, both change and thus, your future self and vision are realized. How soon will this future be realized? Well, the universe works in its own ways and remember, time is not real. We tend to measure everything by clock time and make the mistake of thinking of everything in these terms.

To fully manifest your visions, it is essential for you to adopt faith and to accept whatever comes, while still taking action from an intentional, purposeful place. The key quality to all of this is thus, patience.

PATIENCE

The hardest part of anything is the wait. Time once again plays tricks on us and reminds us of how it isn't real when we're forced to wait for something we want desperately. When you were a kid, waiting to unwrap your presents for the following Christmas morning was intolerable. You couldn't wait for night to be over and wake up the next morning to open up your gifts from under the tree. Odds are, this was the only day you managed to wake up early as well.

The same pattern plays out when you make your choice and then wait for it to manifest. You focus on your intention and carry out the tasks that will take you toward your goals. Then a month goes by. Then another. And nothing changes. You're still in the same place, dealing with the same things and putting up with the same crap that you wish to get away from in the first place.

So what's going on here? Well, first off, when making a choice, a lot of people stumble and choose things they wish to avoid. In other words, instead of wishing to become wealthy, for example, they wish to be "not poor." Choices don't work like that. You see, by choosing the opposite of something, while your language implies a desire to move away from it, your attention is doing the exact opposite.

Think of it this way. When running away from say, a bear in the wilderness, your attention is focused on the bear despite the fact that you're running away from it. This is out of necessity since you need to know where it is and how close it is to you, especially if it's chasing you. However, in situations that are not life-threatening and when dealing with metaphysical realities, focusing your attention on what you don't want doesn't save you from it. It only puts you in a pattern of constantly avoiding it, narrowly.

This is why you should focus on the positive aspect of anything rather than the negative. Avoiding some discomfort is still focusing on the discomfort, and instead of directing that energy toward your solution, you are paying more energy to your obstacle and hence encountering more of that. To illustrate the correct approach, let's use the example of a race car driver.

A fundamental instruction that competitive racers receive is that when the vehicle slides out of control, instead of looking at where the vehicle is headed, look to where you want the vehicle to go instead. Thus, when a car loses grip in a corner and begins to slide towards the wall, you'll always see the driver looking at the corner and not the barrier.

Similarly, when taking a corner, you'll notice that racers never look at the corner but always a few feet ahead of it, at the path they wish to guide their vehicle along. Use the same principle in your life. Always look at where you want to go instead of what you wish to avoid.

If you're doing this properly and you find that the thing you desire still isn't manifesting, then you simply need to wait. Remember that you do not have the full body of knowledge in your sights. You don't know what the universe has planned for you along the path you have chosen, and it is simply a matter of time before you find out.

Your choice is like planting a seed in the soil. Digging up the seed after a week or a month because it is doing nothing, despite you watering and caring for it, is the height of irrationality. Yet, we do this so often in our own lives.

Make your choice and nurture it consistently by maintaining discipline and visualizing your goals. Carry out all your tasks with the right intention, and you'll find that you'll manifest your vision before you know it. The key is to maintain your attention on the journey and not on the goal for the most part. Remain in journey mode and focus on where you wish to go within the next few steps.

This way, you'll cultivate patience automatically and live a purposeful life.

THE JONAH COMPLEX

The story of Jonah from the Bible is one of running away from one's true destiny and the repercussions of that. Now, I'm not pushing a religious angle here, just that it's a great story with a good nugget of wisdom. In case you aren't familiar with it, this is how it goes. God delivers a message to Jonah, a prophet. The message is that Jonah needs to travel to the city of Nineveh and deliver a prophecy of doom should its inhabitants continue along their current path of excess.

Jonah, who abhors Nineveh and considers its doom predestined, resists providing Nineveh's citizens this warning because he wishes to guarantee what he thinks ought to happen. He sails away on a ship to avoid his task, but soon a storm strikes and Jonah is thrown overboard, willingly by his shipmates. He's swallowed by a whale and is transported to dry land where he delivers his prophecy. Much to his surprise, the people of Nineveh repented and escaped destruction.

There are a lot of lessons here but for the purpose of our discussion, let's focus on the ignorance of divine calling and its futility. No matter how much Jonah resists, he is pulled back toward his purpose, and when he does carry it out, he finds greater wisdom than he originally supposed.

Your purpose and you have a similar relationship. A lot of us are afraid or unwilling to carry it out and journey towards it thanks to presupposed ideas often held by those around us. Abraham Maslow observed this effect and mentioned in his works that human beings are often afraid of their own potential. How many of you reading this have it in you to compose the most beautiful musical symphonies? How many of you can change the world and global eradicate poverty?

Answering 'yes' to those questions in the moment is one thing. Constantly believing in it is another. Doubts will creep up, the inner voice will ask "Who, you?" in response to your goals and slowly, but surely, we'll downsize our goals to something more palatable and believable. We'll begin seeking security and comfort which stems from conformity and satisfy ourselves with attaining exactly what everyone else around us wants — what they think is possible for us, what they believe is possible for us — what they themselves desire.

There's nothing wrong in wanting what everyone else desires. Things such as money, comfort, a soul mate, children, and so on. However, these are things that the universe provides to you as long as you set your intentions toward them. Your purpose is usually a very different beast. It scares you because of how grand it is and when you glimpse it, even if for a brief moment, you stand in awe of how inspiring and motivating it is.

That same awe also works in the other direction, pushing you down once the initial feeling subsides because none of us see ourselves as anything close to perfect. We often compare our flaws to other people's perfections. Hence, when we even dare to get a glimpse of the perfect nature of our purpose, we can't help but highlight our flaws. How can someone who barely understands music rival Beethoven, who managed to compose ethereally beautiful and life-changing musical symphonies despite being deaf?

Opening yourself up to your purpose is simply bringing yourself closer to divine energy — an energy we cannot comprehend. You have been placed in the scheme of things with a mission. A mission in which you distribute your gift to the world. Your gift is simply the realization of your purpose. Thus, you owe it to yourself and to the world to pursue it.

So, stop running away from what you were meant to do and who you were meant to be. Go ahead and engage with life to the fullest. Ironically, this is when you'll be the most alive and in greatest touch with who you truly are.

CONCLUSION

How does one live their best life? This has been the underlying topic throughout this book. We began by exploring the true nature of reality and ended by examining how to truly live life at its fullest. The energy that courses through you is the same as what courses through everything else in this world. You are a part of everything as much as everything is a part of you.

Your life is really just a series of choices, and every possible choice is available to you, right now, in this very moment. Much like a tree with infinite branches, you choose your way to the purpose that is important to you. Once your choice is made, sit back and get into journey mode. By journey mode, I mean to say that your focus should be on the everyday tasks and goals you need to implement and achieve in order to bring your journey into fruition.

Along the way, you will encounter obstacles and this is necessary. Everything has a justification for existing and the knowledge that brought the obstacle into reality isn't fully available to us, and neither is it necessary. What is required, however, is a focus on our path and where we wish to go. The universe works through balance, the forces within it will make sure to restore balance wherever there is excess energy being stored and generated.

These forces will usually result in negative consequences for you, so maintaining balance is paramount. Using the power of intentions and goal setting, you can remain on your path and maintain focus on your journey. While it is good to visualize yourself as arriving at your chosen destination, constantly living in the future is like missing the beauty of the entire forest. Much like a train journey through beautiful scenery, if you focus on merely arriving at your destination, you'll miss out on a lot in between. Stop caring so much about your destination and instead know that you will arrive when you need to. Meanwhile, focus on the path you're taking and listen to the universe as it speaks to you.

You may speak with words, but remember, the universe speaks through emotion and intuition. Your heart is your connection to the universe and its wisdom. It has access to infinite intelligence and knows what is best for you. Often, the messages of fear and intuition are confusing. Remember that time does not exist and that fear needs time in order to function.

Examine your feelings, and if you find that they have a dimension of time attached to them, then this is merely your ego driving things. Your ego requires time, and the contrast it provides is so it can function and thrive. Emotional drama, usually negativity, is what nourishes the ego. Press the brakes on it by simply focusing on the present, the now, which is the only moment anyone really has.

The current moment is boundless and exists forever. You need not worry about it coming to an end and can simply focus on what it is you need to do. Intuition lives in the present moment and is accompanied by a feeling of comfort, even if it doesn't always make sense. Listen to it and trust its voice.

Once you achieve synchronicity between your heart and mind, it is time to get out of your own way. Detach yourself from your goals and develop the attitude of faith in everything. Remember to differentiate between the attitudes of faith and belief. Belief is rigid and is simply a product of the ego. Belief requires you to reject faith only asks that you accept if possible.

Faith is an open state of mind and asks for acceptance of things that are beyond our control. Maintaining a state of faith, as opposed to belief, is what will put you in line with the way the universe works. Yield to the path of least resistance which will make itself available to you, thanks to your connection with the infinite. Follow the lead of your intuition and heart.

The relationship between universal laws and quantum physics is well established. Reality exists on a plane that we cannot fully comprehend and it is faith that sustains us as we move along the path of truth. Everything in our universe has an energetic vibration, and in order to achieve resonance with anything, we need to vibrate at its frequency. Thus, in order to change your life, changing your thoughts —which are just vibrations — is essential.

Thought patterns are vibrations we put out into the universe, and the energy we dispel is what we receive in return. Similar to the classical third law of motion in Newtonian physics, every action has an equal and opposite reaction. The effects of this law can be seen in the quantum field as well and in our lives. Striving to live life to the fullest is the only true way to live, embracing the awe it produces within us.

Designing our lives is a matter of changing what is within us and manifesting it in our outer environment. Changing our environment produces an equal change within us, and this relationship exists as a feedback loop. Thus, respecting our environment and engineering it to be as supportive of our cause is crucial. Respect what is around you, and you will find yourself becoming better and bettering it in return. This is the reality of all things and the interconnectedness that exists everywhere.

The purpose of life is to pursue wealth — the wealth of mind, body, spirit, and of course, material wealth. Wealth is a very different thing from money, and understanding the differences is crucial. Remember that nothing, including money, is bad. As chemists often say, it is the dosage that is the difference between medicine and poison. Money provides comfort, but do not mistake it to be a source of happiness. Wealth brings happiness, while excess money brings pleasure. Both are a part of one another and are as necessary as one another. Maintain a balance between this relationship and see your life blossom.

Lastly, remember that you are the supreme creation of the infinite. You are the most evolved and creative of all species of life on this planet. Stop running away from who you are meant to be and live life to the fullest. Engage with that which speaks to you and listen to your heart and trust it infinitely.

REFERENCES

Almeida, F. (2019). Being and Design: Anne-Marie Willis on the hermeneutics of our creations. Retrieved 30 July 2019, from https://www.pantagruelista.com/blogeng/being-and-design

Cho, W. (2017). The Jonah Complex — Fear of your own greatness. Retrieved 30 July 2019, from https://mystudentvoices.com/the-jonah-complex-fear-of-your-own-greatness-47d9e8d41ab5?gi=a514f580acce

Energetic Communication. (2019). Retrieved 6 August 2019, from https://www.heartmath.org/research/science-of-the-heart/energetic-communication/

Fraser, J. (2017). How The Human Body Creates Electromagnetic Fields. Retrieved 30 July 2019, from https://www.forbes.com/sites/quora/2017/11/03/how-the-human-body-creates-electromagnetic-fields/#72add80256ea

How Beliefs Are Formed and How to Change Them. (2019). Retrieved 30 July 2019, from http://www.skilledatlife.com/how-beliefs-are-formed-and-how-to-change-them/

Loeffler, J. (2018). Niels Bohr's Quantum Mechanics and Philosophy of Physics. Retrieved 30 July 2019, from https://interestingengineering.com/niels-bohrs-quantum-mechanics-and-philosophy-of-physics

Medrut, F. (2017). 25 Henry Ford Quotes to Make You Feel Like You Can Achieve Anything | Goalcast. Retrieved 30 July 2019, from https://www.goalcast.com/2017/12/24/henry-ford-quotes/

Munnangi S, Angus LD. Placebo Effect. [Updated 2019 Mar 23]. In: StatPearls [Internet]. Treasure Island (FL): StatPearls Publishing; 2019 Jan- . Available from: https://www.ncbi.nlm.nih.gov/books/NBK513296/

Oppong, T. (2018). Ikigai: The Japanese Secret to a Long and Happy Life Might Just Help You Live a More Fulfilling Life. Retrieved 30 July 2019, from https://medium.com/thrive-global/ikigai-the-japanese-secret-to-a-long-and-happy-life-might-just-help-you-live-a-more-fulfilling-9871d01992b7

Sarah Knapton. (2017). Mothers and babies brain waves synchronize when they gaze at each other, scientists find. Retrieved 30 July 2019, from https://www.telegraph.co.uk/science/2017/11/29/mothers-babies-brainwaves-snychronise-gaze-scientists-find/

Sasson, R. (2019). How Many Thoughts Does Your Mind Think in One Hour?. Retrieved 7 August 2019, from https://www.successconsciousness.com/blog/inner-peace/how-many-thoughts-does-your-mind-think-in-one-hour/

Science of Water. (2019). Retrieved 30 July 2019, from https://www.masaru-emoto.net/en/science-of-messages-from-water/

The Information Interpretation of Quantum Mechanics. (2016). Retrieved 30 July 2019, from http://www.informationphilosopher.com/introduction/physics/interpretation/

Thum, M. (2008). Clock Time vs. Psychological Time. Retrieved 30 July 2019, from https://www.myrkothum.com/the-difference-of-clock-time-and-psychological-time/

THE **MAGIC** OF **MANIFESTING** MONEY

15 Advanced Manifestation Techniques to
Attract Wealth, Success, and Abundance
WITHOUT HARD WORK

Introduction

Does every day seem to bring the same old problems for you? You wake up in the morning dreading how you're going to pay for this month's rent, or how you're going to get rid of that debt that's constantly creeping up on you. You drive to a job you don't like, but keep doing it because it's your only way to put food on the table.

Life, it seems, has you stuck on a hamster wheel where the more you move, the more you remain right in place. Money is one of the biggest issues that everyone in the world faces. To be more accurate, a lack of it is what causes problems. Money might not make us happy, but it sure does make life a whole lot easier.

Thus, naturally, a lack of money seemingly makes everything that much harder. For instance, do you know that people who have less money end up paying more for everything? From overdraft fees on your checking account to higher interest rates caused by poor credit scores. Despite this seemingly being a fact, living like this doesn't have to be your reality.

We're taught from a very young age that money only comes to those that either put in the hard work or are naturally talented. Society has created this construct that limits our potential to achieve financial freedom and abundance. They tell us that getting a college degree is the safest way to succeed in life, then you're told to work your life away as you trade your time for money until you retire at an old age, only to realize you never got the chance to fulfill your dreams or live your life to the fullest.

People see the world of money through a lens that blocks money from coming into their lives. They place limiting beliefs about how money is acquired, and if they don't fit in accordance with these beliefs, then they are destined to lack money for the rest of their lives. But, the truth is, an abundance of money is available to everyone from every walk of life.

You've taken a huge step forward by deciding to read this book. I'm here to tell you that all of these experiences you're going through are temporary. You're going to gain a new perspective around money that will enable you to effortlessly attract it into your life.

Whether you are new to the law of attraction, or a seasoned veteran, this book will have everything you need when it comes to manifesting more money. On top of the new perspectives you'll gain, you'll also be given 15 advanced techniques that are going to help you realize the financial freedom you've always wanted.

We have the power to create an entirely different world for ourselves. Whether you want more money, more prosperity, or whatever strikes you, it's all there to be received.

The idea behind this book is to align your perspective in a way so you never have to do hard work to manifest money ever again. It'll come to your life with more flow and ease than ever before. In other words, you will no longer live as a slave to money. Instead, it'll be like your life companion that helps you strive for your purpose and best life.

Shifting your perspective to this line of thought might seem like it's coming from way out in the left-field at first. After all, we've been so heavily conditioned to believe in the opposite that reading these words might seem like it's too good to be true. If you have any doubts, guess what? You're exactly the kind of person who's in dire need of this book.

Your Biggest Obstacle

How often recently have you woken up with a cold sweat or felt anxious thinking about the future? Have you been asleep, and then out of nowhere, began thinking about a lack of money and then started sweating? Do you begin to feel scared and lose sleep over your bank balance? Does it feel as if you're about to drown in your anxiety?

As unpleasant as it seems, your mind has just created a reality for you. It has rushed into the future, thanks to the way it's conditioned, and has conjured an image that is nightmarish to you. It then convinced you that all of that was real and you began to believe it. Your emotions started to flare up and you started experiencing your future in that exact moment. Once you experienced it fully in your heart and mind, it's only logical for it to show up in your physical reality.

This negative energy you built-up internally is the reason why things never seem to go right externally. You start defining your life based on what your five senses tell you, instead of defining it from within.

There was once a young man who dreamed of being a comedian on the silver screen. He thought he was pretty funny, but hadn't really stood out amongst his peers. His father was a pretty funny guy and loved performing on stage, but didn't have the courage to follow his dreams. The young man grew up watching his father work as an accountant.

He vowed to follow his dreams, since he figured if he was going to fail at something, he might as well fail doing what he loved the most. His career progressed little by little, and despite not setting the stage on fire, he kept believing in what he truly wanted. One day, he wrote himself a check worth $10 million and placed it in his wallet.

I must mention that at the time, the young man had less than $10 in his wallet, let alone $10 million. Despite this, exactly 10 years later, the young man landed a starring role in a major blockbuster movie and got paid $10 million for his services.

This isn't a fictional story. It's the story of how Jim Carrey went from being an obscure Canadian comic to one of the biggest comedic stars of his generation. Carrey is a huge believer in the law of attraction and in having the power to manifest one's own destiny. Given his life story, it's easy to see why; after all, he's living proof that it works.

The universe is abundant and kind. This is something all of us know when we're children. Thanks to the vagaries of growing up and due to the stresses we experience, we forget this information. The knowledge contained in this book will be your stepping stone to unleashing your inner child and wonder.

Human beings are creators, and we have the power to manifest everything we desire into reality. We literally create our own world. Around 200 years ago, people would have laughed at you if you told them that one day we would carry little devices that allowed us to connect with other people who were halfway across the globe, and that we would be able to see their faces and talk to them as if they were right next to us. A person born in the 1800s would not have been able to imagine any of this, and yet, here we are walking around with smartphones. The smartphone was once a dream in someone's mind. It was willed into reality through the power of imagination and belief.

You have the power to create your own reality. Everything you need is already within you. You just haven't been taught how to master it yet. Instead, thanks to external conditioning, you've been busy creating nightmares for yourself. This happens unconsciously because you're simply not aware of the innate potential you have to live a life of financial freedom.

I'm here to show you how to become the master of your reality and get you in touch with the immense power you have contained within you. This is the power of manifestation, the power to create and shift between realities to live in one that is in alignment with your true self. We're born with this power not so we can live in lack, but so we can live in abundance.

Who am I?

My foremost calling in life has been to function as a spiritual consultant. I started off in far more practical circles though. I used to work as a counselor in a government agency. My pay was capped and despite the work being satisfying, it was hard to ignore the lack of freedom in my life.

Stagnation was the word I associated the most with the work, and one day, I decided that I could not ignore my heart's calling anymore. I started seeing my clients after office hours and the satisfaction and financial resources that this act gave me convinced me to quit my job and start my own business.

My mission was to help people live in accordance with their dreams, and to manifest into reality everything they wanted. Whether it was money, a partner, new opportunities, or even something specific like a car or a new home, I was focused on helping them tap into their own creative abilities by aligning them energetically with their desires. These days, I live in a state of complete financial freedom with my family and I cannot recall what it was like to ever worry about money.

My understanding of money for the past 20+ years is that it's abundant. Whenever a situation arises, and a large sum of money is needed, it is present. There were times in the beginning when I didn't have the financial security that I do now, but it didn't matter. Money was still present, despite it not physically being in my bank account. It was just hidden in the opportunities available to me.

I recall a situation like this back in 1989, when I was still living in Japan. I had just graduated from university and began working for the government agency. I always strived to own my own business, so I spent most of my free time acquiring the knowledge necessary through books. Then one day, an old man approached me and offered me consulting services to help me understand the ways of business.

I had a substantial amount of debt at the time from going to university, so it was tough to spend any more on education. Despite this, I still went through with the offer. I thought at the time, "this is the moment I've been waiting for, it's a gift from the universe." However, it didn't work out like that at first.

I was meeting up with him a few times a week to talk about how to strategically move from my regular job to becoming a business owner.

He was someone that had previous success with investing and business opportunities, so I learned quite a lot from him. At the time, Japan was recovering from a huge economic crash, but according to him, it was only a slight bump in the road, or so I thought.

Around 10 weeks into the consulting services, he had to move out of town for a new business opportunity that arose. I felt slightly disappointed, as I had invested quite a lot in him helping me, but I did learn quite a few things about the business world. Despite this, I struggled to make the move out of my job and start the business.

I had more knowledge, but why was I still hesitant to make the move? The truth is, I still struggled with debt, and after these consulting sessions, I had even more. I found myself with more knowledge than I ever had before, yet I was still making the same money.

Was all of that for nothing? Did I put myself in a worse situation than before? I reflected on these questions, then it dawned on me. I was asking the wrong questions.

I had a fair amount of understanding of the laws of life through the spiritual teachings and books I read throughout my younger years, so I decided to apply them here. "What positives can I take from this situation?" and "Where is the opportunity that came from those meetings?" were the new questions I found myself asking.

I started to realize that I didn't need to start a business to make more money. All I needed were more clients. And if I started to see clients outside of my government work, just as that man was seeing me, then I would make more money. This was my "aha" moment.

I began getting referrals from clients I worked with at the government agency, and started working with them outside my office and on the weekends. This was the boost I needed to pay off the debt I had and start saving to launch my business.

The lesson to take from this is that money-making opportunities are indeed available to you. Limiting yourself on how you attract the money will stop you from seeing the infinite universal possibilities that are out there.

I've been where you're at right now, and I completely understand your doubts as to whether all this manifestation and attraction stuff will work. It's ironic, but the only way to truly experience the power of these universal laws is to live it. It requires a leap of faith and only by making this leap can you truly access this power.

Along my journey I figured out what money and wealth really means. We tend to place these things on a pedestal and worship them as if they're holy grails of some kind. Unconsciously, we let these ideas manipulate us into doing things we have no interest in doing. Some of us even sacrifice our morals and happiness for it.

You are not your money, and it is no reflection of you. It was when I finally understood that money and happiness are different things that I began manifesting more of it in my life. Financial abundance occurs when you understand the true nature of money and its function in your life.

The fact is that you don't need to go out and "make" money. What you need to do instead is "allow" it to come to you. If this is hard to understand, don't worry – we're going to cover the art of allowing which is much easier than trying to "make" money.

So, come travel with me as we take an exhilarating journey towards helping you discover financial freedom, wealth, and abundance. Those days of constantly worrying about where money is going to come from are soon going to be banished into the past.

You don't need to conduct "hard work" to attract money to you. You may need to work hard, but this doesn't mean that the work needs to be unenjoyable or soulless. Instead, you're going to learn how to connect with the divine universe that all of us have access to. You're about to embark on a journey of uncovering the truth behind how to manifest money and it's place in the universe.

Are you excited yet?

CHAPTER 1

The Secret Science of Attracting Money

"By being receptive, we can avail ourselves of the spiritual wealth available to us. By being open, we can receive things beyond what we ourselves might imagine."

- Ming-Dao Deng

In order to learn how to attract money, you're going to need to learn all about what money is. This is often a troublesome and an emotionally charged topic. You see, most of us grow up with a ton of misinformation about money. We don't truly understand what it's all about, and thus we walk around with limiting beliefs that stop us from attracting the benefits that come with money.

In many cultures, wealth and money are only something that comes in abundance to those that are of higher social standing. The kings and queens of our past were known for being the wealthiest humans on the planet when it came to money. We've grown to know money as this extremely valuable and limited resource that's incomparable to everything else. However, this isn't the truth. Like everything in the universe, money is just energy.

The only difference money has to everything else we have in our lives is the meaning we put behind it. When this meaning represents everything from freedom, security, and even happiness to some people, it's no wonder the absence of money causes so much emotional and mental turmoil.

The sad fact is that most of these limiting beliefs are carried around in the subconscious part of the brain. Most people would believe that our conscious mind contains all the information we have in our brain when the fact is that it composes less than 10% of our thoughts (Kluger, 2015). The overwhelming majority of our thoughts and behaviors are influenced by neural connections that happen behind the scenes, and most people are completely oblivious to this fact.

Becoming aware of your unconscious thoughts and behaviors is definitely a good first step in the right direction. However, if awareness empties our cup of false knowledge, we need to make sure we refill with truthful wisdom. In other words, awareness alone isn't enough; it needs to be paired with understanding. When we combine the two, our understanding of the reality of money becomes aligned with universal truth, and thus we begin to recognize what it really takes to manifest more of it into our lives.

THE HIDDEN TRUTHS OF MONEY

Back in ancient times, the world was a lot simpler. The average person knew all about the land and the world that surrounded them in a radius of a few square miles.

There was no notion of casual travel, and those that did travel faced perils of an unimaginable character. One of the positives of this small world was that trade was extremely simple. If you wanted rice and had an abundance of clothes, it was pretty simple to find someone who needed clothes and who could give you rice.

In economic terms, this is called the Double Coincidence of Wants. It refers to two people participating in an exchange where both of them have what the other wants. As long as this condition is satisfied, everyone's happy and bartering proceeds smoothly.

As you can imagine, as the world grew bigger and as new goods began making themselves known in the markets, this coincidence of wants began to evaporate. Suddenly, people did not have what the other wanted. A new system of exchange needed to be created, and this is what led to the creation of money.

The first forms of money were simply copper, silver, or gold. What began as a simple medium of exchange has since morphed into an uncontrollable, complex, and manipulative source of energy that differs in perspective from one religion and culture to the next.

Money does make exchange of goods easier. It does give you access to better things in life. These things bring you satisfaction and help ease the burden the world places on you by quite a lot. However, it is merely a source of energy that we've agreed upon this lifetime to use as a form of value exchange. Labeling it as anything else would go against universal truth.

When it comes to manifestation, attachment to any ideas that limit your potential for creation goes against the natural flow of all things. If everything in the universe is infinitely expanding, why does your financial status need to be any different?

Our Connection With Money

The ordinary way people look at money is as a source of accumulation. If I were to give you $10,000 right now, what is the first thing that pops into your head? Do you think about all the bills you could repay, all the debt you could pay down, and how much would be leftover for you to buy fancy clothes or a new TV set?

Or do you simply smile and continue doing what you're doing? The former is a particularly addictive cycle of thought. The limiting beliefs surrounding money convince us that it is an extension of who we are. The more money we have, the more things we can buy, and thus the more value others will see in us. When money becomes the main metric at which people define their identity, all connection with their limitless source is lost.

The power of choice is what frees us. The shape of your perspective around your current financial situation is what will determine your destined reality. When it comes to money, you can view it from one of two places:

lack or abundance. Often, two people can carry out the same action but the perspective behind those actions could be very different.

Let's contrast the perspective of two people who lack the physical accumulation of money in their lives. They visit a jewelry store and see a fancy pair of ear rings. They would love to buy them, but they're already $100 over their spending limit. The first person decides to move on and tells themselves that not being able to buy the ear rings isn't the end of the world.

The second person also decides to not buy the ear rings, but before doing so reminds themselves of how unfortunate they are that they can't afford them. Heaving a sigh, they move on and look at the other things they've bought with a lack of enthusiasm.

The vibrations that radiate from these two people are caused by each person's perspective around their financial situation. While there is a lot more going on here, there's no doubt that the way they deal with the lack of money is what will determine their future reality around it.

You see, money might be a valuable resource in the physical realm but in the non-physical one, it's just energy. It is something that holds a particular vibrational frequency to it. You have a choice when it comes to dictating whether you're in alignment with this frequency or not.

When we look at it from this perspective, doesn't the idea of money feel more relatable? Like it's all of a sudden more accessible to us? Everything in the universe is made up of energy, and all of these energies are interconnected in the quantum field. The quantum field is an invisible energy field containing all of the non-physical electromagnetic information that governs the laws of nature and attraction. The moment you realize that the energy of money is no different from the energy of everything else, you'll begin to manifest more of it into your reality.

The Truth Behind The Value of Money

Central to the economic thesis of money is value. Those that provide others with a ton of perceived value receive their share of money. The value that someone provides is always subjective. Therefore, there is never a concrete definition for how valuable money really is.

For example, let's say a world-renowned chef and restaurant owner created a lottery to see who gets to have dinner with them in one of their finest restaurants for free. During this dinner, they will talk about what it's like to run a restaurant, how they became such an excellent chef, what their most important lessons are, and how they would do it again if they were to start back from zero.

Now let's take a look at two different people that could win this lottery. The first person is the aspiring chef that just started culinary school and has a dream of becoming a popular chef in their hometown and owning their own restaurant. Getting the chance to meet one of their idols would elevate their knowledge of the industry and propel them towards fulfilling their dream.

The other person is a mechanic that can't really distinguish the difference in taste between burger meat at a fast-food restaurant and sirloin steak at a steak house. For him, food is food, and he couldn't care less about what the famous chef has to say.

Notice the difference in perceived value of the lottery prize. For one person, it could be a life-changing experience that they would pay thousands of dollars to partake in. The other has no connection with the chef and finds no value in the experience besides the free food.

The reason why I'm giving you this example is to remove the idea that money has a certain level of value out of your head because, in reality, it doesn't. This just makes it that much more important to get in alignment with your desires and stop worrying about the money itself. If you're unable to radiate perceived value in your service, product, or offer, no amount of actual value will get through to the customer or client, therefore, they won't pay you the money.

In order to create perceived value, you need to understand people's desires. This is what drives the flow of money and exchange. Money is not valuable just because it's money. Money is valuable because it means something for the individual that desires it. For many people, it means freedom, security, comfort, and even happiness. These intrinsic meanings people place behind money is exactly what stops them from manifesting it into their lives.

If you don't have money, does this mean you have no freedom, security, comfort, and happiness? If this is your belief, then this is exactly what will reflect in your reality. If you believe you can have freedom, security, comfort, and happiness regardless if you need money for it or not, then that's exactly what you will experience.

Money is just a tool and it only magnifies what is already present within you. If you happen to be miserable before having a lot money, you're going to be even more miserable after you accumulate it. Money will make it easier for you to be miserable, in fact, you can literally buy your way to more misery!

All in all, focus on the intrinsic value that money can provide for you because this is what puts you in alignment vibrationally with your desires. Placing your focus on the accumulation of a piece of paper will forever keep you out of alignment with your truth.

THE MANIFESTATION OF MONEY

In the last sub-chapter, we talked about two new perspectives on money. The first being that money is energy and its value is nothing more or less than subjective. Now let's talk about where the money (or anything) that you want to manifest comes from.

If you've ever read anything surrounding the law of attraction or manifestation, chances are that you're probably carrying a few incorrect beliefs in your mind as to what these really are and how they work. Many people try to manifest something in their lives and look at this as the process of creating something that doesn't exist.

The very statement "We are creators" implies that you can create using what's already available to you, not that you need to create from scratch. Sometimes our limiting beliefs come about because our language doesn't have adequate words to truly express the intention behind them.

The truth of our existence is that we're currently experiencing a single reality from an infinite number of them. The area of quantum physics isn't fully understood. However, what we do know is that in the quantum scale of things past, present, and future exist all at once.

Niels Bohr was the first scientist to discover and study the behavior of particles that exist in the quantum field (Skibba, 2018). This field refers to particles that are infinitesimally small. Up to that point, physics functioned on the basis of Newtonian laws.

I'm not going to get into the specifics of these laws, since they're beyond the scope of this book. In short, Newtonian physics works because our basic assumption of particles existing in space is that their position can be pinpointed. Think of a large planet of the solar system. In space, it is possible to point to it and say that it exists.

However, these large bodies are composed of much smaller particles. As we begin to dive deeper into their structure, we begin to see that Newtonian physics breaks down. Bohr observed that the deeper one goes into the structure of things, the more one finds the existence of vibration.

Atoms, molecules, and various subatomic particles vibrate constantly. They vibrate so fast that they exist in multiple places all at once. Think of a rubber band that has been stretched. If you were to pull one of the bands and let it go, the band will begin vibrating. Watch the band closely and you will see that it vibrates so quickly that it seems to exist in two places at once.

Now imagine a subatomic particle vibrating at speeds a million times faster than this. Now consider that our bodies and everything else we see in front of us are composed of these vibrating particles. In short, we appear solid but actually aren't. We're just a huge mass of vibrating particles that are present in different points all at once.

The Field

If we're a mass of vibrating subatomic particles, this means we're presently experiencing multiple realities at once. Our brains are receiving one of these realities, but the truth is that our perception is just one small part of an infinite number of realities. Through the power of choice, we can choose to perceive another reality that is just as valid as the one we choose to ignore.

There is a simultaneous reality where you have all the money you want and are living the life you desire. There is one where you don't have everything you desire but have enough money. There is one where you're even worse off than you are now. Through the power of choice, we perceive these different realities and bring them into our current existence.

This is what manifestation and attraction is. We can only bring into reality things that already exist. The money you seek is already out there. The past, present, and future all exist simultaneously in the present moment. By harnessing your power to focus, which is really a power of choice, you create your present reality.

The holocaust remains one of the most evil acts perpetrated by human beings upon one another. The famous psychologist Viktor Frankl was a survivor, and in his book, he recalls observing something curious about all of his fellow survivors (Frankl, 1992). Frankl initially put his escape and that of his fellow inmates down to blind luck.

However, he noticed that everyone who escaped their horrors believed deep down that they were meant to survive, that their life meant something, and that they would make it out of hell. He does not discount the role luck played, but he concludes that without this belief that they will survive, without the choice to focus on this instead of the horrors that were playing themselves out around them, none of them would have made it out alive.

Even in the worst of times, you have a choice. When it comes to money, you can always choose to focus what is already existing in another version of your reality. This isn't about creating wealth in your life. It's about shifting your focus to the wealth that is already present in your life.

That is what true manifestation is; it's a subtle shift in mindset that you need to carry out in order to be successful. There is infinite potential in the field. We can't perceive it because our minds are not designed or haven't evolved enough to be able to comprehend multiple realities at once.

We're still slaves to time and live according to the clock. However, the reality of the universe is that time is not real. According to Einstein's theory of relativity, a person who travels through space at the speed of light will experience time very differently from someone back on earth (Redd, 2017).

You don't need to be a student of physics to understand this. Think back to the moment when you were completely absorbed in what you were doing. You weren't thinking consciously but were simply being. It could have been when you were doing something you love or when you were watching a TV show you enjoy.

Did time exist? Were you conscious of how the clock was moving? Did you look up at the clock and think how did time fly by so quickly? Alternatively, did you look at everything you managed to get done and realize that time had barely passed? That you had completed an hour's worth of work in 15 minutes?

Time is elastic and depends on our perception. It is simply a dimension of our world, much like distance is. You could be on the other side of the planet from someone you love and still be close to them. You could stand on the ground and look at the distance between two points as being large. Or you could stand on top of a building and watch that distance shrink to nothing.

Focus is what matters. Choice is how we exercise focus, and this moves us into different realities that already exist. Manifestation is simply a process of exercising our choice to move into these infinite realities and realizing all the positives and negatives inherent in each reality.

If you choose to live with wealth, don't sit around waiting for it to manifest. Instead, be someone who has wealth. Live according to this reality. I'm not saying you should start going out and spending your money unscrupulously. This is not what defines wealth. Wealth is the recognition that you have an abundance of resources at your disposal. Choosing to live in this reality will inevitably open your eyes to opportunities, partnerships, and people that contain within them hidden money miracles.

THE REALITY LOOP

Once you start making better choices you will begin to see that your life, indeed everyone's lives, exists in a loop. This loop keeps moving us between our perceptions, emotions, and actions. This reality loop is what defines the universal framework within which we experience our lives.

Henry Ford once said that if you think you can or if you think you can't, you're absolutely right. This quote is profound in many ways and hints at how the reality loop works. Given that it's a loop, it can be tough to figure out where to begin analyzing it. Let us start with our current physical reality.

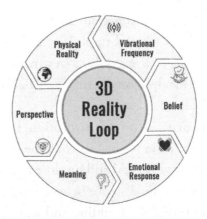

Current Physical Reality

This is your everyday life. It is your current reality that has sprung from the way you've been conditioned thus far. Our physical reality is shaped by our beliefs about our world and also influences how we continue to think, feel, and act.

Perspective

Everyone's perspective of reality is slightly different from one another, even if you've lived similar lives. We are all a unique expression of the universe, therefore no two people will perceive of something in the exact same way. Words can never describe the differences you can find in each person's perspective. The only way to understand what someone is thinking, feeling, and perceiving is by being that person. The key here is to create a perspective that benefits you in your own unique situation. This is what we will be focusing on throughout this book.

Meaning

Before physical manifestation changes your beliefs, you unconsciously place a meaning onto it based on the perspective that you have. You define the world in a certain way based on how you were taught to view it while growing up. How you see things is how you define them. If you look at a box head-on, you will see a square. If you tilt your point of view, you will see a cube. Perspective is simply another word for choice. Your power of choice is an essential part of shifting your reality around money. You can choose to hold onto the meaning you place on things or you can choose to change its meaning, simply by changing how you look at it.

Emotional Response

In this section of the reality loop your inner being, the essence of who you really are, is processing what is going on in your brain. In other words, it's considering whether your true self is in alignment with the thoughts and perspectives that you have. In the case where your thoughts are limiting and self-sabotaging, you will feel negative emotions. If your thoughts and perspectives reinforce the inner guide within you, you'll feel positive emotions, and thus you'll be living in alignment and with more flow.

Beliefs

Beliefs are nothing but thoughts that have been engraved in our brain over time by our emotions. They are solidified ideas that have been strengthened over and over again based on our emotional response to the perspectives we have and the meanings we put onto our physical reality. When we receive confirmation of these beliefs, they become stronger as time goes on. Beliefs are hard to challenge because they are usually attached to an egoic identity. To go against a belief is to go against the identity that resonates with such belief. Although they are difficult to change, it is not impossible.

Vibrational Frequency

You've already learned how all of us are vibrational beings. We're made up of atoms and subatomic particles that vibrate at certain frequencies. Our thoughts and emotions create our unique vibrational signature. This is the section of the reality loop that is responsible for attracting the physical manifestations of our desires into our lives. However, our vibration can only shift once our beliefs about our physical reality and the meanings we give it change.

Physical Manifestation

Your vibrational frequency helps you move from one reality to another. In the field, everything is vibrating, and infinite realities are already present. The way to physically move from one reality into another is to vibrate at its frequency. This is according to a law in physics called resonance.

Resonance is a phenomenon where an object can be induced into movement by placing it close to something else that is vibrating at its natural frequency. For example, a bridge that runs between two points has a natural vibrational frequency. When armies march over bridges, they are ordered to break march and to walk in an unsynchronized pattern. This is because the boots marching at the same frequency as the bridge have the potential to trigger it to collapse.

One of the most notorious bridge disasters in the United States occurred when the Tacoma Narrows bridge in Washington began to twist and turn all by itself. This happened because the wind was vibrating at a frequency that was equal to the resonant frequency of the bridge. Thus, the bridge began moving of its own accord and ended up twisting itself out of shape and collapsing.

In order to manifest a reality, you have to vibrate at its resonant frequency. When you do this with your desired one, synchronicities and opportunities start to show up. It will be unexpected, hidden, and often very difficult to recognize. This is why awareness and focus is so important. If you're focused on your desired manifestations, you'll notice them when they appear.

Reinforced Beliefs

Now that your reality is beginning to change, your beliefs are starting to shift. This is how reality reinforces itself, and why it can seem as if you're stuck in a never-ending financial struggle. It is also why when good things happen to you, they seem to happen continuously as if you're on a roll. This repeated cycle creates what's called momentum.

Limiting beliefs will create a limited reality. These internal beliefs will constantly be reinforced because of what's being confirmed in external reality. This is why breaking free of this momentum is so difficult. Once you start thinking limitlessly, your reality will test you. It will reflect back to you the beliefs and vibrations of your old identity.

One way to break free from this is to recognize that physical manifestations have a delay. In other words, your desired reality will most of the time not manifest instantly. You need to walk past a couple of realities that were a reflection of the old you, before you begin to experience reflections of the new you. We'll talk more about this in the next chapter.

For now, recognize that walking into different realities takes place only in the present moment. If you're operating from the past, you will never take the right steps into the reality you desire. Be present with your beliefs and perspectives, recognize the existence of infinite realities, and begin shifting yourself from within so you can begin thinking, feeling, and acting in accordance to the new reality you want to experience.

CHAPTER 2

The Hidden Money Blocks Stopping You From Financial Freedom

"We are kept from our goals, not by obstacles,
but by a clear path to a lesser goal."

- **Robert Breault**

Now that you've learned about reality loops and how manifestation truly works, you might be wondering, why is it so hard to shift your reality? Why does your brain and body fight back and not assist you with the process? The fact is that all of us have hidden blocks that prevent us from manifesting our dreams and alternate realities.

Some of these blocks occur due to poor conditioning. Everybody was raised a certain way, experienced certain traumas, and lived through many ups and downs in their lives. Our minds and emotions picked up on everything we've experienced. Most people are unconsciously carrying years of baggage that goes unnoticed most of the time, but influences our decisions and feelings on a daily basis. This has a tremendous effect on our perspective, beliefs, vibration, and as a result, the reality we experience.

There are three specific roadblocks that stop you from harnessing the true power of manifestation. These are:

1. Negative emotions
2. Scarcity mindset
3. Old patterns

All of these are connected to one another, and form a tangled web of limitations that keeps you trapped in the same reality that you wish to exit. They also come together to convince you that the only true reality that exists is the one in which you're in right now.

As humans, we were naturally born with a high vibrational frequency. Our purest form is seen in our younger years. When we were kids, we felt no shame or guilt for who we were because we hadn't yet built a false identity to fit into the expectations of society. We used to dream big and never had any limitations for what was possible. This is when we were *unconditioned* by external reality. In other words, before we were conditioned by our parents, teachers, friends, media and other external entities, we were unlimited in our thinking – unhindered by thoughts and beliefs of limitation. As we grew up, this way of being changed.

Negative emotions and thoughts are linked with circumstances and traumas that you may have experienced in the past. As you go through these experiences you start to develop a false identity, as well as beliefs that confirm the importance and existence of those events. You start to resonate vibrationally with these events because if you can sense it with your five senses, then it must be true and it must be what defines you. This is a faulty way of thinking.

As we've discussed in the previous chapter, you have the power to choose a new reality that no longer resonates with the old ones you've experienced. Your identity is flexible for change and not permanent to one way of being. This process is often difficult because it goes against the old identity that is constantly trying to confirm its existence through what you see in the physical reality. The goal is to become aware of these negative emotions, thoughts, and patterns, then shift the perspective around them in order to begin breeding a new sense of self that no longer resonates with the poverty mentality, limited ways of thinking, and impulsive reactive behaviors that are out of alignment with who you want to become.

NEGATIVE EMOTIONS

Our emotions play a fundamental role in manifesting the reality we want to experience. Emotions come in a multitude of flavors but can break down into just two: positive and negative. While no one has a problem with positive emotions, negative emotions are a different subject. Most people turn to the law of attraction and try to manifest a new reality as a means of getting rid of negative emotion.

However, in doing this they misunderstand one of the fundamental truths about the universe: the quantum field and the universe exist in a state of vibration. The things that vibrate at similar frequencies attract one another. Negative emotions are responsible for generating your vibration. So manifesting under negative emotion will only lead to more negative emotion.

Negative emotions such as sadness, frustration and anger rise due to a fundamental misalignment between where you currently are and where you want to be. This is called contradicting energy. Contradictions in energy create resistance, and resistance creates tension, stress, and stagnation.

As we've mentioned before, your natural and unconditioned self already operates at a high vibrational frequency, meaning it already knows how to feel good and what it wants. The problem comes when conditioned mental filters start limiting the potential our inner being is wanting so eagerly to express. Whenever you're misaligned with your inner being, negative emotions will inevitably come as a result. This is why working at a job you're not passionate about doesn't feel good and creates a lot of resistance.

When you are conditioned to think that money is scarce, your resources are limited, and your potential is small, it obviously doesn't feel good because your inner being believes the complete opposite. However, we stand behind these beliefs because it allows us to conform to the expectations and reality of other people. Our human instinct is to follow the tribe and fit in with everyone else. If you start thinking big and feeling abundant, most people around you will start to question your beliefs because it questions theirs. This can sometimes make you feel lonely, which can lead to yet another negative emotion if you allow it to.

The key to mastering your negative emotions is to take them as feedback from the universe. If you're feeling frustrated, sad, or doubtful in your ability to manifest money, your focus is simply misaligned. Instead of labeling them as something bad, use them as a reminder that you're an infinite spiritual being veering off track from your purpose and fulfillment. Much like a GPS notification that goes off when you drive down the wrong road, negative emotions are simply guide rails. Mistake them for being something greater and you will plunge yourself into a negative spiral, taking you into a greater state of energy contradiction between your egoic and spiritual self.

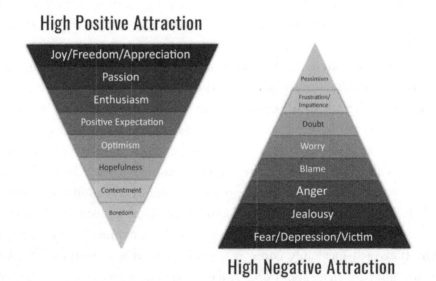

The good news is that if emotions can spiral negatively, they can do so positively as well.

For example, if a situation arises at work where someone loses a client or they receive negative complaints from a customer, the natural response for people with misaligned thoughts and patterns is to see it as a negative. They start thinking that the business is going downhill and they start to expect more to come. These are feelings of guilt or unworthiness that rank really low on the emotional scale.

When someone has aligned thoughts and patterns, they'll take this negative situation and turn it into a positive one. They'll start asking questions like "How did this happen?" which reflects feelings of disappointment and frustration. Then they might ask "How can we prevent this from happening in the future?" which reflects feelings of hopefulness and optimism. This is how you slowly raise your vibration given a negative circumstance that occurred in your life.

Focus on moving up the emotional scale one step at a time and don't ignore or think of negative emotions as being invalid. Instead, accept them and work to reduce their degree by consciously choosing to feel better. Aim for just one emotional feeling notch above what you feel and slowly work your way up.

SCARCITY MINDSET

Why are we so attached to limiting beliefs? Why are we so attracted to negativity in the news, in our relationships, and in our lives? The reason is that the brain has learned of the pleasure that a scarcity mindset brings. It seems odd to use the word pleasure in conjunction with something negative, but it's true. You will not engage in any behavior that you don't find pleasurable. Like a masochist, you've trained your brain to derive pleasure from negativity.

Scarcity is the idea that there isn't enough to go around. The focus is more on "taking" rather than "giving." This mindset not only cuts off the perspective of abundance, but it also causes us to make rash decisions and not see the decisions that are available and more in line with what we want. We're always looking for the path of instant gratification.

An example of this is gambling. Instead of recognizing that we have the potential to create our own wealth and abundance, we look for quick fixes and pleasures. This usually leads to disappointment because these quick fixes and pleasures are never sustainable. Money will only come and stay with those who recognize their own abundance in their lives. If you don't recognize the abundance of money, you will never attract it or have it for too long.

Being the Victim

It's easy to want to think of ourselves as a victim. If we're powerless to change our situation, then obviously there's nothing we can do. We're not to blame for our lives. It's all someone else's fault. If we didn't try our best in some situations then it was because of excuses A, B, and C.

Spend too long being a victim and you will forget that you're the creator of your reality. When positive emotions do come up, we don't allow them to stay too long. Why? Because they don't match with our physical reality. This is the contradicting energy that we talked about before.

Take the case of someone offering a service to you for free. You may take it as a sign of abundance, or you can look at it as a sign that someone is trying to convince you of something. This kind of mentality blocks out opportunities because it frames them from a perspective of lack. You view it from an identity that's not aligned with an abundant mindset.

Perhaps the person offering you something for free wants something from you, and is trying to manipulate you into doing something. Sometimes, people inject large doses of negativity into situations and end up hurting those around them even when everything was positive.

The scarcity mindset is particularly insidious because it's so convincing. It has the most rational and logical arguments, and so there's no denying its claims. The only way to beat it is to be irrational. Or, seemingly irrational. In a bad situation, this means focusing on the positives or hanging onto your belief that everything will work out. You might not know how or might not know when the tide will turn. You just know it will.

Many people who try to practice the law of attraction end up validating their scarcity mindset. The reason you picked up this book is because you're feeling a lack of money in your life. If you were to try to manifest money from such a place, you will only end up manifesting more lack.

Instead, you need to first believe and educate your mind to the wonders of abundance in this world. This is why I made it a point to emphasize in the previous chapter that the money you need is already here. All you need to do is align yourself with the possibility of you manifesting what money can bring you. You don't need to know about the how, what, where, and when just yet.

OLD PATTERNS

The reason people continue repeating the same acts, feeling the same emotions, and thinking the same thoughts is because they've become accustomed to it. Doing what you've always done your whole life is a lot easier than striving for change. With change, comes more challenges than you already face, new obstacles to overcome, and resistance from outside forces. If change was easy, everybody would be living their best life, but that's far from the case.

Our brains are very receptive when we're children and at that age, they don't discriminate between the information that they receive. We're completely dependent on our parents and caregivers at that age and we don't question their words; we simply absorb and mimic everything they tell us. This is a survival mechanism that has kept humans going for centuries. Little do parents know, their bad habits are rubbing off on their kids, even if they have the best of intentions.

As we grow up we begin to discern between good and bad information and exercise a great degree of control over what thoughts are worth thinking. This is the journey we all know as personal development. However, despite our best efforts, the initial information that embedded itself in our minds during our younger years is still present and colors everything we do. It is these patterns that often end up sabotaging us when we least expect them to. Our environment and experiences have an inordinate amount of influence in who we are and strive to become.

The subconscious mind is the storeroom for all of our unconscious beliefs, behaviors, and habits. This is also known as our paradigm. A paradigm is simply a collection of beliefs about who you think you are and your perspective on your life.

If you grew up in a low-income household, chances are you probably developed a scarcity and limited mindset. However, people are unpredictable beings. Some of us use this as fuel to redefine our destiny and strive for greatness whilst others continue the path their parents and guardians followed. A former client of mine, let's call him Tom, grew up in a household where money was scarce. He developed a paradigm that defined himself as a poor person.

It seemingly didn't matter whether he was earning a lot of money or earning too little. Tom was always financially broken. The money he did earn disappeared faster than he knew what to do with it. It wasn't in his identity to have too much money in his possession. It was uncomfortable for him to have money because the idea wasn't aligning with his beliefs.

You might have developed paradigms surrounding what it takes to earn money. Perhaps you believe that you need to do hard work, graduate from the best college, find yourself a great job, and so on. Religion might have caused you to develop beliefs that money is the root of all evil.

These paradigms have huge control over us because they speak to our desire to fit in and be a part of a community. Unfortunately, our mind often mistakes poverty and lack as being the markers of a community that fits us perfectly. This is often why most poor people remain poor and most rich people remain rich.

This kind of cultural conditioning creates a false sense of self, also known as our ego. It's merely a pattern of artificial reactions and habits that other people have taught us to embody.

Building awareness around your current paradigm is essential if you want to shift into a new one. If you're not self-aware, you're vulnerable to external influences that have nothing to do with your point of attraction. Your mind is both the only problem and the only solution in your journey to manifesting financial abundance.

Forcefully trying to convince your mind to make the shift in your perspectives and beliefs will never work. Our brains are way too smart for that. They're built like this solely due to survival purposes. If they weren't so glued to the instinct of fear, avoidance, and familiarity, humans would have been extinct a long time ago. The thing is, we're in the 21st century now. These instincts are hardly ever beneficial and are mostly detrimental.

Instead of trying to convince your mind to think differently, try proving to it that what you want to accomplish is possible. You can only do this by stepping into the unknown. If you're constantly in the known, you will only be showing your brain what it already knows, and thus nothing will change.

To start making the shift, step into unfamiliar territory by surrounding yourself with more successful people, start doing the things these people do, and start optimizing your environment to show your brain what's possible for you. Gain new perspective, place new meanings on your reality, feel the emotion that comes with this, engrave these thoughts and emotions in your mind until you have fully embodied the experience of being the new you, and let the universe take care of your external reality to fit this new identity.

HEALING YOUR RELATIONSHIP WITH MONEY

The process of reprogramming yourself to think differently is the same as healing your relationship with money. The interesting thing is that your relationship with money often reflects your relationship with yourself. Reality is simply a reflection of how we think about ourselves and the outside world. If you've identified with thoughts of lack or scarcity, then it's inevitable that you will experience this in your life. Using money to form a sense of self-worth indicates a fraught relationship between you and your perception of who you are.

It's the scarcity mindset expressing itself through your perception of a lack of money in your life. If you're completely happy with who you are and are living the life you want, would you ever think about money or the lack of it? It's only the things that are wrong in our life that we spend time pondering over.

Instead of pondering over lack, we need to retrain our minds to focus on what is present in our lives. You might not be rolling around in money, but do you have something in your life to be thankful for? Of course you do! The very fact that you're made up of the same energy that makes the world go round should be something to be thankful for. This gives you power.

Know this: All the fears that you have regarding money are simply an illusion. These fears have been ingrained deeply into your subconscious mind, and are dictating your perception of reality. It is limiting you to think only inside of a closed box. Little do you know, you have the potential to break free from this cubicle that life has put you in and strive for a life of great financial success and abundance.

The greatest perspective you can have around money is the perspective of your inner being. Since your inner being cannot be changed or altered, the only thing you need to do is focus on removing the illusions that are placed on top of it.

The process of healing your relationship with money isn't one of addition; instead, it is one of subtraction. You need to chip away at those limiting thoughts, old beliefs, and conditioned paradigms that are keeping you rooted at the wrong end of the emotional scale. Empty your cup first before you fill it up with new life.

The spiritual being that lies deep within you is naturally abundant and knows everything it needs to know. You've inadvertently been covering it up with negative filters and false beliefs. Remove these and your inner self will naturally come to light. This will allow you to display your creativity and energy in full flow, and money and prosperity will come rushing to you as a result. Once you begin the process of destroying these filters, you will be amazed at how abundant and replete with opportunity the world truly is.

Now that we have covered how negative emotions, old patterns, and limiting beliefs can hinder you from attracting the financial abundance you want to manifest into your life, let's finally get into the 15 techniques that will help you get there.

TECHNIQUE #1: FENG SHUI FOR MANIFESTATION

For the first technique, I'd like to introduce the idea of Feng Shui. This ancient practice originated in China over 6,000 years ago. The word roughly translates to the English word "Geomancy," however, the words individually translate to "Wind" (Feng) and "Water" (Shui).

The original idea behind this technique is to bring about happiness, harmony, and alignment in areas where family, friends, and workers reside. This can include, but is not limited to, your living room, bedroom, co-working space, office, or even your bathroom. The idea is to rearrange the items and furniture in relations to the flow of natural energy (Qi). Characteristics such as color, material, framework, and structure are also taken under consideration. The practice and methods of Feng Shui were hidden for many years from the public eye and were strictly known only by nobles and government officials.

Lucky for us, we have access to these ancient secrets. But how does this work to help us manifest money? Since we've learned in the last two chapters that money is energy and old patterns are the reason for our "stuckness" financially, wouldn't it make sense to rearrange the items and furniture in our home to align with this new idea of abundance and wealth? Do you think the rich man/woman across the street keeps their house messy, dirty, and void of natural light? If we're going to align ourselves with the energy of riches, aligning the items around us can serve to not only declutter our mind of scattered energy, but also build a new environment where new energies can thrive. The changes do not need to be drastic (buying new furniture or moving out) and they also don't need to be too specific (buying crystals, Chinese coins, or expensive decorations).

Here are my steps to reaching optimal Feng Shui for manifesting money:

Step 1: Clear out or cover up all of your broken items.

Step 2: Keep things organized and in their place. Scattered items equal scattered energy.

Step 3: Open up and clear the space. Move big items toward the walls or get rid of them. Give space to allow the energy to flow.

Step 4: Invite nature to take part. Open up to natural sunlight and keep a plant or two around.

Step 5: Implement the Money Jar Method. This process requires you to get however many jars you'd like (ideally 3-5) for all the places you frequent the most throughout the day. Label each of these jars with a phrase such as "I am abundant in money and in wealth" or "I am connected to infinite money abundance." Fill these jars with real money, checks, and symbols of wealth, and let your subconscious mind do the rest. Every time you notice the jar, you're reminded of your abundance.

TECHNIQUE #2: GENERALIZATION TECHNIQUE

For this next technique, inspired by Abraham-Hicks, we're going to be touching upon the negative emotions you have around money. Whether this be anxiety around your next bill payment, depression due to the lack of financial freedom, or jealousy of fellow coworkers or friends that are having some success.

The idea behind the generalization technique is to generalize these negative emotions. In other words, you do not need to give them a specific meaning. Giving meaning to negative emotions creates attachment. When you create attachment, you get stuck with them. This can create negative momentum that spirals out of control. What ends up happening is you end up manifesting your misery. More money problems start to pop up and thus the cycle continues.

Generalizing your negative emotions will slow down this momentum, giving you the power to respond in a more proactive manner that's more in alignment with how you want to feel. When you focus on the emotion itself rather than on the story that created it, you will find it easier to shift into a more positive state. Consider doing it in this order:

Step 1: Accept the current circumstances that may have caused these negative emotions to arise. Acknowledge that these negative emotions are present and be aware of how they make you feel.

Step 2: Take these negative emotions as a sign that your beliefs are out of alignment with what you want to attract. If you're feeling worried or jealous, it's because you're operating from a state of lack. View these feelings as an important wakeup call that helps you come to the realization that you need to shift your focus.

Step 3: Generalize the negative emotion and slowly begin to move up the emotional scale one step at a time. For example: Move from worried → overwhelmed → bored → content → hopeful → enthusiastic → joyful.

For example, if you're constantly *worried* about how you're going to pay the bills, choose a slightly better feeling vibration such as *overwhelm*. Feeling overwhelmed from the extra work you might have to indulge in is a higher vibrational feeling than worry. The goal here is to gradually work your way up the emotional scale. Generalize it even more by not labeling the extra work as something negative or positive. Instead, recognize it just for what it is, extra work. Be *content* that you have the opportunity to indulge in this work. It's not the best thing in the world, but it's not too bad either. You might be learning something new or helping other people with their problems. As you begin embracing the extra work, you start realizing that you're about to earn enough to pay off your bills. Your first paycheck comes in and now you're *enthusiastic* about finishing it all up. Finally, you're *joyful* for the fact that you were able to pull it off and pay your bills on time. This is how you slowly shift your perspective and vibration. Take it one step at a time.

TECHNIQUE #3:
TUNING INTO FREEDOM

For the final technique of this chapter, inspired by Nick Breau, I'll be introducing to you the vibration of freedom. What is the first thing that comes to mind when you think about an abundance of money? For most people, it usually includes never having to worry about finances, living wherever you want to live, having the choice to purchase from the highest quality products or services, feeling empowered, and always having enough to help and support those in need.

These thoughts, ideas, and feelings all correlate to the vibration of freedom. What we truly want is not the money, but the freedom that it gives us. In order to tap into the vibration of abundance, we need to start tuning into freedom.

Start being aware of the freedom that you currently have in your life, even if it's the smallest of things. Practice consciously tuning into this vibration and it will carry over to your finances. For example, you have the freedom to go take a walk outside, to eat the food that you eat, to have the things that you have, and to do the things that you do. Tap into the vibration of freedom and you will start noticing more freedom in the form of money coming your way.

CHAPTER 3

A Broke Millionaire's Mindset

"If you change the way you look at things, the things you look at change."
- Dr. Wayne Dyer

One of the things that most people stumble upon is the thought that their dreams don't match their reality. They practice the law of attraction, mindfulness, and all sorts of techniques, yet they still seem to get the same results. This leads them to doubt their potential and the infinite abundance that's available to each and every one of us.

They carry this feeling of doubt throughout all areas of their lives and as a result end up sabotaging themselves. Their old selves start to confirm their doubts by having a third dimensional perspective of their life. In other words, they're not operating from the quantum field, but from physical reality.

This tragedy plays out over and over again. Such people often attend tons of personal development courses and seminars, and read all the information that is out there on the topic. They think they're *doing* something wrong, but the truth is their *identity* is not where it needs to be.

As I've already mentioned, choice and recognizing your power to direct it is critical for your success. Most people adopt a powerless position upon entering the world of self-help and aren't willing to let go of the victim mentality. However, the truth is that this is just one reality of existence. You have the power to choose another reality and live according to it.

Your mindset determines how long you will exist in that reality. When you make the decision to change your beliefs and perspectives, your old identity is going to do its best to pull you back. After all, you're comfortable there. Your brain knows what to expect and there are no surprises. A lack of surprises means the brain can function on autopilot and doesn't have to expend much effort, even if it causes you misery.

In order to ensure you remain in the identity that conforms to your new life, you need to train your mind to think differently. So how do you do this? Well, this is what I'm going to teach you in this chapter. It might be titled "The Broke Millionaire's Mindset," but the attitude is anything but broke!

THE ABUNDANT MINDSET

Your mindset determines your world. This much is true. The universe's sole mission is to deliver to you exactly what you want, and your mindset is a reflection of whether you're allowing this to happen or not. Many people use their words in a positive manner and think that this qualifies as communication with the infinite consciousness that is the universe.

However, the universe listens to more than just your thoughts and emotions. In fact, this is where most people get it wrong. You can think the right thoughts and feel the right emotions at certain moments, but if you're not *embodying* the combination of the two, you're not undergoing a real and sustainable transformation. These positive thoughts and emotions should be your new normal. An abundant mindset is the realization that the universe is capable of manifesting anything you want. All it takes is for you to become aware of it.

Infinite Realities and the Receiving Mode

You've learned about the presence of infinite realities from Chapter 1. You've learned how the universe functions on the basis of vibration, and that choosing a new reality is simply a matter of choosing to vibrate at the frequency that matches your desire.

The underlying idea behind the abundant mindset is to recognize that everything you're ever going to need is available for you right here and right now. This is why living in the present moment is so essential. If you were to live from the past you would only get the same results you have right now. Living too much in the future will keep you unaware of the opportunities that are in front of you. Avoid trying to escape the present moment by reminiscing on the past or wishing for a better future. This is the only moment we have, and in order to realize our dreams, we need to live fully in it.

Scientifically, the present is the only time that truly exists. It is the door to the quantum field where infinite creation is possible. There is no ego in the quantum field, therefore there is no past nor future identity, there is only now. This freedom allows your thoughts and emotions to flow and open up to more possibilities than you ever thought possible. Presence is the key to limitless creation.

When you begin to think in this way and embrace the present moment, you've entered a state that is called the receiving mode. It's where you're in full communication with the universe and the infinite intelligence it possesses. You start gaining clarity and insight that you never would have thought of with your conscious mind.

Because the present moment doesn't take into account the ego and the identity you've created for yourself, this is also where you take the leaps necessary to change your identity. You can only choose to act, think, and feel different right now. If you keep waiting for things to change, you're not creating. If you're not creating, then things aren't changing. When you allow yourself to fully embrace your limitless potential to create your own reality, this is when the magic starts to happen.

Everyone has access to this magic. Unfortunately, we've become so accustomed to cluttering our mind and emotions with fears, worries, "what if" statements, and limiting beliefs that we fail to open our eyes to the wonders of the present moment.

The wealthiest person on the planet, Jeff Bezos of Amazon, is no different from you and I. Bezos isn't some alien, even if he might behave like one occasionally. He just thinks differently from you. The fact that he has additional zeros to his name doesn't change the fact that he's a human being as well and that he's worked with all the resources he's had access to.

"Frugality drives innovation, just like constraints do. One of the only ways to get out of a tight box is to invent your way out."
– Jeff Bezos

Your job is to do your best with the things you have been given. No matter how small, you always have something to build on. This is the essence of the abundant mindset. While on the surface, it's about believing that you have enough of what you desire, when you get down to it, it's also about believing that you have a lot of things to build on and are never lacking resources.

Bring your focus to what's available to you right now rather than what's missing. Instead of working your way out of lack, work your way towards abundance. It might be a small distinction, but it proves to make a world of difference.

Just like how the peak of Mount Everest is never going anywhere, the abundance of resources at your disposal will not either. Your destination awaits you. Start your journey working with what you have first, and the universe will thank you with dividends for appreciating what it has given to you. This leads us to our next topic.

APPRECIATION

When you're in the right mindset, do you think you'll waste time fretting about how terrible things are in your life? Life will not be perfect when you have money. After all, you'll still be human and you'll still be a part of this world, which means you'll still be dealing with problems.

However, do you think you'll spend your entire day sitting around and moping about how unfair everything is in your life? Or do you think you'll take a look around you and appreciate where you've reached in life? Appreciate where you are and the possibility you have to go wherever you want to go in relation to your goals and aspirations.

Many self-help books encourage you to be thankful and to have gratitude (mine included), but I prefer to take it a step further. Appreciation as an emotion is far more powerful than gratitude. Appreciation involves acknowledging the abundance in the universe. It implies your recognition of the infinite possibilities that exist in the field. While gratitude is still a positive emotion, there is an element to it that is still attached to feelings of lack. You are recognizing the possibility that things could be worse for you. You compare to those that don't have what you have.

Don't misunderstand what I'm saying here. Gratitude is great. However, if you have the ability to go higher up the emotional scale, then you owe it to yourself to do so. Don't just merely thank the universe for what it has brought to you. Go ahead and appreciate it wholeheartedly.

Look with wonder at the things that are around you and appreciate both the abundance of opportunity you have as well as your own ability to manifest the reality of your dreams. Appreciate not just your surroundings but also who you're becoming. Celebrate your will to create this new reality and appreciate how strong you've become.

"Be content with what you have; rejoice in the way things are. When you realize there is nothing lacking, the whole world belongs to you."
- **Lao Tzu**

Appreciation isn't something you indulge in when things have gone your way. As much as possible, you should cultivate it even in your current situation. No matter how much money you manifest you're always going to want more. If you want to manifest 10k per month, once you reach that you will want 15k per month. There is never an end point to manifestation, even if the desire shifts. After making the desired 10k per month, you might decide to want to spend more time with your family, and thus another desire is born.

So no matter at what stage you are in life, you must appreciate it for what it is. If you don't, not only will it make the journey unenjoyable, but it'll take longer to manifest what you think you want. Feel good about going somewhere instead of feeling bad that you are not there.

Your choice to focus on the positives in your life deserves appreciation. How many people have the strength to focus on these even when things are falling apart around them? Not many! Whenever you feel happy and light, look around you and make it a point to appreciate your surroundings and these emotions. Keep practicing this behavior consistently and you will have no problem believing in the abundant universe.

THE MILLIONAIRE SELF

It can seem as if being positive is the very opposite of what you ought to do in such situations. The way to override these paradigms is to instead create a self-image that supports your new reality and underlines your chosen behaviors. The way to believe in abundance isn't to simply parrot a few lines to yourself over and over again.

Instead, you need to move into a new reality, and this means you will need to become the person who lives in that new reality. In short, you will need to develop a new self-image. The money you want is there for you to receive, thanks to the wonders of the quantum field. However, in order to align with the reality you want, you need to become the person that is in a vibrational match with it.

I've used the analogy of climbing Everest before, so let's stick with it. You cannot climb to the peak unless you train beforehand and practice all of the skills you will need to execute the climb. You can't roll out of bed and simply expect to succeed at this task. Try this, and you will almost certainly experience humbling failures without useful feedback.

Instead, in order to achieve the goal of climbing Everest, you need to become someone who can climb it. You need to train and study, but you also need to think and move like someone who is capable of climbing Everest.

Awareness

Awareness is like a headlamp you can use to navigate the wilderness at night. Every time you step outside of your current reality and try to manifest something new in your life, you're moving into the unknown. Your mind fears this, since it does not wish to change. Often, the fear of change is far worse than the event itself.

There are many ways of cultivating awareness, and being aware is a habit just like everything else. It begins with you establishing your intention to be aware of your thoughts, feelings, and impulses. This is as simple as taking a "mental step back" from all the conscious movement that's going on inside your head, and taking a deep breath. Review the thoughts, emotions, and actions you were just taking and decide whether these thoughts, emotions, and actions are in alignment with what you want to experience.

The first habit that you will notice about yourself when you become aware of your old identity is you will start to judge it. This is a form of egoic thinking and goes against what we're trying to accomplish. This is what causes people who want to be confident to go from being shy to arrogant. Instead of getting angry, judging, or labeling your old self, focus on accepting it for what it is and gently guiding it towards your new behaviors.

Habits and Repetition

Your aim is to match vibrationally with what it is you desire. When you operate at the new frequency and practice your new habits, your new paradigms will be reinforced in your mind. Because of the work you did to believe in the potential of your new paradigm, your habits will receive positive reinforcement to confirm these beliefs. Thus, creating positive momentum towards the new version of yourself.

This work takes time to have an impact. Although you can choose to identify as a new version of yourself now, it isn't as if you'll wake up tomorrow and be a changed person. Expectations of this kind are not a true reflection of the transformation you're trying to achieve. Instead, focus on repetition. Repetition creates habits and habits build who you are.

This may seem exhausting at first, but only because you're operating from the old sense of self. To ensure you take the right steps forward towards your new identity, practice altering your physical environment to strengthen it. Start off by slowly changing the things in your immediate environment. The people you hang out with to the stuff you own. Notice the things you talk about that are still attached to your old poverty-stricken perspective. The will to move into a new reality will help you take the right action and enforce the new behavior you want to install.

The idea here is not to drop everything for an identity that doesn't resonate with your authentic self. Remember, expressing your authentic self is already naturally aligned with all of your desires. You do not need to become someone you aren't in order to get to where you want to go. Focus simply on removing the filters that are covering up your authentic expression and creation. The best way to do this is through repetition.

As you begin to enact change in your life, you'll notice yourself disconnecting from your old environment, or the things that conform to your old self-image. This is normal, and you should expect some resistance from the people and things around you. They will say things you might not like, and your old impulses will get harder to contain, however, with time, this will all go away.

What is the fastest way to learn French? Is it to learn it online from a teacher or is it to actually live somewhere in France where no one speaks English? While the first method is great, there's no denying that the immersion the second method provides will force you to learn a lot faster.

Repetition and immersing yourself in the environment get the ball rolling, and the elevated emotions this brings will win the game.

TECHNIQUE #4: APPRECIATION MEDITATION

For this technique, you're going to do a mindfulness meditation and fusing it with the act of appreciation. In order to do this, find a comfortable and quiet place to sit either in the morning, during your lunch break, or in the evening. Take a couple of deep breaths to tune you into the present moment.

After you've tuned in, think about a person or an object who has recently supported your journey towards financial freedom, security, and abundance. This could be something as small as a pencil you use to write, or as relevant as a financial consultant who's helping you deal with a few issues.

The subject matter is not important. What is important is that you express appreciation to it/them both logically and emotionally. Let's take a look at the example of the pencil. Logically, the pencil is helping you write down your intentions for the day, thus helping you carry out your work with more vibrational resonance. Emotionally, the pencil is helping you take one step closer to manifesting the financial freedom you desire.

This is a very powerful technique because the vibration it builds can carry to other areas of your life. When practiced daily, this creates momentum and can lead to days on end of high vibration, which can result in faster manifestations. Work your way into abundance, and not out of lack.

TECHNIQUE #5: CONTENT SHIFT

The Content Shift is a technique that is more in line with this 21st century way of living. We have more access to information today than ever before in human history. This can cause our minds to clutter with useless information or be influenced by news, opinions, and events that ultimately lower our vibration.

In a world where politicians, corporations, and government officials control everything you see on the screen, it's important to filter out what doesn't serve you and your purpose. When it comes to negativity related to local or national politics or economics, only give enough attention to be informed but not enough attention to be consumed.

The idea behind this technique is to simply be aware of the content that you consume and the time that you put into it. Ideally, you want to be consuming content that benefits you vibrationally. In other words, content that makes you feel good, inspired, motivated, creative, and aligned with who you're becoming. Rather than putting your focus on things that don't benefit you, put your focus on things that do.

CHAPTER 4

A Dollar Bill's Relationship Advice: How to Make Yourself Attractive to Money

"When I chased after money, I never had enough.
When I got my life on purpose and focused on giving of myself and everything
that arrived into my life, then I was prosperous."
- **D r .   W a y n e   D y e r**

You've already learned how the regular notions of "making" money are invalid. The money you desire is here, waiting for you to allow it to come into your life. Your job is to shift your paradigm and match with it vibrationally. By doing this, you'll effortlessly align with the idea of it and attract it into your life.

I discussed habits in the previous chapter and how these are the bedrock of your new reality. What are some of these habits and paradigms that allow you to attract money? I briefly hinted at some of them, but in this chapter, you're going to learn four very important perspectives.

These perspectives can be seen as paradigms or behaviors that will help you align with the manifestation of money from multiple different streams. Don't look at them as things to do necessarily. Instead, look at them as ways of being. These methods will help clarify to you how one needs to perceive money in order to attract more of it into their lives.

ALLOWING VS FORCING

The first method or way of being is the act of allowing. Think back to when you've received something desirable in your life. Did you feel as if you had to force it to come to you? Or did you simply desire it and allow it to come into your life?

Chances are the latter is what happened. When we want something desperately, we make the mistake of chasing it and trying to force it to come to us. We want a beautiful partner, so we chase them and try to convince them of how amazing they are and how happy we would be with them.

All the while, the person being pursued is building greater resistance towards us. If you've ever been pursued by such a person, you know exactly how this feels. The very act of chasing implies lack. Think about it. Does a whole and complete person go around trying to convince people that they're a great person to be with? Do they run around trying to get people to be friends with them? Or do they simply relax and be who they are and allow friendships to develop?

Allowing is something that most people who have grown up in Western society do not understand. The education systems have convinced people that in order to achieve something, we need to go out there and take it through hard work and persistence. This act of "taking it" is heavily misconstrued.

Think of yourself as a vortex that attracts everything you want in life. The spinning of this vortex is working in your favor as you align vibrationally with the frequency of your desire. The more you are in alignment, the stronger the spinning, and thus the more you will attract.

Now, imagine sticking your arms out to reach for your desire. As you stick your arms out, you begin to disrupt the flow of the vortex. Instead of allowing the vortex to attract your desire, you're forcefully trying to reach out and grab it. This slows down the spinning and thus leads you to misalignment with your point of attraction.

Forcefully pushing yourself towards your desires is only going to distract you from what's really important, the process. All of life is a journey and the goal itself is nowhere near as important as what you undertake to achieve it. When your focus is on the process, you're in the present moment. We've touched at how important this is in the last chapter.

Ask successful people or those who have achieved their goals and they'll tell you that the journey was far more enjoyable than achieving the goal itself. While the sense of achievement was amazing, the joy of that moment was far shorter lived than the appreciation they have for the journey that got them there.

Fixating your mind over a goal that has to be reached is also believing in the fallacy of time. Your goal is a fixed moment in time and represents a moment when you will be satisfied or be somehow whole. This attitude also convinces you that the current moment isn't good enough and just like that your appreciation for it vanishes.

Allowing is extremely powerful because you become more receptive to alternative routes toward where you want to go. Remember when we talked about infinite realities in Chapter 1? The manifestation of money will not come in a way that's 100% predictable. Manifestations come from the unknown. In other words, from a pool of infinite possibilities. Understand that manifestation is not a fixed process.

Be open to any detours or delays. Trust that everything is conspiring to help you towards your dream. Allow yourself to relax in the present and go with the flow. Every action you take should reinforce your vibration and thus bring you closer to your destination!

Consider the example of a consultant who is scarce in their mindset. All they can see is the lucrativeness of one on one consultations. However, a consultant who is abundant will realize that there is more than one way of making money. They can make money from speaking opportunities, personal branding, creating courses, conducting private group coaching, writing books, and so on.

There are many ways to reach your financial goal and you cannot possibly envision all of them. So sit back and allow yourself to align vibrationally with new opportunities and ideas that will lead you toward your desired manifestation.

THE NON-IMPORTANCE OF MONEY

The power of choice is the most important thing that all of us possess. Being able to consciously direct your focus to things that bring you joy and happiness is a super power. We've talked plenty about this already, however, it's important to know exactly what are the specific perspectives we should be choosing to focus on.

Consider the following situation: A large group of people are milling around and suddenly, dollar bills start showering upon all of them. All of them begin to rush around trying to grab as much money as they can. They push and shove one another out of the way in an attempt to collect as much money as possible.

All except for one person. This person looks on with bemusement. They might pluck a few bills that land on their head or shoulder, but they aren't crawling around and acting desperate. They're completely secure with their position and are unwilling to let the promise of free money swerve them out of alignment with who they are becoming.

Recognize that you have the choice to stay in alignment with who you are becoming, however, it requires you to have a certain perspective about yourself and your reality. Life will test you and your new way of being. It will bring up opportunities that poke at the habitual impulses of the old you. Standing your ground is essential if you truly want to experience self-transformation.

Imagine hiring someone for a position in your company. The first person is a people pleaser and is willing to do anything to make you feel good. The other person carries themselves with a sense of self-worth and stands behind their values. Who are you going to respect more? Who will you direct more of your attention towards?

Your relationship with money is the same in many ways. In order to attract money to you, you need to treat it as your equal. It is energy like everything else. You own a pencil, a car, a couch, and some money. It is no different from anything else. Become servile to it and it will disrespect you and force you to demean yourself in order to attain it. Eventually, this leads to burnout, depression, and a wasted life chasing instead of living.

I want to stress that when talking of how money is "non-important," I'm not saying it's not a necessity. If you reject money just for the sake of rejecting money, then you're rejecting your dreams. We live in a world where money is indeed necessary if you want to express your highest potential, however, it's not necessary enough for you to sacrifice your values and vibration to earn it. Become a "partner" to money rather than being its "servant" or "master."

Treat your money like you are walking a dog. Give it the freedom to walk around the neighborhood and experience growth, but make sure you have a leash on it or you will spend the rest of your days chasing. A neutral perspective of money is essential if you don't want it to manipulate how you think, feel, and act. Detach it from sense of self-worth. Treat it as an equal and you will find it flowing to you with more ease.

Where to Focus

Money is energy, and this also provides us with a clue with regards to where your focus ought to be directed. In every encounter you have in your life, focus on the energy being exchanged. Are your interactions resulting in an increase of energy within you and within those around you? Are you involved in a process of creation or deterioration?

Money is made when value is provided. This is just another way of saying that when the energy of something is increased, money flows towards the entity that worked to increase it. Focus on the energy you are putting out into the universe and it will reward you with the necessary tools to continue doing what you're doing.

Thinking in this manner will be tough at first, since we're so used to focusing on money as being an object to collect. If you give it this meaning, you'll give it too much importance. It goes from being a simple form of exchange into your main goal. This stops you from being focused on the process, and thus removes you from the present moment.

There are an infinite number of ways to generate money, and you have more than enough within you to make it happen in your life. Work into abundance at all times by searching and being aware of the opportunities that surround you right now. This could be at your current job or through some idea you came up with.

Focus on creation and expansion using what you have and the universe will automatically register your efforts and push you towards even more abundance. It isn't just money you will attract, but prosperity in all areas.

THE LAW OF INCREASE

Central to the point of focusing your energy on creation is the truth that the universe is always expanding. This has been proved scientifically (*What Does It Mean When They Say the Universe Is Expanding?*, 2019). Since the moment it came into existence, the universe we live in is growing in size.

Physically speaking, this means there is always going to be more space for us to express ourselves and live through our natural state of being. It also means that the energy surrounding us is constantly increasing. Most people have a backwards idea of value despite the physical evidence that is right in front of their eyes. They believe that they can give value only when they receive something first.

It simply doesn't work that way. Holding onto this belief implies that the universe is scarce and that it isn't infinitely abundant. When you're dealing with abundance, you're firmly stating that the more you give the more you get. There is no limit to how much you can give or receive as a result.

Think about a relationship in your life. The more love you give or display towards the other person, the more you receive in return. There's no limit to how much you can love someone. Neither does displaying affection and love reduce anything within you. In fact, the opposite is true: the more value you provide to the universe and to those around you, the more of it you receive in return. This allows you to expand and to move in line with the natural flow of the universe. Why else does every successful person constantly invest in learning and in bettering themselves?

Contrast this behavior with an unsuccessful person. What is the first word that springs to mind when you think of someone who does the same thing at a job they hate, day in and day out, waiting for their paycheck at the end of the week? Words such as stagnation, restriction, and deterioration spring to mind. All of these words imply a lack of movement and the absence of expansion. In other words, they're out of alignment with the natural flow of the universe. How can they expect to receive anything when they're against the flow?

Another way of applying the law of increase is by raising the vibration of everything you come in touch with. In other words, you're in the act of creation through others. A good example of this are the motivational speakers and coaches. They bring the best out of you so you can go create and expand more things in your own reality.

Generosity is the key to happiness. What is this but another way of saying that by increasing the wellbeing and the positive vibration of those around you, you raise yourself as well? Attracting wealth and prosperity is an alchemical process wherein you better yourself, and better the world as a result.

This is why many spiritual leaders constantly advise us to share our gifts with the world. All of us have been blessed with skills and gifts that will make the world a better place. You could hold onto it and try to keep it all for yourself but this will only result in stagnation.

The more you focus on creation and expansion, the more you increase prosperity, and this is right in line with the way the universe behaves. The natural conclusion of this law is that you will attract more of what you want into your life.

Focus your energy on not only feeling good yourself, but on helping others feel good as well. The key here is to do it from a place of sincerity and not from a place of "if I do this then I'll get that." It won't work if you do the latter. Every action you take has a vibration behind it, and when your vibration is out of alignment with the action you're taking, no matter how many times you perform that action, it'll never serve you in a positive way.

Avoid this by embracing the law of increase as part of your identity. You naturally want to help people just for the sake of helping them. You don't have to take responsibility for what someone else feels, but you can do your best to help them better themselves without placing expectations on them. For example, you can advise someone as to the best course of action but leave it up to them to walk that path.

Placing expectations over them to behave in a certain way is trying to control the outcomes of the universe. It removes you from the mode of allowing things to happen. Remember that you're not in control of your reality, you're only in control of how you respond to it.

TECHNIQUE #6 -
DAILY VIBRATIONAL INCREASE

This technique will resonate with those that want more in their life. Not just more money, but more relationships, friends, passion, connection, and impact. It's a part of life for us to always want more. We are naturally looking to expand just as everything else in the universe does. Your vibration is either increasing or decreasing. This means you are either experiencing more of what life has to offer, or less of it. You are never stagnant. However, many people are unconsciously allowing their vibration to drop because they're unaware of this.

The idea behind this technique is to focus on increasing the vibration of yourself, others, and your environment on a daily basis. Some examples include cleaning up your house, complimenting someone, donating, listening, being a good friend, etc.

It does not matter what action is entailed. What matters is the intention behind it. By increasing the vibration of things around you, you are inevitably increasing your own vibration. When this happens, you become more aligned with the law of increase. Simple acts done on a consistent basis can produce extraordinary results. Live by this and opportunities to grow your finances will come.

CHAPTER 5

The Easiest and Fastest Way to Build Wealth

"If you say that money is the most important thing, you'll spend your life completely wasting your time. You'll be doing things you don't like doing in order to go on living, that is, in order to go on doing things you don't like doing..."
- Alan Watts

If you're reading a book such as this one, you no doubt want to manifest money in your life as quickly as possible. No one wants to sit around waiting until they're of old age for wealth to show up! Wanting money to enter your life as quickly as possible isn't unrealistic or impossible.

Remember that all the wealth in the world already exists and is available to you. Yet, many people who practice the law of attraction don't realize success they expected to. Why is this? In short, it has everything to do with alignment. Alignment is the harmony between the heart, mind, and soul. When we're in alignment, we're a vibrational match to our desires.

You've already learned that everything in this universe is energy. While we have material forms, what we really are is a bunch of vibrating subatomic particles that emit energy at a certain frequency. The more you vibrate at the frequency of what you want, the more your dreams will manifest in your life.

You can generate as many positive thoughts as you want, but if you happen to be misaligned with your purpose in life, you won't realize the type of wealth that you're truly after. Feeling fulfilled from building a certain level of wealth is more important than manifesting the money that comes with it. When speaking of purpose, a lot of people become scared and retreat into their shells.

This is because our true purpose is a pure and raw reflection of our inner being. Recall how you earlier learned that everyone has a gift that they can impart to the universe to make it better and to help it expand. For most people, thinking in such terms is scary. After all, we're talking about the meaning of life itself!

What they instead do is aim smaller or adopt someone else's goals. This is why "making a million dollars" is a trending search topic no matter where you look. Most people want the best-looking partner in their lives, to be rich, famous, and on the cover of glossy magazines.

But hardly anyone pauses to ask: What makes me happy?

YOUR VISION AND PURPOSE

In order to align yourself with the ideal scenario you wish to manifest, you need to clarify or construct two pillars in it. These are your vision and your purpose. Your vision refers to how you see your life unfolding and specifying what it is you're in this world for. Everything that you do is subordinate to your vision.

Your purpose defines the impact you want to make. This is the mark that you will leave behind in the world. These are not puny questions to answer. Over the course of our lives, our vision and purpose might change. In fact, a person who grows over the course of their lifetime will inevitably move onto bigger and broader purposes.

Everyone on this planet has their own path to walk. The origins of this journey are not known. No matter what your beliefs are, there's no denying that our lives are a journey in and of themselves. We learn things about the world and about ourselves and are given opportunities to become bigger and better versions of ourselves.

Our knowledge and resolve are tested every step of the way and it only makes us stronger. Having a vision for everything you do helps put everything in your life into better context. It answers the seemingly simple question: Why am I doing this?

We do many things in our lives that don't make sense to us. Why do we spend time at work when we really want to be spending time with our kids? Why do we treat our loved ones more harshly than we treat strangers? Why are we harshest towards ourselves? These behaviors typically occur due to a lack of a vision.

Make it a point to ask yourself the biggest question of them all: Why do you want more money? Now there are two ways to answer this question. You can either answer it through your egoic mind or through your inner being. One is an illusionary answer and the other is the truth.

The first answer will involve aspects around strengthening an egoic identity that is attached to past and possible future experiences. As we know by now, the past and future do not exist. The past and future are inaccurate definitions of an experience that doesn't exist because the only moment that really exists is now. Experience is momentary, therefore, wanting more money to fill a need from the past or in the future is flawed thinking. This will always keep you wanting more and never being satisfied enough to appreciate your life experience. It's as if you're eating a burger today while thinking of the sushi you want to eat tomorrow. When tomorrow comes and you're eating the sushi, you'll start thinking about the next day's meal without ever fully embracing the sushi that you're having right now.

The second answer will involve aspects around authentic expression of life experience. In other words, all your inner being wants is to fully express itself without limitations. This entails fully embracing the present experience. What this means is you will never need anything external to ever feel fulfilled within. Sure, you want things in your life, but you don't need them. It's by radiating this kind of energy out into the world that will attract all the things you want. If you need something out there to feel good in here, you'll never match with it vibrationally. It's like someone gifting you a car, but you don't know how to drive. If you don't know how to drive, then the car is useless to you. Master your internal experience and the external one will naturally fall into place.

Back in the early 1900s, there was a man who had figured out his purpose and his vision and brought an entire empire to its knees. His name was Mahatma Gandhi, and he managed to free the Indian subcontinent from the British empire without firing a single bullet.

He was imprisoned, derided as a half-naked monk and was mocked for organizing salt marches across the subcontinent. However, despite all the mockery and despite all the taunting, he won. Do you think Gandhi cared about the money he made in his lifetime?

This fact is less known, but he was a highly educated lawyer. Prior to taking part in the Indian freedom struggle, he was an activist in South Africa where he protested the racist policies of the Apartheid era government in that country. He was even thrown out of a train and jailed for all his troubles. He could have led a comfortable life as an educated lawyer.

This wasn't aligned with his purpose though. Gandhi's aim was to rid his homeland from the oppression of the British. When he set about trying to achieve his purpose, there was no way he could have known how it would play out. He did it anyway.

The grand scale of his vision and purpose should have scared him. He had no money to speak of and owned less than ten possessions. Nonetheless, he achieved what he set out to do step by step, piece by piece.

In the beginning, you're not going to know how you will manage to get from A to B. Your purpose should scare you a little. This means you're doing it right. New experiences will always come from the unknown. It won't be easy to let go of everything and step into the darkness. Dropping all external expectations for how you should be living is the number one key to getting into alignment with what you want out of life. It's as if you dropped a 9-5 job you hated that paid you six-figures, to start working on your dream whilst living in a studio apartment. Choosing happiness over money will always lead to a fulfilled present moment, the only moment in time that exists.

It's never too late to make the switch from your unenjoyable 9-5 job to following your passion. Do not let societies faulty expectations tell you what you should and shouldn't do. If you ever decide to take this leap of faith, be sure you're doing it with a conscious state of mind. If you're only dipping your toes or quitting your job just to quit your job, you'll never get the results you'd expect because most of you is still attached to the old identity. Follow your heart, plan with your brain, and align yourself vibrationally to the point where your emotions are so elevated the universe will begin to shower you with opportunities, people, and money like you've never experienced before.

My purpose with this book is to help you manifest wealth in alignment with who you really are. You may start off in that studio apartment, but if you're in alignment, if you're optimistic about what you're creating, if you're happy with the process even if it entails near impossible challenges, you will succeed. This is to adopt the path of least resistance and is what will cause you to manifest money into your life and build the financial wealth you've always desired.

PASSIONATE VS HARD WORK

There is a lie that is extremely prevalent in our societies. We venerate people that call themselves hustlers and refer to "the hustle" as being something that ought to be rewarded. To make it clear, there's nothing wrong in working hard towards a cause. Someone who is passionate will expend a lot of energy towards building their vision.

The danger arises when you buy into the lie that in order to make your dreams come true, you have to hustle and nothing else matters - that you have to give up everything else in order to make it a reality - that sacrifice and suffering is a necessary part of your journey. That is a complete lie.

People like Elon Musk regularly make comments about how he works 120-hour weeks and that the best way to defeat the competition is to simply outwork them. He also openly admits that he cannot sleep without Ambien and that his vision has cost him two marriages and has placed untold amounts of stress on him.

He sometimes refers to these events with a hint of pride, as if his vision is large enough to make these things justifiable. Let's take a step back and consider the relationship we have to the field or to the universe, which is one and the same thing. The universe's purpose is to nurture life. It's why we've received the gift of existence on this planet.

More than any other part of the known universe, this singular planet is at a perfect distance from the sun so as to create warmth but not burn us to a crisp. It has a layer of air that protects us from the sun and filters only the life creating aspects of it. It has deep oceans that regulate the air temperature and provide us with food.

The entire ecosystem of this planet is balanced in a way so that the entire system prospers when just one portion of it is healthy and nourished. If the universe were personified, you would conclude that these are the actions of an immensely kind and benevolent being.

This being wants us to achieve our purpose because when we do this, the universe grows richer. It is ready to give us all that we need. Do you think such a being would want you to exhaust yourself and punish yourself in pursuit of your goals? If you have a child, is this what you would want for him or her?

Yet, we believe that hustle is the only way to get there. The truth is, it's not impossible to get rich by hard work alone. Plenty of people have done it before, including Elon Musk. If you believe it takes hard work to be successful, then it'll take hard work to be successful, thus making that statement true.

You are that powerful. You create your own reality through the power of your own beliefs. If you believe that success can come with more flow, ease, and alignment, then it'll come with more flow, ease, and alignment.

Remember that the energy that you put out into the world is what you will attract back to you. A person that regularly punishes themselves in the name of achieving their goals will attract nothing but more punishment, even if they manage to achieve it. Imagine working all your life for a single purpose and then finding out that it makes you even more miserable!

This is because when you work out of alignment with yourself, you're creating even more resistance in your life. You need to expend more effort to overcome this resistance and this creates even more resistance. It's a bit like trying to swim upstream for no reason other than being convinced that this is the only way.

Acting out of alignment is to display supreme arrogance in your knowledge and it is to say that your ego knows better than your inner being. Society often backs up this sort of thinking because we haven't evolved beyond our three-dimensional way of viewing reality.

We look at a person's results and think that copying whatever they do must be the right way of doing things. The right way to evaluate a situation is to look at the energy inherent in it. A person who exhausts and punishes themselves in the name of their purpose doesn't contribute to the energy of the world, they end up sucking more out of it. They place a burden on the ones they love and on those who work for them. Instead of spreading their vision as a gift, they end up spreading misery.

Is it worth achieving your purpose at such a cost? Working from real passion is all about increasing the vibrational energy of everything around you. This leads to more freedom and flow when it comes to how you operate at work. Ironically, this helps you achieve your goals a lot faster. This is because when you love what you do, you work on it just for the sheer joy of working on it. You'll work harder than someone that isn't in love with the process. This is the difference between hard work and working hard. If you don't love what you do, it's hard work, if you love what you do, you'll work hard for it.

This doesn't mean you should quit your job and sit meditating under a tree. That is a childish conclusion. Instead, you should work because you want to work, and not because you need to. There is an intelligence far greater than you that is on your side. When you ignore it's guidance, you're prolonging the manifestation of your success. Work from a place of inspiration rather than motivation.

Inspiration Impulse

The inspiration impulse is an impulse that moves you to take action on a particular task in accordance to the wants of your inner being. This is an action you're taking just for the joy of taking the action. It feels almost like there is a universal force moving you to take that action. There is an absence of urgency, neediness, anxiety, and stress when taking this type of action.

The importance behind the inspiration impulse is that when it happens, you're usually at a high vibrational frequency. This means that the action that you're taking is coming from a place of joy, love, happiness, and inspiration. This leads to more efficiency and better work.

Take the music industry for example. There are artists that release 10s of 100s of songs a year, yet they still struggle to reach the masses and climb the charts. Then there are the artists that release two or three songs and one of them ends up being a big hit. The song then proceeds to climb the charts, the artist gains more recognition, and before they know it, they're a superstar.

This is the power of taking action through inspiration rather than through effort. If your actions require effort, then there is resistance when taking this action. This means that you are out of alignment with what you want. You will never feel bad about what it is you desire. This is precisely why feeling bad while taking action to manifest a desire will move you out of vibrational alignment with it. Work that is performed from effort rarely produces results, and if it does, the progress is minuscule.

Putting in hard work leads to burnout and drained energy. If effort correlated with the amount of money someone made, construction workers would be millionaires. However, this is obviously not the case. The amount of money that you make is only correlated to the vibration behind the actions you take to make that money. This is why following your passion and purpose is such an important step in your journey to effortless success. Reaching monetary success that isn't in alignment with your passion is not real success. Real success has to come from within.

Resistances arises when we ignore these impulses simply because we do not logically understand them. The brain will never speak the language of the heart, however, recognizing that both have a role to play in your transformation is essential.

Consider the brain as a lightning rod that receives information from either your ego or infinite intelligence. Your heart is the decision maker on whether these bits of information that you're receiving are in alignment with who you are and what you want. Let the brain translate the information for you and let the heart choose what will serve you best.

The path of least resistance is the path guided by your inner being. Following this path can be confusing, uncomfortable, and strange because it goes against all the conditioned thoughts you have about who you are and how the world is supposed to be. Ask yourself whether you would like to swim against the current or with it. The path of least resistance will put you in the direction of the current in your life and will bring the physical manifestation of your purpose and vision that much quicker to you.

This is why "hard work" is weak work. It requires you to go against your true self and to then overcome all the obstacles that emanate as a result of that resistance. Working in alignment is far more powerful. There's no reason for you to tackle obstacles that you create for yourself after all!

Vibrational Productivity

Often times people have trouble finding out what their passions are or lack the necessary connection to have the inspiration impulse we mentioned above. What should you do then?

The answer is simple: Move into a state of higher vibration.

Accept that the inspiration hasn't manifested within you yet and move on. This is a crucial step because there are two ways of accepting the absence of your inspiration. You either focus on the lack of it, which goes against everything we've talked about so far, or you focus on what can possibly trigger this inspiration.

If inspiration arises from your passion, fulfillment, and happiness, then do things that are in alignment with this. If you have a passion for cooking, but lack the inspiration for a new dish, start cooking!

It can be anything that puts you in alignment. Inspiration in the dictionary is defined as: "a feeling of enthusiasm you get from someone or something that gives you new and creative ideas." The key word here is "new." Inspiration doesn't come from your old ways of thinking. It comes from this infinite consciousness we call the universe. It comes from the unknown.

When ideas, thoughts, and actions arise from the unknown, they carry a heavier weight. They come from an intelligence beyond you and me. One step of inspired creation can get you farther than one hundred steps of misaligned and effortful action.

Another way to get in alignment with an inspiring idea or impulse is to focus on why you're performing the action. If you dislike your job or you have a distaste for your boss, shift your focus. See where the positive aspects lie in the work that you do. Who are you helping? Who benefits from what you do? How does your job influence the vibration of other beings?

Most of the time, you're working to make people's lives easier and better. So why not focus on that? This will inevitably raise your vibration, increase your productivity levels, and put you in a state where you perform a higher-level quality of work, thus leading you to more inspired ideas, and as a result, more money manifestation.

TECHNIQUE #7 - YOUR PERFECT DAY

The Perfect Day exercise is a classic that never goes out of fashion simply because it's so effective. Creating your perfect day helps you outline exactly how you want your life to look like. The idea behind it is to create this perfect day without any limitations. Do not put your focus on the "how," instead, put it on the "what."

Your perfect day should be a few pages of what you want your average day to look like in the next 5, 10, or 20 years. This technique involves reading it as often as you can to help align you energetically to that which you desire. If you write exactly what you want out of life, there is no reason why it shouldn't raise your vibration. Pick it up every morning, be present, and give it a quick read to remind you of your purpose and vision of what you want to experience and who you want to become.

Because you're human, your values are constantly changing. Your perfect day will also change with time, so don't worry if you're not resonating with it after a few months. Re-write it and continue doing the exercise. I've compiled a collection of questions that I used (and still use) to create my perfect day. I read it every morning as part of my routine as soon as I wake up. Every few months I change a few things here and there, but the overall vision is the same.

Consider the following questions when writing out your perfect day:

- At what time do you wake up?
- Who do you wake up with?
- What does your house look like?
- What city are you living in?
- What does your morning routine look like?
- What are you having for breakfast?
- What's the weather like today?
- How do you feel throughout the morning?

- What kind of passion projects are you working on?
- How much are you making every month?
  Every year?
- What kind of people do you work with?
  Describe them individually.
- How long do you work for?
- Where are you going for lunch?
- What's your daily mode of transportation?
- What kind of people do you spend your time with?
  Describe them individually.
- How do you feel around these people?
- What activities do you do throughout the
  afternoon?
- How do you speak and act?
- Where are you going for dinner?
- How do you feel after living out 2/3 of your perfect day?
- What activities do you do throughout the evening?
- What is your nighttime routine?
- What time do you go to sleep?
- How do you feel when falling asleep?

TECHNIQUE #8 – PURPOSE FINDING

Now that we've talked extensively about why pursuing your passion and purpose is essential for manifesting money quickly and easily, let's focus on how to actually find these things. Most people do not know what their true passion or purpose is. This is where the Purpose Finding technique comes in. If your work feels more like play, there's no reason why you wouldn't manifest money with it, especially if it involves providing value to other people.

The Purpose Finding technique involves three simple steps. They are the following:

Step 1: Set the intention of finding your passion. Put energy behind this endeavor. Most people never find their passions because they never go out to look for it. Become more aware of the things that draw you in and how you can provide value in this field.

Step 2: Do things you enjoy doing. The definition of passion is: "An intense desire or enthusiasm for something." Follow that which lights the fire within you in this very moment. It's important that you don't follow any future or past feelings. Follow what feels good right now.

Step 3: Seek new experiences. Sometimes, you may not even know what you enjoy doing or how you can turn it into something monetized. This is where this step comes in. Trying new things will get the creative juices flowing and keep you constantly expanding your horizons. This will help you connect dots you never knew you could connect.

CHAPTER 6

The Truth Behind Visualization

"Know that faith is like a seed planted in the ground;
it grows after its kind. Plant the idea (seed) in your mind, water and fertilize
with expectancy, and it will manifest."
– Joseph Murphy

Visualization is one of the most powerful ways of ensuring your vision comes to fruition. How does one go about performing it, though? The fact is that visualization triggers many positive things, along with one major negative. You're going to learn all about the proper way to visualize your dreams in this chapter.

All visualization starts with a desire. If you're reading this book, you wish to manifest more money in your life. The thing about visualization is that desire alone isn't enough. It needs to be backed by an expectation that this desire will come true to really lend it some weight.

Expectation

Why is expectation so crucial? Put simply, expecting your desires to come true is an act of faith. It is an act of placing your trust in the universe and in the way it works. This isn't a particularly new concept; every religious book and treatise has spoken about placing trust in a supreme being and praying as if your wish has already been granted.

This goes to show that the knowledge about how the universe works is pretty ancient indeed. Whether you're religious or not, there is no denying that we are a part of the infinite cosmos. Thanks to this, we have direct access to its consciousness. While we might not be able to comprehend it at all times, there's no denying that we are nurtured by it.

Visualization prepares your mind to live in the future and shed the memories of the past. Those paradigms that hold you back do so because they keep referring back to certain memories that justify their existence. For example, if you believe that money is evil, there is a memory within you that pertains to this belief. Perhaps your parents told you this, or you suffered through some experience in your life that validates this thought. Visualization is a method of using this memory referencing for your benefit and helps you create new beliefs and paradigms. The mind cannot tell the difference between a real experience and an imagined one (Hanson & Mendius, 2009).

The more connected you are to your visualization and the more you embody it, the more your mind will believe that it is a real experience. With repetition and intention, you'll manage to have this new paradigm override the old one. Lending the new paradigm weight, and your visualization along with it, is the expectation that your desire will come to fruition.

The key here is to expect your desire to manifest without needing it to manifest. In other words, you will not be swayed whether it manifests or not. Keep in mind that your primary focus should be to stay in alignment at all times in the present moment as if it already did manifest. You can use expectation to put you into alignment, but don't let it move you out of it.

When you expect your desire to manifest, you unconsciously align with it vibrationally. Let's say you want to travel to Europe for 6 months as an example. If you expect this to happen, what first steps would you take? You would probably start looking up hotels, flight dates, tourist attractions, or contacting relatives and friends that live in these places. You'll start doing things that imply that your desired manifestation is already on its way. Expect the experience, and let the universe take care of the details.

This is an extremely powerful way to manifest, however, there are a few pitfalls that people can fall into during this process. It's okay to stay connected with your visualization and desire, but do not be attached to it.

Attachment

One of the biggest pitfalls you can fall prey to is getting attached to the outcome. Attachment implies movement beyond mere expectation. The state of expectation is characterized by you eagerly allowing the arrival of something you know is coming. Attachment implies tying your entire self-worth to its arrival.

There's a fine line between expectation and being attached to the outcome. Attachment is simply another way of escaping lack when what you should be doing is moving towards abundance. The key to note here is the place where your focus is directed. Anyone escaping lack is simply looking backwards; they care more about avoiding something bad than gaining a desirable outcome.

Often times, when we have expectations, we subtly give room for our ego to start thinking about the details. This includes the how-to's of manifesting a desired outcome. This "muddles up" the energy and thus creates resistance rather than trusting the process and trusting that there is an infinite scale of energy that is in the works. The "how" is not your problem.

When things go wrong, the ego will try to convince you that your dreams are impossible and that staying where you are is more suitable. This is why expecting details is never a good idea. It gives room for the ego to judge your manifestation just because it wasn't "perfect". Become more aware of your doubtful beliefs and you will start to recognize just how absurd they are. The ego is always trying to hold onto an identity, predict an outcome, and create from a known state of being. In other words, the ego solely operates from the past.

Prosperity and money can come to us in a million ways. We cannot possibly know the permutations and combinations that lie ahead of us.

Only the infinite knows that. Keep your focus on the present moment and on the timeless wisdom you have access to. This keeps your ego at bay. One of the reasons why locking ourselves into one single way of manifesting doesn't work is because creation is a joint process. It takes two to tango and creation is no different.

Co-Creation

Despite the large part we play in creating our reality, the truth is that we're still a part of a larger ecosystem. Everything that you have created has a portion of reality that has been created by someone else. If you're working a job and visualize earning a higher salary, you need your boss to cooperate with your vision to grant you higher pay, whether they know it or not.

They are co-creators in your vision. Given the infinite number of ways in which people interact with one another, this means there are an infinite number of ways in which money can come to you. Attaching yourself to one particular vision or expectation thus removes this infinite possibility from your life.

It's a bit like the universe saying that you have all of these options, but you stubbornly cling onto a single one because you think you know best. This creates resistance and moves you out of alignment with your abundant self.

Everyone on this planet and in this universe is a part of a unified field, with all of us interacting and creating each other's dreams. This is what creates life in our existence. So let go of the need for one particular outcome to manifest and instead allow the universe to give you what you desire.

Focus on the experience and not on the physical manifestation of money. In other words, don't visualize your bank account growing larger. This doesn't mean anything without the feeling of security and freedom that it brings. Therefore, focus on that instead. I've already detailed the myriad number of reasons why you should be focusing on this.

There is one other thing you should be aware of. Your dreams will not manifest immediately. This is because you need to experience them in the fourth dimension before you see them physically in the third dimension.

Fourth Dimensional Reality

The idea of experiencing your dreams in the fourth-dimension ties back to having faith that the universe is ready to give you everything you want. It goes back to believing in your ability as a creator. Only when you've fully experienced gaining your desired sum of money vibrationally will you see it manifest physically in your life.

Why does the universe do this? If it's ready to give you everything you want, why not simply give it to you? The reality is that most of us are not ready to receive what we desperately want. A large sum of money might cause you more harm when showered upon you all of a sudden.

The universe ensures you're prepared for what you want by wanting you to vibrationally match the experience first. This is how the universe works. You must emit a vibration that fits in accordance to the physical reality you want to experience. You will never be mentally or emotionally ready to experience it because you haven't experienced it, but vibrationally, you did, because you believed it and allowed it to be a possibility in your life. This is why you feel nervous, or should I say excited, the first-time you buy a new home, land your dream job, or reach a 6-figure month in your business.

People who expect their emotions to follow physical manifestation are doing it backwards. They're failing the test that the universe is placing before them. If you want money in your life, you need to already feel rich. If you wish to meet your special soulmate, you need to already be in love.

As Gandhi said, you need to be the change you wish to see. Only then does the universe send experiences that match the vibrational frequency you're emitting. This is a universal truth and is the very basis for manifestation.

The reason why manifestation takes so long to happen is because physical matter is extremely dense, while thoughts and emotions are fluid and flexible. They both make up the same kind of energy that can be found across the cosmos. However, they are simply expressed from a different perspective.

The third dimension is where the ego thrives. This is where everything is seen as fixed and where duality is perceived. This is what allows us to differentiate from good and bad, up and down, and light and dark. A lot of contradictions happen here. It can feel very real to notice the difference between various expressions of matter. The key is to know that everything you perceive with your five senses is all connected and an expression of the same thing.

Reality is very flexible. We only perceive that reality is solid, fixed, and permanent because we may still be operating from a third dimensional level of consciousness. Your identity and your physical reality is very much malleable. This brings us to the fourth dimension.

Think of the fourth dimension like a dream world. Everything is very flexible, easy to manipulate, and things manifest instantly. Understanding this should give you enough inspiration to believe that you are the creator of your own reality. When we begin tapping into the fourth dimension, we consciously start deciding who we want to become and what we want to experience in life. Instead of allowing life to control us, we control our lives.

The existence and the importance of the fourth dimension is essential for the manifestation of your desires. So go ahead and visualize all of your dreams in detail. Don't stop there, though. Continue and live your chosen reality with your eyes open and be aware that nothing is permanent, and anything can change if you choose to perceive that possibility.

TECHNIQUE #9: FOURTH DIMENSIONAL MANIFESTING

This is a technique that focuses on primarily manifesting in the fourth dimension. In other words, we'll be focusing on manifesting in the quantum field. This will help you experience the freedom you're after before it's reached the third dimension. The steps are as follows:

Step 1: Be aware that the only moment is the present moment. Everything you've ever desired can be experienced here. This is the door to the fourth dimension.

Step 2: Choose what it is you truly desire. The possibilities are infinite. Refer back to the Perfect Day exercise if you need to.

Step 3: Find something that implies that this reality that you desire already exists in the third dimension. In other words, find an object or experience that confirms that which you want is possible for you. Something you can touch is often more powerful. For example: If you desire to live in a beach house, go to the beach to experience it. If you want to travel more, grab the bookbag you'd travel with.

Step 4: Shift your focus from the physical into the meta-physical. Bring your focus to the feeling of experiencing your desire like it's happening right now. Go for a ride in your imagination and let it roam free. Some may call this "day-dreaming."

Step 5: Carry this feeling throughout the rest of your day. If you feel out of alignment, refer back to steps 1-4 and bring yourself back to your desired state. Do this technique until it comes natural to you.

TECHNIQUE #10: MANIFESTATION CONFIRMATION BIAS

For this next technique, we're going to confirm that your manifestations are happening, whether this be in the form of an opportunity, person, or money that unexpectedly came to you. This will especially help those that find it hard to trust the universe due to a negative filter that block them from seeing the magic that's happening to them on a daily basis. This technique will focus on removing these negative filters.

The idea behind this technique is to become aware of the confirmation that you are manifesting. Even if it's the tiniest little thing. Recognize proof when you see the manifestation of the money, wealth, and abundance you desire.

A good example could be finding a penny on the floor. Most people would completely ignore it or think of it as useless. If you want the universe to give you the big things, you need to appreciate it when it gives you the little things too. Everything is energy. A penny has the same energy as a $10,000 check. The only thing that changes is the meaning you put behind it. Give the penny a meaning of freedom, security, and abundance that you would give to any other amount of money because after all, you don't want money, you want what money brings you. Focus on the experience of being the person that is accustomed to attracting money.

Point out the little things, and you will find yourself having more faith in the universe as time goes on. Letting go of doubt is one of the most powerful things you can do for manifestation.

CHAPTER 7

Manifestation Bullseye: Nailing 100% of Your Money-Making Decisions

"Intuition is the whisper of the soul."
- **Jiddu Krishnamurti.**

Most of us consider ourselves to be poor at handling money and financial decisions. Perhaps it's the numbers that scare us, or the thought of deciphering incomprehensible financial jargon. Wouldn't it be great if you had a built-in mechanism that automatically signaled a yes or no decision for you?

What if I told you that such a mechanism exists within you, and has existed since your birth? This mechanism is your intuition, and as I briefly mentioned earlier, it's your connection to the infinite. Intuition is a largely misunderstood thing, and in this chapter, you're going to learn all about how it works and what its voice sounds like.

The simplest definition of intuition is that it is our guide. It is the inner voice that tells us what is right or what is wrong. To be more precise, it tells us what "feels" right and what doesn't. Feelings are the mode of communication of the universe, and this is why it's essential for you to become more comfortable with them.

If intuition is divine instruction, then it stands to reason that it exists only in the present moment. This is something that a lot of people miss. The common thought process around intuition is that it illuminates the path ahead of you. This is not necessarily the case. The best way of stating this is to say that intuition illuminates what is directly ahead of you. If you're on step one of your process, it shows you how to get to step two. It will not show you how to go from step one to step 100 directly.

UNDERSTANDING INTUITION

Intuition goes beyond thought, ideas, and words. The greatest minds in history always came up with the most revolutionary ideas not by thinking from the past, but by viewing from the present. By truly experiencing the present moment, you'll allow your mind to fully connect with all the information in the universe. You'll be drawing information directly from the unknown where an infinite number of possibilities have already been mapped out.

As great as this sounds, the voice of intuition can be drowned out easily. The voice of intuition is very subtle, and truth be told, most of us aren't accustomed to hearing it. Think of it as eating food that is very mild in flavor right after eating food that is full of spices and tickles your tongue in every way imaginable.

Most likely, you'll not be able to detect subtle flavors because your taste buds have adapted to the stronger flavor profile. Now imagine doing this over and over for however long you've lived. Chances are it'll take you many months or even years to start noticing more subtle flavors in food.

In the same manner, your mind has become accustomed to thinking loudly. "Loud" in this sense means it's become used to time traveling. It's become used to trying to figure out how to go from step one to 100 and doesn't consider all the steps in between. It hasn't been trained to view the wisdom inherent in the journey and only sees the end goal.

When the mind speaks to you in practical and logical terms, it is valid to consider it. However, it can be quite detrimental if it is the only thing you consider. Your intuition is just as important as any other part of your guidance system. Rational thoughts are just as valuable as irrational thoughts. To separate the two would be like to read the lyrics and notes of a song without hearing the singer and instruments.

Whenever you try to stray away from the mind's logical way of thinking, it'll normally experience some sort of resistance. Putting trust in the unknown wisdom of intuition is "risky" when you compare it to the rules of how you're supposed to do things. Trusting your intuition is only risky if you mistake it for your compulsions.

Compulsions are nothing but the old thoughts and behaviors of our minds. They are loud, stubborn, and operate from known ways of thinking. These are the urges, cravings, and addictions you have to external stimulation. If we're ever going to maximize the potential of our intuition, we need to recognize that both are present.

If you're unsure of how to distinguish between the voice of your compulsions and your intuition, consider the element of time within them. If the voice is time-traveling far into the future or is telling you stories from the past, then this is most certainly a compulsion. Intuition does not concern itself beyond the present moment.

Your intuition proposes a course of action and leaves it up to you to follow through on it. It needs action on your behalf for it to speak to you. Some people think of using their intuition by simply sitting back and dreaming about it. That's not how it works!

You need to build momentum in order to build your receptivity on the part of intuition. Momentum is built by creation. Whether this be the creation of new thoughts, feelings, or actions. Do whatever you know and begin executing whatever ideas you have. By doing this you're giving the universe some material to work with. You're allowing it to help you.

Scientific evidence points to the fact that listening to our intuitions is highly beneficial for not only decision making but for guiding our lives down the path we're in most alignment with. There are two kinds of intuitive listening, in scientific terms. The first is emotion-based and the other is experience-based (Kutsch, 2019). Most researchers seem to agree that listening to experience-based intuition usually results in better decisions. This is because experience is simply another measure of how much momentum we've built in a certain area. It is the result of actions repeated over long periods of time, and as a result, the universe has plenty of material to work with and provides you with the right information at the right time.

Don't make the mistake of thinking that emotion-based intuition is invalid, though. Emotions are the expression of your inner being. Be aware of them when you're making decisions as they will tell you whether moving forward with this decision is something that will keep you in or out of alignment.

Getting good at distinguishing between these voices is a matter of repetition and awareness. Never question your hunches, especially if they make you step outside your comfort zone. Stay present, receptive, and open and the universe will channel to you your truth.

ENERGY MANAGEMENT

All of us are obsessed with managing our time. We live by the movement of our clocks. However, you've learned that money and everything else in this universe is simply energy. It stands to reason that if you're experiencing a lack of money in your life, what you're really experiencing is a lack of energy.

Therefore, the way to increase the amount of energy you have is to manage it better. In other words, let go of time management and instead focus on managing your energy. Intuition plays a huge role in helping you do this. It speaks to you and tells you what you ought to do next, whether it is taking a break or spurring you into more action.

Einstein and Newton used a famous technique called the "micro nap," which helped them manage their energy. Given the intensely theoretical nature of their work, they needed their minds to be in peak form. When things became too heavy, they would take a power nap that lasted for no more than 20 minutes.

The painter Salvador Dali had an even more effective technique. He would nap holding a set of keys. As soon as his mind shut down and his hand let go of the keys, they'd clang on a plate and wake him up. Dali would then resume his work fully refreshed, having provided his mind with the exact amount of rest it needed.

Energy can also come from the rituals and practices you do on a daily basis. Do you exercise regularly? Do you meditate? Do you read books? Do you spend time in nature? These are all excellent ways of managing your energy. In fact, if you're able to master just one of the habits I've listed above, you can expect a good return on investment when it comes to how you think, feel, and act.

Exercise can release stress hormones and reduce the tension and stagnate energy around your body. Meditation is a great way of training your brain to stay present and mindful about your current circumstance. Reading books will open you up to different perspectives, thus giving you a wider scope of untapped creativity and imagination. Spending time in nature will keep you grounded and connected to the essence of life. Managing your energy on a daily basis is crucial if you ever want to find any success in managing your money.

Energy Investment

Where are you currently investing your energy? Are you investing it into drama and negativity? Are you investing it into a poverty-stricken self-image that convinces you that you cannot hang onto money or make any?

Around 70% of lottery winner go broke because they didn't have the self-image of someone that could handle the energy that came with money.

Managing your energy output is essential if you're ever going to fully take control of your financial life. If you need to buy a new laptop to execute your plans to earn more money, then pick one that suits your budget. If you expect your financial desires to manifest, why rush things right now? Move at your pace, with the means you currently have. You do not need to overindulge yourself superficially to prove that what you have is coming.

Your compulsions will act from a place of lack. They'll try to convince you that the present moment is unbearable if you don't spend it on fancy items. It uses the existence of your future riches as a pretext to get you to act from a scarcity mindset. The media is one of the main mediums of communication responsible for this type of conditioning. If we're not seen with the latest shoes, clothes, car, or jewelry, than we don't qualify as rich or successful. This is a superficial form of expressing riches that only keeps you more stuck in poverty.

Warren Buffet still lives in the same home he bought for $31,500 in 1958. Mark Zuckerberg still wears a t-shirt, hoodie, and jeans as his uniform to any social event or meeting. Richard Branson doesn't enjoy spending more than ten euros on a bottle of wine.

I'm not saying you shouldn't buy luxury items when you have money to do so. What I am saying is you shouldn't buy luxury items in order to fill a void within or strengthen an identity that is not who you really are. Invest your money on who you want to become, rather than feeding an identity you're trying to escape.

There is another perspective that can be seen on the other side of the coin. This one relates to people that hold onto their money for dear life. Most of the time, this is because they've been ripped off in the past or never got their money back from an investment they made. When this happens, it leaves a mark in your subconscious mind. You start believing that no matter where you spend your money, it's always going to be a waste. You avoid taking the risks you need to take to move forward, and this keeps you stuck.

Saving your money just for the sake of saving it is not a good investment because money is energy. If you're not planning on investing it in the future, it needs to go into something today. It needs to move and circulate in order to grow and help you generate more money. When you invest money and it doesn't work out, it wasn't because you invested the money, it was because you invested the money poorly.

Stagnate energy will keep you stuck. For you to make more money, you cannot be afraid of letting it go. If you are afraid of letting it go, you've either built an attachment to the money itself or you fear losing it. Discovering how you can use your intuition to get out of this viscous cycle will help you tremendously on your journey to manifesting wealth.

TECHNIQUE #11: WHOLE BODY YES

The Whole Body Yes technique comes from the Conscious Leadership Group led by Jim Dethmer, Diana Chapman, and Kaley Warner Klemp. Since discovering this technique I've noticed a huge positive shift when it comes to how I handle business and relationship decisions. Not only do I find myself being right more often, but it also leads me to be more aware of certain situations and to see them from a new perspective.

The Whole Body Yes is divided into three separate sections. These sections are the head, heart, and gut. Let's break them down individually.

Head: Think of the logical side based on the research, feedback, and information you've gathered on a certain topic. This is where experience-based intuition comes in. Review these things and confirm that they make sense or don't make sense.

Heart: Now let's view this decision from an emotional view. Refer back to a time when you felt your heart was fully in it. Try to remember what it felt like when you fully committed your emotions. This is when the heart was speaking to you. With every decision, notice if this same feeling arises.

Gut: This is the perspective of your inner being, in other words, the purest form of intuition. For this one, recall back to previous intuitive hunches you've had and notice if you're feeling the same during this decision.

A Whole Body Yes is meant to ensure that you are 100% committed and correct about your decision. The more often you recognize the difference between a "yes" and a "no", the easier it'll be for you to make decisions.

TECHNIQUE #12: ENERGY HABITS

For this next technique, we'll be focusing on the habits that you have. The idea behind the Energy Habits Process technique is simply to build positive habits that raise your energy and vibration. Activities such as exercise, meditation, reading, or journaling can all be examples of habits that move you into alignment with what you desire.

As previously mentioned in this chapter, if we're ever going to manage our money the right way, we need to understand how we manage our energy. I've created a step-by-step process to help outline all of your habits, how your energy flows when you perform these habits, and what new habits you can start to implement.

Step 1: Write down all of the habits that you have right now. These are actions you do on a daily basis without even thinking about it.

Step 2: Consider if these habits are in alignment with your purpose and the vision you have for your life. Do they waste your energy, or do they increase it? Write down "yes" or "no" next to each one.

Step 3: Write down all the habits that you have in your vision. Refer back to the Perfect Day exercise if you need to.

Step 4: Optimize your habits by removing the ones that move you out of alignment and introduce the new habits that move you into alignment. Here are two tips to help you build positive habits and break bad ones: Start small and adjust your environment accordingly to help with the execution of the habit.

With this newfound self-discipline, you'll find it easier to manage your energy, and as a result, you'll find it easier to manage your money.

CHAPTER 8

The Language of Success

"Money is only a tool. It will take you wherever you wish,
but it will not replace you as the driver."
- Ayn Rand

What is a clear indicator of the kind of mindset you're currently choosing to live with? In short, it's the language you use to describe your situation and various events in your life. The universe is a constant feedback loop in that it always gives you what you want, whether you're conscious of it or not.

We attract more of the things we focus our energy on. Focus on lack and you will attract more lack. The universe also checks in with you constantly to evaluate whether you're receiving everything you asked for. One of the ways it does this is by monitoring the language you use to describe your reality.

THE POWER OF WORDS

Have you ever met someone who springs out of bed every morning telling themselves "Today is a special day!" every single day you've known them? "How many special days can a person possibly have?" you might have thought to yourself. Well, it doesn't really matter because that person has chosen to believe in their abundance and that the universe manifests what they choose accordingly.

Your language, both spoken and unspoken, reveals what you truly desire. Are you reading this book because you're "sick of being poor and want to learn how to make money" or are you reading this to "figure out how to increase your wealth"? Both of those statements are two sides of the same coin.

Duality exists in everything in the universe, and your language is no exception. Wealthy people talk about money, and their reality very differently from those that perceive a lack in their lives. Shifting your focus from lack to abundance also means you need to consciously monitor your language.

Your words are influenced by your beliefs and as you've learned previously, your physical reality exists in a constant feedback loop that incorporates these two items. Since this is a loop we're talking about, it stands to reason that your words, the choices you make when fully conscious of them, also influences your beliefs.

If you wander around the aisles of your local supermarket telling yourself you can't afford this and can only pay for that, you're creating a belief in your mind that you're poor and lack money. If you're moving through reality in a state of abundance, you'll frame these spending choices as being aligned with your goals or not.

That box of premium cereal might feel right to buy now, but your mindset of lack tells you that you can't afford it and it costs too much. This might be true, but it's in situations like this where you can flip the equation to your favor. What if you didn't want to buy it because you'd rather spend the money on your passion project? Or you'd rather buy a brand that has less sugar? Change the stories you tell yourself and notice your reality will change with it.

Trusting in your sense of lack is simply being penny wise and pound foolish. You save a little money today only to blow a lot more down the road. The language that you use to frame these choices is a sure marker of which way you're headed. The great news is that language is easy to change.

All it takes to change your language is awareness and choice. Become aware of how you communicate and set your intention of changing the language surrounding your thoughts. Understand that language is energy, and by focusing on negative language, you're draining energy out of yourself. You're manifesting a reality that doesn't resonate with the frequency of your desires.

A lack of money is simply a reflection of your perception of your reality. It isn't the only thing that will be missing. Happiness, love, freedom, security, etc. are all feelings that you will lack because your language won't translate to their abundance.

Language is an expression of your perspective. This goes back to what you learned in Chapter 3 about the reality loop. Your perspective eventually frames your reality. Start speaking like you're abundant and watch your thoughts, emotions, and actions reflect these words.

CONSCIOUS VS UNCONSCIOUS SUCCESS

When it comes to success in anything, there are two ways of manifesting it into your reality. You can either manifest it consciously or unconsciously. Let's break down what I mean by this.

Conscious success means that it was expected based on the prior thoughts, feelings, and actions you chose to express in order to achieve the desired outcome. It's a sustainable way of reaching success. It's a way of shifting your identity to fit into the reality of what you desire. This is when your vibration is in perfect alignment and your life is the perfect reflection of it.

By reading this book, it's exactly what you are trying to do. You are trying to consciously create the success that you want in life. By applying the principles and techniques outlined here, you will eventually find this success. The only obstacle is yourself. In order to experience a new reality, you need to embody a new identity. You do not embody a new identity simply by adding more to the current one you have now. The real process is to remove that which is covering up the potential that is already inside of you. This is a far more "difficult" path to success, however, it's the most sustainable one in the long-term.

Unconscious success occurs when someone reaches a certain level of financial, career, or professional success without consciously knowing how they did it. This happens when they've had positive conditioning in their life. They've unconsciously embodied an identity that resonates with this kind of outcome. This is usually the case for the sons and daughters of the wealthy. Because they've spent most of their life around successful people (their parents), they grow up being taught about the "secrets" to success and with the probable financial backing and support.

Although this looks like a far easier path to the top, it's not very sustainable. With more success, comes more problems. If you're unconscious about how you should overcome these problems, it can lead to severe anxiety and depression. This can be seen amongst hundreds of celebrity and public figures around the world.

Recognizing that there are two kinds of success is essential because it will help clear up a lot of the "how" in your journey. Everyone finds success in their own way. Whether you were born into a single parent and low-income household or as the child of a famous politician, we all have our own unique path to take.

Judging how others are taking their path will only create resistance within yourself because it implies that you don't have the power within you to achieve the same level of success. If you judge others, you're really judging yourself. Be aware of this, because it can be far too easy to get caught up on the latest social media post of their new car.

Being aware and conscious of your journey to success is not a handicap. In fact, it's a gift. It'll make the process that much more enjoyable and transformational. You'll experience more than you ever would if you started from the top. Appreciate the chance you have to face all the failures, setbacks, and obstacles that will inevitably come your way. They will help build a stronger internal foundation that will skyrocket your ability to manifest more success than you could ever imagine.

A Chinese bamboo tree takes around five years to reach full maturity. For the first four years or so, it only reaches a few feet above the ground. During the fifth year, in the space of six weeks, a Chinese bamboo tree can grow up to 90 feet in height. Consider getting reassurance from this ancient plant next time you think your success is "taking too long." Focus on your roots, and your height will come with time.

CHILD-LIKE PLAY

Something that all successful people embody is a curiosity for what comes next. I'm talking about the child-like wonder that keeps our excitement roaring every hour of every day of every week. This is a vibration that keeps you receptive to the hidden opportunities and creative ideas that life throws at you. Being in a playful state while in the process of building wealth is essential if you're ever going to align with the desire that comes with it.

It's no secret that all human beings love playing fun games. Observe a child learning new information and you will notice that the only way to get them to focus is when they're playing. Children are the epitome of perfect alignment with desire.

They wake everyday like it's the very first day of their life. What seems mundane and normal for a 40-year-old mind can be an opportunity for creation for a 6-year-old one. It doesn't need to be the creation of something physical. It can be the creation of a new perspective. This is where imagination comes in. An action figure can be a superhero one day and a farmer the next. The child embraces its power to choose what their character will be dressed up today. Nobody can convince them otherwise.

It's this state of limitlessness that radiates vibrations that attract people, things, and opportunities into our lives. The younger we are, the less conditioned our minds are. Unfortunately, as we grow older, we start developing certain beliefs about who we can and can't be. This can lead down a negative spiral because it goes against everything our inner child wants to express.

Play puts us in an automatic state of joy and abundance. It makes us feel good because it jogs both the rational and creative faculties of our minds. It removes all resistance to learning and places us immediately in the flow state or on the path of least resistance. The fact that we enjoy the state of play is the surest evidence that feeling good is the best marker of aligned vibration.

A mental state of play is essential for you to maintain if you wish to manifest your dreams into reality. I'm not talking of being frivolous or of shirking your responsibilities. Nor am I talking about indulging in childish behavior. Instead, it is to maintain a sense of humor and freedom throughout whatever life throws at you. It is about choosing to be cheerful, no matter the circumstances that you are facing.

"This is the real secret of life – to be completely engaged with what you are doing in the here and now. And instead of calling it work, realize it is play."
- Alan Watts

A lot of people buy into the popular notions of being "driven" and of focusing "singularly" on their goal. There is no problem with this if their journey to achieving their goal is thoroughly enjoyable and fun to them. The problem comes when their journey to success becomes more of a need rather than a want. If you *need* to become successful, it will be very hard to.

If you *want* to, but do not mind not having the physical manifestation of it right now, then you're in the perfect vibration to attract it.

Living in a playful state will help you remove all of the resistance that comes with your career, business, and road to financial freedom. Money is a very serious topic in the minds of many. This is justifiable given the world that we live in today. However, making the accumulation of money your primary reason for living in this moment will only move you farther away from it.

This is because you will end up sacrificing your own vibration in order to achieve it. Moving yourself out of alignment like this will make it very difficult to manifest the experiences that come with money. Even if (and this is a big if) you achieve your money goal, you'll have sacrificed so many things that keep you in a positive vibration, that it'll feel like it was all for nothing. Your priority should always be your vibration. This is the path of least resistance and it is the path most sustainable for true happiness in the long and short-term.

Imagine what it feels like to be happy before and after you're financially successful. Viewing the manifestation of your reality as playful puts you in this state automatically. Who has ever been miserable playing a game they love? It's the opposite of being intense.

Intensity implies effort, hard work, and struggle. When you let go of this idea, you let go of the notion that obstacles are meant to stop you, when the truth is they are there to help you grow. The very fact that you find obstacles annoying to overcome indicates that you aren't enjoying the process.

How can you expect to manifest your reality in such a state? Be playful with the universe and have fun living the life you live. To consciously move towards success is to understand that success doesn't need to be about intensity, unenjoyable effort, and seriousness. It's about getting enjoyment out of every step in the process and feeling successful as a result. This is the key to living and manifesting success with flow and ease.

TECHNIQUE #13 - MEDITATIVE WRITING AND JOURNALING

This is a technique that was inspired by Elizabeth Gilbert, author of *Eat Pray Love*, and it involves putting your mind in a meditative state through the act of writing. I've noticed this myself when I'm writing out notes, ideas, and topics for a new book in my journal. Before I know it, I write 4 pages worth of content in just 30 minutes. Time seems to fly, and ideas flow effortlessly.

Some people might call this the "flow state," Elizabeth calls it "wordless oneness", and others may call it "the zone." During these times, your brain is in optimal conditions to be creative and intuitive. This is the state where you begin to connect all the dots that have been accumulating in your subconscious mind.

With the Meditative Writing and Journaling technique, you can achieve this state of timelessness and flow. It also helps you lay out all your thoughts, feelings, ideas, and hunches onto a piece of paper so you can refer back to it whenever you want. Your next big opportunity, decision, or idea that leads to financial success might just come from one of these sessions.

Here are the steps to Meditative Writing and Journaling:

Step 1: Take a few minutes to settle in a space of silence. Focus on your breath or on the subtle movement of energy on the surface levels of your body. Set the intention of being fully open with yourself and receptive to ANY thoughts that come to mind.

Step 2: Set a timer for 10-15 minutes and begin free writing without stopping. Do not waste your time trying to edit, reflect, or fix anything throughout this process. Simply be present in the moment, relax, and express your thoughts in the form of writing.

Step 3: When the timer goes off, take a deep breath, and review what you've written. Underline anything that catches your eye or intrigues you some way. You don't need to ask why it intrigues, just accept that it does.

Step 4: Use these new ideas and thoughts that you underlined as a prompt for your next session. Express appreciation for the connections that you made and the positive aspects you pulled out of it.

CHAPTER 9

Money Manifestation Mistakes: 3 Unconscious Reasons Why You're Not Manifesting Money

"Dollars aren't the root of happiness, but they are not the root of evil either. They are the result of how somebody lines up the energy."
- Abraham Hicks

People often wonder why their physical manifestations are taking as long as they are. The universe takes its time manifesting your new reality physically, and given that it knows far more than we can ever comprehend, it stands to reason that everything will happen in its own time, when you're vibrationally ready. There's nothing to be worried about.

Worry drives people to perform actions that end up blocking the abundance that is coming their way. They sabotage themselves, and even worse, continue to believe they're living from a state of abundance when they're clearly not. This chapter is going to spotlight three of the most common mistakes that people make.

Most of these mistakes portray a superficial view of reality. In other words, they are a perspective that only takes into account the physical part of reality. You are not living with presence and in alignment with every moment of your day, rather you are chasing something that is outside of you. Again, the first step to changing these behaviors and patterns is to become aware of them.

MISTAKE #1- ACTING AND NOT BEING

One of the most repeated mantras of success is "acting as if." Everyone from rappers to movie stars advise people to act as if they're already where they want to be. This is both true and false. What's more important is that a person "be" who they need to be in order to successfully manifest. If they're in this state then they won't just be acting, but they will be behaving in line with the reality that they desire.

If they aren't being, then acting takes on a negative connotation. It implies that you need to hide your true reality and superimpose a fake persona in order to convince the world you're someone else. This is a hard thing to do! Moreover, it's a viewpoint that is focused on the outside world and isn't centered around your inner compass.

It removes you from listening to the universe and to your intuition because you're busy listening to what someone else is telling you. How could you possibly manifest anything from this state? The only possible result is that you will end up unhappy because you will either notice the lack of your desired manifestation physically or you will lose yourself trying to please everyone else around you.

Being is far more important than acting. Being implies your beliefs, perspective, actions and reality are in alignment and you're receiving the full flow of information from the infinite. You've chosen to be a certain way, and this means the outer reality is not as important as the inner one.

Change always occurs from the inside out, not the other way around. We make the mistake of looking at other people's results and think that the results are why they're successful. The fact is that the fancy car is a result of them being a certain way. It isn't the cause of it.

As an example, let's say you wish to manifest a new BMW for yourself. Sticking a BMW label on your Honda isn't going to turn it into something it isn't. The interiors are the same, the shape of the body is the same as is the engine and the transmission. Slapping a label onto the Honda is a bit like "*acting as if*" without the power of "*being as if.*"

Financially successful people get that way because of who they are and how they view themselves. They are rich on the inside and thus vibrationally align themselves with the frequency of money. They view it as a natural state of being. Those who moan about their lack of physical money, focus on the absence of it, and thus vibrationally align themselves with the frequency of lack.

So focus on being, not acting. Surface level actions get you nowhere. It's the change on the inside that really counts and removes all the negative filters from your old identity. Positive thoughts allied with elevated emotions followed by inspired actions is what attracts your desired manifestation to you.

MISTAKE #2- JUDGMENT

There are a whole host of issues that emanate from an attitude of judgment. Judgment itself implies that you're imposing your views upon a certain situation that is acting outside of you. It implies that instead of being and remaining in the moment, you're rushing to process the information through your perspectives and beliefs.

More often than not, judgment leads us down wrong paths. For example, if you see someone who is financially wealthy with a nice car and clothes, your mind, or better yet ego, will immediately start comparing what you have to what they have.

On the inside, this can start generating negative emotions or patterns that enforce a perspective of lack upon yourself. In such times, it's important to remember that you always have a choice. Tapping into your intuitive hunch to believe in your own potential to be happy and successful has nothing to do with what's going on in someone else's life.

You have full control over your own reaction to external events. You don't have control over the external event itself. A lot of people try to control the external. We wish that those around us would behave a certain way so that we can be content. We wish for others to carry out certain actions that will result in greater prosperity for ourselves.

In order to enforce this point of view, we judge their behaviors and actions. What we miss is that by doing so we're giving up our choice of reacting to the external positively. We're giving away our power to the external and are falling into the trap of acting instead of being.

Your only choice is to talk to the external and choose your own reality. Judgment is a way of giving up this choice and power. It is trying to live in a fantasy world where you have full control over the external, when you don't. Allow your reality to change by choosing what you want instead of trying to make it happen and pushing away what you don't want.

MISTAKE #3- IMPATIENCE

Patience is a huge sign of abundance. If you dig a little deeper, you'll understand why. When you are patient, you are expressing your belief that everything is happening according to the universe's plans for you and that everything will take as long as it needs to take. After all, the universe is in control of the external events in your life, so there's no need to worry about how, when, and where your desire will manifest.

Let's say you're stuck in traffic on your way to an important meeting. This meeting is between you and a client who is ready to sign a lucrative contract that will bring you a ton of money. Naturally, you want to get there on time and not sabotage your chances. Being stuck in traffic might breed impatience within you.

Where does this impatience come from? When it comes down to it, it stems from a belief that you're going to lose this contract if you're not on time or that you're not going to achieve your desired reality of making more money. It's from a place of lack. You believe that the money this client is going to pay you is the only money that is available to you in the world and that the universe has no more in store for you.

Let's take a step further back and examine the implications of these beliefs. First off, how could you possibly know that this traffic jam is going to cause you to be late? How can you know that the client is going to decline signing a contract with you because you were late? How could you know that the jam is a bad thing?

Perhaps there's an accident that's about to occur down the road that would put you in the hospital. Would you rather be late due to a traffic jam or late due to needing hospitalization? When you struggle against your external world by expressing impatience, you're building resistance within your reality. You're leaving the serene world of the present and are time-traveling into the future and past. You're giving your power away to something that isn't in your control and judgment soon follows. "I should have anticipated this traffic jam," "This is why I'll never be successful," "Bad things always happen to me right when something good is about to take place", and on and on.

Impatience causes us to make rash decisions and to assume that we know better than the universe. It only breeds more frustration and sets us on a negative spiral. Break out of this by shifting your awareness back into the present moment and by choosing to respond to your environment instead of reacting to it.

It's important to note that there is a difference between being patient and being complacent. Being patient means that you're working to better yourself internally, because the better you feel with yourself despite the situation, the more your reality will reflect this. If you're complacent, you're not really changing your reality. What you're doing is waiting for reality to change for you. This is yet another superficial perspective that contradicts the science of manifestation. If you're waiting for reality to change, you're not in the process of creation, and if you're not in the process of creation, your reality is not changing.

Be comfortable with not being in control and recognize that the universe is always connected to the vibrations that you're emitting. All you need to do is continue creating from an aligned state and be patient!

TECHNIQUE #14 - NEUTRALIZATION

The Neutralization technique is very similar to the Generalization Technique we talked about in Chapter 2. The only difference is that this neutralization technique works in relationship to your external intentions and desires. In other words, we're going to be focusing on detaching you from the outcome and helping you view life through the present moment.

Before I explain how it works, I'd like to highlight the difference between neutrality and complacency. Neutrality is the absence of strong or extreme expressions of something. Complacency is the act of being overly content or uncritically satisfied. The difference between the two is that neutrality takes into consideration the access we have to infinite abundance, while complacency doesn't.

The idea behind the Neutralization technique is to simply be neutral to all the ideas, opportunities, desires, and situations that arise in your life. A state of neutrality removes you from the egoic way of thinking. The ego is constantly needing and chasing after something that validates its identity. This way of thinking ends up repelling all of the evidence that you're looking for in your physical reality. The goal here is to simply keep your eyes open and allow the opportunity, the evidence, or the manifestation to show itself to you rather than going out there to look for it.

"Stop trying to leave, and you will arrive. Stop seeking, and you will see. Stop running away, and you will be found."
– Lao Tzu

CHAPTER 10

How to Make Your Money Manifestation Inevitable

"If you will assume your desire and live there as though it were true, no power on earth can stop it from becoming a fact."
- Neville Goddard

Your mindset is a key determinant of how much money you will attract and wealth you will build in your life. As you've learned throughout this book, it will come under attack from external sources. Most people react to this attack by trying to control their external reality, but as you've learned, doing this is futile.

Instead, it's far better to build a mindset that is impervious to such attacks and is resilient. No matter the negativity surrounding you, a strong mindset will help you sail through those difficulties and will reduce them to impermanent states as opposed to a permanent state of reality.

There are three shifts that you can execute right now to ensure a strong mindset. Let's take a look at them one by one.

MONEY ZEN

The first mindset shift to make is to view reality from yet another perspective that we will look into. What is the biggest source of unhappiness in your life? Your first instinct might be to say the lack of money, or the lack of prosperity, and so on. These are answers that are focused on external causes. Dig a little deeper and you will notice that it isn't the external that is causing problems, but rather the internal judgment of those external events that is creating suffering within you.

Let's say you witness a minor car accident. If one of those vehicles happens to be yours, how would you react? Your first thought would be on the amount of money it's going to cost you to fix it, how much time it's going to take, and how unlucky you are, and so on. Now let's assume the car that was involved in the accident was not yours.

Not so angry now, are you? Both scenarios involved the same outer reality (car crash), but your reactions were polar opposites. This is because your perception was based on external conditions rather than internal state. While it's impossible to control external circumstances, it goes to show that you can always choose to respond however you want to what you witness and experience.

Being in a state of Zen with regards to money is the perspective that everything that is happening to you is for the best, that these things make you stronger and are guiding you towards a higher goal that will result in higher degrees of happiness.

It is to believe that the universe is abundant and is therefore incapable of leading you astray. You might perceive the current situation or the choices in front of you as being bad but this is only because you aren't aware of the divine plans the universe has in store for you. You cannot directly see the consequences of all of your actions in the field and thus cannot see the long-term ramifications of something seemingly negative in the short term.

By framing everything that happens to you as helping you, you remove the possibility of being disappointed or frustrated with your situation. You place your awareness fully with your choice to respond in accordance with what you want to take out of the situation, rather than on what the situation is taking away from you. This not only leads to more happiness, but a lot less resistance when it comes to the vibration you're emitting to the universe.

In this path, there are minimal possibilities for guilt, frustration, or sadness to exist. This path only leads to more internal growth. How can any negativity exist in a world that's always working in your favor?

THE UNIVERSAL FEEDBACK LOOP

All of your actions and words, indeed your entire state of being, is monitored by the universe. Don't mistake this for a judgmental frame of mind. The universe does not judge and is impartial towards everyone. Its sole concern lies in giving everyone exactly what they want. In order to know what they want, it's important for them to know what they don't want. The same is true about how you're thinking, feeling, and acting. If you're not thinking, feeling, and acting in accordance with what you want, the universe will show you this.

You can think of this loop as being a mirror. What you put out there is what you will receive back in kind. If you dress yourself well and look into a mirror, you'll see a positive reflection of yourself. Dress yourself haphazardly and you won't like what you see.

The universe reflects back to us what we're putting into it. If you choose to radiate negativity and scarcity, that's all you will receive back. The great news about this fundamental truth is that you can shift your reality based on the energy you choose to put into the universe.

Let's say you view evidence of poverty around where you live. You see run down housing and other signs of people struggling to make ends meet. If you look at this and think that this is what you deserve, or that this accurately reflects who you are, you're only going to create the same kind of reality for yourself. The things you try to do will not work out and will only reinforce this belief. Instead, if you view the positives in your life despite the evidence of negatives around you, and you choose to believe that you're destined for great things, this is exactly what the universe will provide you with.

I must mention that the universe will give you opportunities to act. You'll still need to have intention with how you think, feel, and act. Using the natural laws of the universe puts you in a position to take advantage of events. It doesn't do them for you. The universal feedback loop is also a great way to check where your mindset is currently at.

If you've been working on something but haven't been receiving evidence of positive manifestation, or better yet, have been receiving more obstacles and roadblocks that you ever anticipated, then take a look at the vibration behind your executions and what perspectives and beliefs you're holding onto.

Your mindset is in direct contact with the metaphysical reality, the fourth dimension. This is where the feedback loop gathers information about your state of being. Focus on radiating positive intentions in everything you do, and you will automatically connect with the laws of attraction. The more in line you are with your desire when it comes to your state of being, the more the universe will shape your reality to fit your desire.

This is why the rich get richer and the poor get poorer. The feedback loops are either ignored or they're reinforced. Everyone's living in the reality that their mindset has created, and this is what determines the level of wealth they create in their lives. Focus on working hand in hand with the universe, and it'll reward you.

TRUSTING THE UNIVERSE

Manifesting what you desire in your life isn't about creation or about visualization. Instead, you need to think of it as a way of living. The things you desire will come to you only when you truly become the kind of person who's vibrationally resonating with the experience you desire. This takes time because it requires a lot of cleansing from past conditioning.

It is during this time that most people sabotage themselves. They begin to judge their efforts and compare themselves to other people. A huge reason for you to relax into the present moment is that you will be at the door and fully in touch with the infinite quantum field. Your ego cannot exist during this moment in time. Every choice you make is in accordance to who you are being in the exact present moment you are in. You can only choose to embody your old identity if you choose to. If you choose to make a shift into a new identity, you need to start making the choices that resonate with it as you live your life. Make new choices in your focus, thoughts, and feelings. Respond how you choose to your environment rather than reacting based on how you've always done.

Often people become nervous due to the seeming lack of progress in their lives, and they'll begin to try and force situations rather than looking to align with them from within. They visualize with greater "force" and spend more time trying the various techniques that they believe lead to manifestation. In doing all this, they build massive resistance between themselves and the universe.

After all, trying hard to make things happen implies that you have some control over your environment and that you don't trust the universal forces that actually do. You've just learned that this is hardly the case. All you can control is the inner reaction you have to your outer circumstances and nothing else.

People who try to force their manifestations to become real are effectively trying to push a boulder up a steep hill. At some point, you'll run out of energy and the weight of your effort is going to crush you. Is it any surprise then that such people begin to question whether manifestation is real? Believing that your desired manifestation will come from tireless effort and relentless action is pitiful. Sure, it can work if you believe it will.

The only problem is that this way of manifesting creates so much resistance that it won't even feel worth it because you will always want more. In other words, when you sacrifice the present moment, for an imaginary future goal, you're ultimately sacrificing life itself. No matter how much money you manifest and wealth you build, you're always going to want more. It's the natural inclination of human beings. Therefore, why not live like you have it all already? Live in the reality of your manifestation right now instead of chasing an illusion.

If you find yourself in such a situation, relax and acknowledge that you're trying too hard. There is no past or future that needs reassurance, there is only now. Relax into the present moment and remind yourself of the fact that everything that's happening will only contribute to your growth and how you choose to live your life.

TECHNIQUE #15 - QUANTUM LEAPING

The Quantum Leaping technique, inspired by Bob Proctor, is a way of surfing through reality in order to achieve faster and greater manifestation results. As discussed in Chapter 1, we have access to infinite realities in the quantum field. This access comes through tapping into the present moment. Now, believe it or not, every time you make a decision or choice, you are actually moving across different alternate realities.

We usually make these leaps into alternate realities by resonating our energy with other versions of ourselves in those realities. In other words, when we match the energy of another version of ourselves, we move towards the reality they are living in. When we have this strong connection, it's possible for us to gain access to information that can only be found in the other reality. This is what helps us make the necessary decisions to successfully manifest our desires.

Most of society believes that growth only happens linearly, but this is not true. In fact, it's possible for you to achieve your five-year plan in just one year. This is called exponential growth. Now, you may be asking yourself, "How do I consciously quantum leap to the reality of my choice?" Well, the more important question should be how to NOT quantum leap. Removing all the filters that prevent you from living through the intentions of your inner being is essential.

Here's what you need to do:

Step 1: Experience the present moment living as the alternate version of you. In other words, embody the version of you that you want to become. Take actions, think thoughts, and feel feelings that are in alignment with this version of you.

Step 2: Eliminate all feelings of doubt, disbelief, and disempowerment. You need to be receptive to everything that the universe has to offer and accept that it is possible for you to get that which you desire, no matter how big it is. Closing access to even the fewest possibilities will lead to more challenges and obstacles, and thus doubt and disbelief follows.

Step 3: Realize that quantum leaps rely on unknown forces. There is no way of you knowing how it will happen. Accept this and be receptive to all possibilities.

Step 4: Think beyond common sense. If you want to make exponential progress towards your financial and career goals, you need to think illogically. There are no limits to what the universe can offer, so until you accept that normal three-dimensional thinking is most of the time irrelevant, you can't make the quantum jump you're expecting.

Step 5: Start setting intentions and making decisions that align with the reality you want to experience, even if you don't feel ready yet. You need to think beyond what you've thought about so far. Appreciate and take advantage of what you have now, and more opportunities and chances will arise. Learn about yourself, grow yourself from within, and expand your horizons by putting intention into becoming a greater version of you.

Step 6: Enjoy the ride and don't try so hard, after all, nothing in this book should be hard to do. It should all flow easily to you. If you're executing steps 1-5, all you need to do is enjoy the process. Play with the universe, turn fear of the unknown into excitement, think and feel in accordance to who you truly are, act towards your passion and purpose, and finally, embody your inner sense of freedom.

Conclusion

You have now learned about "The Magic of Manifesting Money." It is my sincere hope that you have found the new perspectives and 15 advanced techniques to be helpful, and everything else that was discussed about how to attract wealth, success and abundance without hard work. Even if you find just one of the techniques to be helpful, it could make a huge difference in your life. You may have been looking for that one piece of the puzzle that was missing in order to "get the law of attraction" to work for you. And perhaps you found it in this book.

We covered a lot! We started off by discussing how even your environment is a reflection of how the energy is flowing in your life, and how important it is to keep your physical environment neat and tidy. We also discussed the generalization technique, how to tune into the vibration of freedom, the appreciation method, how to content shift from negative to positive media, how to increase your daily vibration, your perfect day (one of my favorites!), how to find your purpose, 4th dimensional manifesting, and ended with how to quantum leap in order to change your reality. From the micro level of quantum physics, to the macro 3rd dimensional level of reality, we discussed all aspects around the manifestation of money.

Changing your life seems daunting at first glance. Money is a big part of that change, and unfortunately, all we think of when we look at our money is lack. This is true of both rich and poor people. Our minds and the universe have the potential to create massive changes in our lifetimes, changes that are unthinkable for most of us.

Consider the story of a boy born to a handloom weaver and a seamstress in 1835 in Scotland. This boy was hardworking and studious, but was born into a situation that was less than ideal. Money was scarce and opportunities even more so. He attended school for four years before his parents decided to move to the new world in search of better opportunities.

They landed in an area that is modern day Pittsburgh. The boy's parents couldn't afford to send him to school, so he got himself a job working at a local cotton mill. He earned a pittance and was often at work when other boys of his age were out playing or studying. He yearned to learn, but could barely read. He was ambitious but was met with pictures of squalor everywhere he turned.

His parents struggled to make ends meet, like most immigrant families, and he often had to sleep on an empty stomach. His belief of the potential for better days began to pay off slowly as he held a variety of jobs. First as a messenger, then as a cotton mill worker, and then finally he landed a great post for someone of his qualifications: the secretary of the manager of the Pittsburgh section of the Pennsylvania railroad.

The job wasn't glamorous, but he made it his own. Now a young man, he had finally achieved a respectable position as a white collar worker. Not bad for a boy with just four years' worth of education! He had taught himself to read in the meantime, and was prosperous enough to afford a few books.

However, the young man had bigger dreams. He was content with where he was, but this didn't mean he wanted to remain there forever. Collecting the little money he had, he began investing into other railroad and industrial companies based on the intuitive hunches the universe was giving him.

Just as the investments began booming in value, he was appointed to be his boss's successor as the railroad division manager. The young man's career now really began to take off. His investments grew rapidly as did his wealth. By 1865, he was rich enough to quit his position with the railroad and founded a bridge building company. He also founded a telegraph company and won key contracts thanks to his agreeable nature and his willingness to work with whatever he was given.

By his mid 30s, the formerly poverty-stricken boy was a wealthy man. He could have retired in this state and no one would have begrudged him anything. However, he wasn't done yet. In 1870, he decided to get into the steel business. He knew nothing about making steel, just as he had once known nothing about running a railroad or running a bridge-building company. He let go of the "how."

Like his previous businesses, the steel company succeeded and attracted the attention of one of America's wealthiest men. This person, a banker of some repute, paid the man $480 million for his company in 1901. This is the equivalent of $12 billion in today's money.

The man then turned around and gave away 90% of his wealth to underprivileged people and other such causes. He founded one of the biggest libraries in the United States and funded a renowned center for the arts in New York City. You might have heard of this center; it's called Carnegie Hall.

Andrew Carnegie was just one of the many people who figured out that the universe was on his side through the course of his life. Not only was it on his side, it was on everyone's side. It was just a matter of aligning oneself with the true purpose of their life. He figured out that all he had to do was energetically align with what he wanted, and the universe would do the rest.

The universe is so abundant and so rich in opportunity that even an unremarkable boy born into poverty and who had known nothing but squalor could rise to become one of the world's wealthiest men. Throughout his life, Carnegie's success was the quintessential American dream come true.

Napoleon Hill featured him as the basis for his famous book "Think and Grow Rich." Carnegie hinted at the existence of the law of attraction and abundance throughout that book's lessons. You now have the entire blueprint in front of you, thanks to the knowledge that he so willingly shared.

It isn't just Carnegie who shared this knowledge. People such as Oprah Winfrey, Jim Carrey, Steve Harvey, and Arnold Schwarzenegger have spoken about it as well. The universe is ready to give you everything you want, and it doesn't matter where you were born or what situation is prevalent in your life.

In order to manifest success, you need to first understand and think about your life in terms of energy. What sort of energy are you putting out in the world and what sort of energy are you allowing within you? Money is simply energy. If you're experiencing a lack of it, it's due to certain blocks you're carrying. Removing these blocks is as easy as moving into abundance and drawing the immense knowledge that the field has.

Your life's purpose, your perspectives, your vision, your goals, your beliefs… All of these play an important role in helping you align with the universe. Once everything is in alignment, like a well-oiled machine, the right energy and money will begin flowing to you.

You might have been misled into thinking that one needs to do "hard" work for their money, that money only comes to those with unique talents, and so on. This is true only for those people who believe in such things. If you believe that you are worthy of money and that it flows to you effortlessly, then guess what? It will do so.

The universal feedback loop is merely a reflection of what's going on within you. Change yourself from within, and the change outside of you will follow.

With the new perspectives and 15 advanced manifestation techniques taught in this book, you've now received the blueprint, understand how the universe works, and have learned the magic of manifesting money. All you need to do now is apply it. Go out there and put all of this knowledge into practice. Remember to prioritize your energy, and not your time or effort. Riches will surely follow as day follows night.

References

A Step-By-Step Process To 4th Dimensional Manifesting. (2019, October 22). Reality Hacker Co. https://www.realityhacker.co/blogs/news/4th-dimenional-manifesting

Breau, N. (2020a). My 2020 Complete Guide to Manifesting Money - Law of Attraction [Inspired by Abraham Hicks] [YouTube Video]. In *YouTube*. https://www.youtube.com/watch?v=Du0l6PTxyuU&list=PLwryVAXS0c4H8kOBnC-2rYE9eXZ5in4GO&index=19&t=389s

Breau, N. (2020b). Law of Attraction Money Manifestation Process The Three Jar Method [YouTube Video]. In *YouTube*. https://www.youtube.com/watch?v=_57HvsK56ZM

Chen, J. (2019). *Are You in the Top One Percent of the World?* Investopedia. https://www.investopedia.com/articles/personal-finance/050615/are-you-top-one-percent-world.asp

Doughty, A. (2020). Find Your Purpose by doing these 3 things and WATCH what happens [YouTube Video]. In *YouTube*. https://www.youtube.com/watch?v=fnDi6081j5Y

Emmer, J. (2018). *What is Feng Shui? A Brief History of Feng Shui | Feng Shui Style.* Feng Shui Style. http://fengshuistyle.us/what-is-feng-shui/history/

Frankl, V. E. (1992). *Man's search for meaning : an introduction to logotherapy.* Buccaneer Books, Inc.

Haltiwanger, J. (2014, December 24). *The Science of Generosity: Why Giving Makes You So Happy*. Elite Daily. https://www.elitedaily.com/life/science-generosity-feels-good-give/890500

Hanson, R., & Mendius, R. (2009). *Buddha's brain : the practical neuroscience of happiness, love & wisdom*. New Harbinger Publications.

Hicks, A. (2019, August 12). *Abraham Hicks Explains How To Respond to Negative Emotions*. The Joy Within. https://thejoywithin.org/authors/abraham-hicks/how-to-respond-to-negative-emotions

How To Manifest Using Mirror Principle: The Mirror Feedback Loop. (2019). YouTube. https://youtu.be/_d2zxmdbXDo?t=538

Hurst, K. (2016, July 13). *Learn How To Move UP The (Vibrational) Emotional Scale*. The Law Of Attraction. https://www.thelawofattraction.com/law-attraction-learning-move-emotional-scale

Kluger, J. (2015, June 26). *Why You're Pretty Much Unconscious All the Time*. Time; Time. https://time.com/3937351/consciousness-unconsciousness-brain/

Kutsch, L. (2019, August 15). *Can We Rely on Our Intuition?* Scientific American. https://www.scientificamerican.com/article/can-we-rely-on-our-intuition/

Manifestation, in. (2018, December 14). *The Importance of Neutrality in Manifestation*. YouTube. https://youtu.be/4xn5EdpSz9c?t=14

Proctor, B. (2020, March 9). *What Causes a Quantum Leap?* Proctor Gallagher Institute. https://www.proctorgallagherinstitute.com/41382/what-causes-a-quantum-leap

Redd, N. (2017, November 7). *Einstein's Theory of General Relativity*. Space. Com. https://www.space.com/17661-theory-general-relativity.html

Robinson, A. (2016, June 8). *Universal Law of Increase* |. Https://Divine-Awakening.Org/. https://divine-awakening.org/2016/06/law-of-increase/

Skibba, R. (2018). *Einstein, Bohr and the war over quantum theory*. Nature. Com. https://www.nature.com/articles/d41586-018-03793-2

Weese, K. (2018, January 25). Why it costs so much to be poor in America. *The Washington Post*. https://www.washingtonpost.com/news/posteverything/wp/2018/01/25/why-it-costs-so-much-to-be-poor-in-america/

What does it mean when they say the universe is expanding? (2019, February 1). Library of Congress, Washington, D.C. 20540 USA. https://www.loc.gov/everyday-mysteries/item/what-does-it-mean-when-they-say-the-universe-is-expanding

Whole Body Yes. (2020). Conscious.Is. https://conscious.is/excercises-guides/whole-body-yes

THE **MAGIC** OF **MANIFESTING** **LOVE**

15 Advanced Manifestation Techniques
to Stop Chasing, Start Attracting, and
Become Magnetic to Your Dream Relationship

Introduction

I t is an innate human need to love and be loved. You have likely heard countless people utter it before. Maybe the words have even sprung from your own mouth … "I just want to find *the one*."

If you are reading this, then chances are someone you thought to be 'the one' turned out to not be so after all, or you have sadly suffered loss in your life from that loved 'one,' and believe there is no other. Alternatively, you are here because you feel a yearning for that connection that can only be shared with what is often referred to in popular modern literature as your *soul mate*. We have all felt it.

Nowadays, though, it may seem very difficult to find the one. To meet that one magical person who will sweep you off your feet like a knight in shining armor, or that unbelievable woman who will soften your heart, smooth your rough edges, and care about you like no one else before. Although a knight in shining armor or a woman who seems too good to be true may be stretching it a bit for anyone's reality, the truth is that it is not impossible.

This book will form an integral part of healing your perspective around love. To do this, you need to know that this will involve healing yourself as well - the most important part. When this personal healing occurs; when you have acknowledged and worked on healing the beliefs you have of yourself; you will have achieved the most important goal. Only then have you overcome the biggest obstacle to truly becoming magnetic and drawing your perfect match towards you.

WHAT IS TRUE LOVE?

It can be the most magical feeling you've ever experienced, or it can turn into the worst nightmare and make you question the reasons for living any further. It can give you the strength and willpower to steer you through the most difficult times imaginable, or it can pull you down, into your darkest, deepest, most depressing lows.

What am I talking about?

Relationships. Love.

Nothing compares to the feeling of being in a caring and loving relationship with someone who sees you as a uniquely wonderful and beautiful person. When you first fall in love, not even the sky is the limit. It may feel like a never-ending daydream where everything feels perfect. Every moment is an eternity, and when you spend time together, it may feel as if you are conversing with a reflection of yourself. One mind in two bodies. A perfect connection.

You rarely notice any flaws because you're in such a high vibration that nothing negative ever crosses your mind. There is no substitute for that feeling. Nothing else compares.

"Love makes possible the miraculous, without labeling it miraculous."
– Dr. David R. Hawkins

The above analogy may be difficult to take in. After all, the fact that you are reading this book likely indicates that the explanation above is what you are searching for in a relationship. The truth is, you deserve to find the relationship of your dreams. You deserve to be happy. You don't have to live life alone or even feel lonely. This book is going to show you how – no matter how 'bad' you think things may be looking right now.

You CAN attract your dream relationship once you know how the universe really works. The journey you are about to take will lead you through all those seemingly hidden rules of the universe. What you will need however, are not only words, but also tools to achieve this seemingly elusive goal that will enable you to attract your soul mate, twin flame, or that perfect connection you have been wanting to manifest.

Like many, you may be going through life believing your past relationships have damaged you beyond repair. What this book will help you to realize is that EVERY SINGLE RELATIONSHIP - both good and bad - that you have ever had, is a blessing in disguise.

Yes – you read that correctly. Even those bad past experiences can actually help you attract your perfect match.

Take a moment and think about it. Can something bad produce anything good? Can a dreadful and heart-wrenching experience give birth to something pure and divine?

Yes, it can.

Together, we are going to dive deep into the practical applications of manifestation, stemming from the principles of the Law of Attraction. You will gain valuable insight on how to become magnetic to the relationship you've always dreamt about.

That's the bottom line. That's the ultimate goal. And I will lay down every single little detail I have learned in my life to help you avoid the pain and struggles that many people go through.

In this book, I'll share everything there is about the hidden secrets behind human attraction. I will share every little thing that enables people (whether consciously or unconsciously) – and that includes YOU - to finally attract that perfect person into their life.

It doesn't matter what gender or race you are. It doesn't matter what your sexual preference is. Your age and the number of past relationships you have been in are irrelevant. If you want to attract that one special person into your life, this is the journey for you.

The same rules of manifestation apply to all of us. What I can tell you with absolute certainty is that when you understand how it all works, others will notice. It will seem to them as if you have the magic touch.

Throughout this book, a secret will be made available to you that not many receive. You see, it all boils down to understanding the true reality behind successful relationships and attraction. In other words, while it may seem like magic to some, to others, it's just life. Because they understand the mechanisms. They know how it works. They are making the mental and emotional effort to change the way they think and feel to, ultimately, take inspired action steps and set it all in motion. After reading this book, you will be much better equipped to do the same.

THE ABUNDANCE OF LOVE

For you to grasp how important this information is, you need to first hear the following somewhat harsh truth. You have to understand that getting involved and being committed to the wrong person for too long can stop you from living at the frequency of your desires.

Such a misdirected commitment limits your ability to attract amazing things into your life - things that exist beyond your relationship. That's exactly what makes this exciting journey so vital for you. It will set your life on a growth trajectory path by helping you avoid making the same mistakes that so many of us made while searching for a loving partner.

Then again, is there just *one* person for you? With over 7,5 billion people on this beautiful planet (divided approximately in half by gender), if you remove a billion of those who are already committed, you end up with well over one billion remaining people, conservatively speaking, waiting in anticipation to finally meet *the one*.

Knowing that, do you believe it's possible to have a "perfect relationship" with .01 percent (or 100,000) of those people? Wouldn't it be fair to say then that you actually have a hundred thousand potential soulmates instead of just one?

That's how you need to start thinking. I want you to realize that there is the potential for more than just one amazing relationship. That a failed relationship does not mean there are no more out there for you.

The word to describe this is *abundance*. An abundance of love and connection *is* possible and available to you, whether you believe it or not. This is where this book comes in. Helping you align and solidify a belief of true and limitless abundance is exactly the perspective you need to not only know and understand, but nurture. It will open you up to a whole new world filled with love. It's all around us. Once you begin believing in your self-fulfilling abundance, you will become aware of the attraction happening all around you.

MAGNETISM AND AVOIDING MISALIGNED MANIFESTATIONS

In reality, the feeling of 'being in love' for many is actually rather an unhealthy attachment to an individual or relationship. Avoiding this pitfall of a pattern of dependency involves setting standards and values from the start, *before* you even attempt to draw someone into your life.

With that said, being very clear as to what your dream relationship looks like is essential for avoiding ambiguity and misaligned manifestations. You have to know who you truly are and what you want. In other words, **set your standards and stick to them**. Do not compromise. This is not about you learning how to see every partner through rose-colored glasses and ignoring everything you don't like about them, or making excuses for them. Instead, this is about being specific as to what you want for yourself deep down so that the universe can do that familiar magic and finally connect the two of you. Your soul mate is out there. He or she is waiting for you to get into that perfect alignment with who you truly are so that the universe can initiate the attraction process.

A key point is this: It may sound rather ironic, but the more you don't *need* a partner, the more attractive you will become to one and the happier you will be in the resulting relationship. The more freedom you give yourself to think, feel, and act in alignment with who you are, the more freedom you give others to do the same. This is what it means to become *magnetic*.

It is my mission to make you embrace your true self; to embody this wonderful, amazing person that you are so that ANYONE would be lucky to have you. I want you to stop fearing being hurt, rejected or disappointed in love, and rather feel good about yourself while simultaneously radiating happiness everywhere you go. Most importantly, I want you to experience this feeling *now* - even without an ideal partner being in your life yet. Removing the victim mentality will be one of the primary goals of this book. When you finally *choose* to become a powerful, magnetic, attractive version of yourself, you'll never feel lonely again.

Does this mean I'm asking you to not really ever love someone? Absolutely not! Quite the contrary. **Once you learn to unconditionally love someone, you are effectively empowering yourself**. When you love without strings or conditions attached, you free yourself from bondage – from the normal relationship fears most people have. If this sounds too complicated or confusing, do not worry. This book will give you everything you need to learn how to do this.

YOUR PART IN MANIFESTING THAT MAGICAL CONNECTION

In working through this book, you will be required to think deeper than usual. You will need to carefully read and contemplate all 15 techniques. Pick a few that resonate with you best, and extract as much good feelings as you can out of them. This is how you feed your soul. This will come with the important realization that you're becoming fully equipped with everything you need to finally manifest that magical connection with another being.

We are going to get into some concepts that are going to challenge your entire central belief system and everything you think you know about attracting love. During this process, be prepared for me to ask you deep, probing questions - the answers of which are necessary to help you get a clear vision of what it truly takes to create your dream relationship. This is a vital part of letting go of the old, to make place for the new.

Before you realize it, you will be able to let go of the past negative relationships that have been keeping you stuck. This will in turn lead you down the path of a new perspective and understanding, resulting in the occurrence of a necessary internal paradigm shift. As a result, you will have enabled yourself to attract the right person. It's going to take a little faith on your part, but once you embrace the new reality, you'll never look at relationships in quite the same way.

If the above sounds familiar to you and intrigues you, I am confident that no matter whom you are; no matter what is going on in your life; no matter how dismal you think your relationship outlook may be - you're going to become the magnetic force you really are with the ability to manifest all of your relationship desires. You will be empowered, your mindset boosted, and ultimately, you will find what you innately seek … **THE ONE.**

"Love is the recognition of oneness in the world of duality. This is the birth of God into the world of form."

— Eckhart Tolle

CHAPTER 1

The Hidden Connections
Between People

Intuitively, we all know that there is a hidden connection between people. Even if only subconsciously; we can feel it in the very fiber of our beings. Usually, the closer the person is to you, the stronger that connection may feel. This is why a mother or a father feels a special bond or a connection to their offspring, and likewise, children to their parents. But this connection is not only limited to families. It can go way beyond that.

You may meet someone for the very first time and feel a powerful, inexplicable bond towards them too – maybe even stronger than those held with family members. It may feel like your souls are somehow intricately linked; like they are at home with each other. How can that be? What could be the source of this? Is the myth of past lives possibly true?

In this chapter, we will explore the hidden connection between all of us. We will cover the connection between humans and the universe, and the most powerful law that brings it all together - the Law of Attraction. Using scientific evidence, we'll be able to explain this connection by examining the nature of how our reality works from a quantum physics perspective. Understanding the 'whys' and 'how's' of your reality will give you a broader view of the concepts you will learn about throughout this book. As a result, you'll be able to apply them with more conviction and confidence, ensuring that you attract the exact relationship you desire.

Before we dive into the connection between each other and the universe however, the most important connection that needs to be considered is the connection between YOU and yourself.

THE MOST IMPORTANT CONNECTION OF ALL

The importance of understanding the relationship you have with yourself cannot be emphasized enough.

All of us have a higher self, an inner being, or a soul, if you will. It is that part of you that could also be referred to as source energy, or the divine. This is the part of you that knows who you truly are and what you truly want. It's the unfiltered and unconditional expression of you.

From the secular perspective, this is called your *intuition*– that part of you that knows things beyond the realms of logical reasoning. This unique calling, that every one of us has, is connected to a wisdom that goes beyond what we can explain simply with mere words. It's infinite. When we recognize and follow this guidance offered by our intuition, we're put on a path which leads towards more synchronicities, success, fulfillment, and love.

This is why life coaches are taught to encourage their clients to "follow their own intuition," or to "go with their gut instinct." They know that this infinite wisdom springs forth from this connection with the source energy within us all, even though they may never really go too deep regarding what its source actually is.

The best way to refer to your unique expression of source energy is as your *inner being*. The term *higher self* is somewhat accurate, but this reference makes it seem like you are less than your higher self, when nothing could be further from the truth. You are indeed your higher self - you just haven't fully embraced it yet. The reason for this, in part, is that we have been raised by a society that limits our potential to consciously be the powerful and deliberate creators of our reality that we are.

For the journey that lies ahead in this book, it is important that you understand who you really are. Through this understanding, you will have the strong foundation needed in order to get the most out of life in every way possible when it comes to manifesting love.

Your inner being loves you more than you know, and it communicates this through your emotions. It is that non-physical, larger, older, and wiser part of you. This spiritual part of you has been with you since your birth. As mentioned earlier, the connection you have with your inner being is the most important connection you can have.

The truth is, if you were living in complete alignment with this part of yourself already, you wouldn't need this book. You would never feel lonely. The idea of lacking love would never cross your mind and express itself as a negative emotion. You would be able to manifest whatever you wanted to, easily and quickly, including a wonderful love relationship. Love would manifest with an ease and flow like you would have never experienced before.

Throughout this book, I am going to assist you to see life through the eyes of your inner being. When you start to see life from *that* perspective, life will become much more gratifying, with less fear of what may lie ahead in your life and relationships.

We will delve into more concepts around this later, but for now, let's talk about the nature of our universal reality. This will support and strengthen your belief around the link between existence and human connection.

THE CONNECTION BETWEEN HUMANS AND THE UNIVERSE

For over two hundred years, quantum physicists have known that the smallest particles known to man, subatomic particles, defy the Newtonian laws of physics in dramatic fashion.

One example of this was through an experiment called the Double Slit Experiment, performed by scientist Thomas Yang in 1801. You are welcome to research more about this experiment, but for the sake of understanding how quantum physics and manifestation are intricately linked, I'll explain some of the basic terms of quantum physics, and the outcome of this experiment in layman's terms.

Quantum physics is the study of the subatomic particles spread across the whole universe. It also explains how physical matter comes into being, as well as how we are able to influence and have direct control of this matter. As these subatomic particles, (of which everything - including you and I, exist), vibrate at a certain frequency, everything in the world is made up of the energy emitted by them. This energy movement creates the illusion of a physical reality, as if everything were a standstill and solid object, when in truth, it's just a collection of non-physical energy emitting a specific signature.

This is why Einstein said *"Everything* is energy." He didn't just say that hypothetically. He said it because that was what they found to be true. As Nikola Tesla also once stated, *"If you want to find the secrets of the universe, think in terms of energy, frequency, and vibration."*

The Double Slit experiment involved seeing how subatomic particles reacted to being forced in a certain direction. The outcome? The particles behaved completely against what the scientists expected to occur. To see why this outcome transpired, they recreated the experiment, this time with a measuring device. The subatomic particles were thus being *observed* – and amazingly, they acted according to the scientist's expectations!

Numerous further developments have been made in quantum physics over the past two centuries. If all of the scientific jargon is removed, some of the outcomes of this initial experiment (confirmed further in studies since then), could be listed as follows:

- Subatomic particles seem to be able to make decisions based on the behaviors of other subatomic particles (they appear to have an instantaneous 'knowing' between them)

- Multiple realities/possibilities exist at the same time
- What the scientist (observer) *observed* offered the *reality* of the outcome, even though the previous (unobserved) outcome was different. In other words, what they observed became the reality created at that time of observation.

So how can this then be linked to manifestation of something desired in your life, such as a meaningful, loving relationship? It is important to remember, in this regard, that we are also made up at a cellular level of subatomic particles – which means that we also have a vibrational frequency that impacts other subatomic particles. Let me narrow it down for you:

- The power of observation offers the reality created. If you can picture a desired outcome, and think, act and speak accordingly (in other words, observe/acknowledge it in all ways) as if you actually have it, then your vibrational frequency will manifest that reality. It will become physical in your reality. It first requires your belief, attention, and focus, as the observer.
- Just as different outcomes occurred in the recreation of the exact same experiment, except that one was observed and the other not, multiple realities exist at the same time. The subatomic particles in the Double Slit experiment could make decisions towards the outcome, based around the movement and intention of other subatomic particles. Similarly, your thoughts, decisions, beliefs, and expectations can and will determine which possibility or reality you experience.
- 'Coincidences' may actually be the manifestation of people, opportunities, and experiences caused by you, being drawn across your path to support you in making your desired outcome a reality. However, if you are not in alignment with this reality, these synchronicities will mean nothing to you and will pass you by as if nothing happened. In other words, the opportunity for the manifestation of your dream relationship could literally be right in front of you, but because you're not a vibrational

match to it, the inspired action necessary to bring the manifestation to fruition would never happen. Remember - all subatomic particles are connected across the time-space continuum in the universe.

Ultimately, what this all means, is that when you set your intention (call it your desire or outcome if you prefer), the vibrational frequency which then emanates from you will influence all subatomic particles to be arranged in such a way that follows your intention. That's right – YOU set things into motion! Now that you know that, we can move onto breaking down the Law of Attraction.

THE LAW OF ATTRACTION AND LOVE

I am certain you are at least slightly familiar with the term 'Law of Attraction.' It is the law that states that things of a similar vibrational frequency are attracted to one another. Vibrational frequency has been mentioned above, and will be expanded on further shortly. For now, let's look at how the Law of Attraction influences our lives, and more importantly, our relationships.

The Law of Attraction is not a once off event. It is a universal law, meaning it is *constantly* in effect. There are moments throughout the day where we notice its effects, sometimes instantaneously. Have you ever thought of someone who you had not thought of in a while, and then suddenly, they called you? Or, have you ever felt really good, and then suddenly started experiencing a momentum of positive manifestations? The opposite is also true. Have you ever gotten out of bed in a bad mood, and then have everything go wrong for the rest of the day?

You have seen the effects of the Law of Attraction. It's an inescapable part of reality, which is why it's so important to truly master the concepts surrounding it if you desire to live your best life. There are many misconceptions around this law and contradicting ideas that lead people to believe it's not true. One of the most important things to understand, though, is that **you attract who you are, and not necessarily what you want.**

How so?

We live in a 'yes-based' universe. What this means is that whatever you focus on, you attract. This is an important idea to understand because if you have tried to get the Law of Attraction to work for you in the past, but it hasn't, this could be why.

What I mean by we live in a 'yes-based' universe is the following: whatever you think about, you bring about, whether you want it or not. The more you shout "No!" to anything in your current reality, the more the universe hears "Yes!" For example, if you shout "No to war!"- the universe hears "Yes to war!" If you shout, "No to bad relationships!" - the universe hears "Yes to bad relationships!"

Can you see why it's so important to understand how it works?

Whatever you shout no to, the universe hears yes. This is why most spiritual gurus will never be against something, but they will always be *for* something. They will not march *against war*, but they will march *for peace*.

Can you see the difference? It's all about what you think and focus on.

This is going to be very important for you to understand when you consider finding true love. The point is, when it comes to relationships, **you must focus more on what you want and less on what you don't want.**

From a practical perspective, what this means is you should avoid, to the best of your ability, talking about and identifying with past negative relationships or experiences. Why? Because once you've tuned into the frequency of that experience, you've begun the process of shifting into a reality that resonates with that experience. This is why it is best to avoid complaining about an ex-partner to a potential new one - it not only activates the old vibration, but you risk closing off the possibility for a new love relationship.

Have you ever noticed how you or your friends seem to attract the same kind of person over and over and over again, even if you don't want to? That's the Law of Attraction in action. This is why understanding vibrational resonance is so important. Once you master your state of being, when it comes to relationships, you'll embody magnetism so powerful that you will inevitably manifest EXACTLY the type of partner you want to attract.

It can be difficult to avoid resonating with a negative past you are so adamantly convinced you need to identify with. You may dread making the same mistakes, and thus be constantly reminding yourself of what you *don't* want to have reoccur in a relationship.

You have to stop those patterns of thought here. You have to get over the urge to constantly rehash those negative bygones. In this book, I will show you how.

VIBRATIONAL FREQUENCY

Vibrational frequency is the foundation of attraction. It is the energy we emit into the world and we attract into our physical experience based on the signature of this energy. Our vibration (energy) has a unique frequency (signature). This is what creates our own unique vibrational frequency that manifests our own unique reality.

Our vibration is determined by two things: our thoughts and emotions. When you think a certain thought, it causes you to have a certain emotion, and when this becomes a habit, the reverse can also occur. Certain memorized emotions will start leading to certain thoughts. These events create a vibrational frequency that is emanated out into the universe.

Something that confuses a lot of people is the idea that a high vibration results in the manifestation of what you truly want, but this is not always the case. A very happy and positive person can be single, just as a very sad person can be in a wonderful relationship. This is why it's so important for you to tune into the right frequency of precisely what you want in order to attract it. The same way a radio station releases electromagnetic waves (vibration) from one signal to another, you need to practice tuning into the station (frequency) that plays the music you want to listen to.

The point is, if you have resistant thoughts about something specific you want to manifest, you can't manifest it, whether you are generally happy or not. Our thoughts play a big role in this and they can be broken down into three sections: beliefs, patterns, and awareness.

Beliefs

In simple terms, a belief is just a thought you keep on thinking. But it's a little more than that. It's also a set of crystallized perspectives that have been confirmed repeatedly from past and current experiences. These experiences then produce an emotional response that leads to a deeply rooted truth about your reality. For example, if you had a negative experience, or multiple experiences, where a person has let you down, you may be convinced that all people will let you down.

The problem is this...

You create your reality based upon what you believe, because when you believe something to be true, you will *unconsciously live* at the frequency of that reality. You start embodying this state of being naturally, and thus your vibrational frequency slowly begins to manifest the reality where all people will let you down.

A belief can also be described as entrenched thinking. It is a set of thoughts that you have thought over so many times that it has now become like a worn pathway through a meadow. In other words, it has become a truth of your life. Although it can be difficult to rewrite this truth, it's not impossible.

Patterns

Patterns of thought are the result of solidified beliefs. They too are perspectives you have thought many times over before. The perfect example of this is driving. Most people drive without any effort at all because they've done it so many times before, it's become second nature. Any thought can become a pattern of thought, if it's repeated enough times. If you find yourself facing the same problems over and over again when it comes to relationships, you may have unconsciously developed a pattern of thought.

Both beliefs and patterns are not necessarily bad things, but they can be if they are strengthening a perspective that isn't in alignment with what you truly want. But just like you can create negative patterns, you can also create positive ones that reinforce the vibrational frequency you want to be emitting. The goal of this book is to redefine your perspectives around love and relationships in order to break free from the patterns that repel them.

The first step to breaking free from the chains of negative beliefs and patterns is through awareness.

Awareness

The advantage human beings have over all other mammals on Earth is we have the ability to be aware of ourselves. We have the ability to be aware of awareness, and aware of who and how we are being, what we are doing, and how it affects us and others around us. It's an amazing ability that should never be taken for granted.

We can practice awareness right here and right now.

Bring awareness to a negative belief you might have. It could be anything. It could be about men or women, dating in general, or relationships. It could be something like "all men hurt me," or, "no woman ever likes me." Whatever it is, shine a light on it. If you can't yet figure out what it is, no worries, let's go through a quick exercise.

The simple act of being aware of what you believe is the first step to making a vibrational change. Once you identify it, then ask yourself the question, "Which of my perspectives is forming this belief?"

Once you've identified the cause, it's time to look at the "why" you hold this belief.

In many ways, beliefs are formed because they serve you in some way. Sometimes beliefs are formed to protect you from getting hurt or from changing who you think you need to be in order to receive love from others. Once you realize a specific belief is something you no longer want to hold onto, you've taken the first step to making the shift.

Your perspective is usually formed from past life experiences, but let me tell you something now. The past is exactly that, the past. And once you start resonating with an experience that no longer serves the manifestation of your current desires, you block yourself off from the natural growth and expansion of the universe. This is what leads to negative emotions and a state of being that is stagnant and completely out of alignment with your inner being.

Resonate with a *future* self now, and make the intention of creating the experience you want consciously, instead of unconsciously letting experience create you.

We'll talk more about the specifics of putting actions into place to let go of these beliefs in a future chapter. For now, let's see what it truly means to manifest a loving relationship.

THE MANIFESTATION OF YOUR DREAM RELATIONSHIP

The manifestation of your dream relationship starts when you realize that **you are the creator of your reality**. If you think otherwise, you'll never allow yourself to play with the magic at your disposal. You'll allow circumstance to define your life and relationships for you. If your circumstance is far from ideal, and you believe that it will never change, then you'll continue manifesting circumstances that are far from ideal. This, in turn, will have an effect on your relationships.

There is no other way to look at it. When your emotional state of being is consistently radiating a certain vibration, you are consistently tuning into a certain frequency. Master your state of being, and you'll master your reality. Your thoughts, emotions, and beliefs play a huge role in this.

Whatever you believe about relationships is what you will create. It's really up to you! This is why it is so important to choose to have good, solid, positive beliefs about relationships.

Judgment, blame, jealousy, guilt and a feeling of unworthiness are all feelings which have negative beliefs as their basis. These will keep you from attracting the relationship you want. Judgment can be either internal or external. Guilt and unworthiness are examples of internal judgment. Blame and jealousy are examples of external judgment. At the end of the day, these all reflect what you think about yourself.

Emotions come in only after you've decided on your new perspective. Emotions are defined as 'energy in motion.' Because of this motion, emotions are never what you might call *stable*. They will always fluctuate up and down. This is especially important to realize because our emotions are what connect us to other human beings. This is why relationships involve such a strong emotional commitment. The goal here is to not hold your emotions in one state forever, but rather to accept and effectively manage them when they arise.

Whenever you are feeling really down, it's impossible to instantly snap out of it and suddenly start feeling joyful and happy. Instead, take small steps up the emotional scale. Choose to view these negative emotions as a sign that you are not in alignment with your inner being. What this means is that your *perspective is misaligned from your truth*. In other words, you're depending on external conditions to make you feel happy, instead of feeling like you have the ability to create or manifest better external conditions. Remember - manifestation starts from within!

You have a *choice* to think and feel how you wish. This is the choice of watering the seeds of your desires.

"To grow your garden (change your reality), you must guide the flow of water (emotions) using the garden hose (thoughts)."
– Ryuu Shinohara

THE FREQUENCY OF LOVE

It is mentioned above that our vibration (energy) has a unique frequency (signature). The frequency of love is very high. It is one of the most sublime feelings we can experience. Many people have tried to define what love is. Regardless of any given definition, we can all agree love is one of the best feelings a person can experience.

The problem with most of us is that we have a distorted view of what love is, based upon our own experiences, and influences from society and the media. Many movies portray love as something external or extrinsic, and that we must 'go out there and find it' in order to be happy and satisfied. Often in movies, a sense of being incomplete is portrayed, until that seemingly perfect match occurs towards the end.

The problem most of us get ourselves into is when we think love is something we *receive* from someone else, rather than *create* within ourselves. When you think of love as an external, conditional entity you must work on in order to have, then you are going against the very tenets of the universal laws that attract it to you.

When you realize that love makes up the underlying non-physical aspects of who you are, with or without another person, then you have understood what love truly is. This understanding will help you to not only attract more of it from others, but *be* more of it as well. Love is the ingredient that makes up your true nature. You do not need to create or find it, because you *are it*.

Haven't you ever noticed how people who seem the most attractive and magnetic don't go around chasing love? What do they do instead? They focus on themselves because they are confident in their own self-worth. This confidence may appear to be arrogance to some people, but the truth is, either knowingly or not, they attract love because they love themselves.

When you love yourself; when you appreciate yourself; when you enjoy your own company; only then will you attract it. That's the law. That's how it works.

Be it and you will attract it.

Feel it, regardless of your circumstance, and you will witness its manifestation.

Most people wait until conditions are right in order to feel good. "I'll be happy when my dream partner arrives. Until then, I choose to be miserable!" is pretty much what they are telling themselves and the universe. But can you now see why this is a fallacy? Do you understand why most people get stuck in a vicious cycle from which they seemingly cannot escape?

When you can love yourself, love life, love others, and love all that is, *regardless* of conditions - then you haven't just mastered the art of love — you have mastered the art of life.

TECHNIQUE #1:
RELATIONSHIP CREATION

Ask yourself the following questions and contemplate the answers:

What do I want from a relationship?

How do I want to feel in a relationship?

For this technique, we're going to be answering these two questions. It's a simple, yet extremely effective technique simply because it puts you in the right vibration every time you do it. Your focus is purely on the wants and positives that will come from your relationship with another person.

The point is to write down not just 1-2 sentences, but rather a full page or two of the kind of relationship you want to attract and how you want to feel in this relationship.

Something you want to consider is how you feel about the different aspects of this person's life. For example, would you be open to playing volleyball if they were someone that enjoyed playing volleyball? Maybe they enjoy their quiet time and staying indoors. Would this be something you could enjoy with them too? **Define your unconditional perception of them.**

You want this person to like you for who you are, not for who you think you are. This is key because if you're not referring to your true self in these writings, you may vibrationally match with someone you don't truly enjoy spending time with. Instead, **write about how they make you feel.**

Be aware that being too attached to the extremely detailed specifics can close you off from infinite possibilities. This is why it's essential to focus on how you resonate with the person on a vibrational and energetic level. Use the details to make you feel a certain way instead of using them to outline a plan or aesthetic picture.

If you feel any doubt or tension while writing out the specifics of what you want to experience, start with general items. Begin with appreciating and believing in your ability to manifest, your connection with the universe, and the contrast that you've witnessed in your life that gave birth to your desire. When you've been thinking about what you've been missing for so long, it can be tough to shift into a whole new line of positive thought.

Start with general thoughts, work your way into more detail, and allow yourself to fully feel what it will be like to experience this relationship. Do not try to rationalize your thoughts, or you'll give room for doubt to creep in. Instead, allow the intuitive flow of your truth express itself through your writing.

Take time now to write these things out.

TECHNIQUE #2: THE RELATIONSHIP FEELING

The Law of Attraction is based on the vibrational frequency you're emitting. Your vibrational frequency is determined by your emotions but guided by your thoughts. For this technique, we're going to be focusing on elevating your emotions so you can enter the positive state of attraction that will allow you to attract the kind of relationship you're after.

The key to manifesting the relationships you want is not about focusing on the physical representation of the relationship, but rather the *idea of the relationship*. "What's the difference?" you might ask. The difference is that one focuses on the manifestation and one focuses on the feeling. Instead of looking at the relationship you want from a place of lack, look at it from a place of abundance. **Allow your imagination to be the reason why you feel good.** You do not need the physical manifestation of it in order to feel what it's like to have it. Here are the three main reasons why getting joy from *the idea* is powerful:

- Prevents you from getting attached to and vibrationally influenced by physical reality.

- It's the easiest way to get into alignment at any moment in time, no matter where you are.

- You will focus less on the 'how' and 'when' aspects of manifestation. This opens you up to infinitely more synchronicities.

Be receptive, open, and allow yourself to receive the manifestation of a new or enriching relationship by becoming a vibrational match to it *now*.

"Every time you are tempted to react in the same old way, ask if you want to be a prisoner of the past or a pioneer of the future."

– Deepak Chopra

CHAPTER 2

Creating Clarity from Chaos

Out of the chaos and contrast in your life, clarity, direction, and resolution are born. When you can see the value of the 'bad things' that happen in your life, including bad relationships, only then will you begin to experience the emotional freedom that comes along with this realization.

Even relationships which had apparent negative outcomes have their own unique type of value. There is value in EVERY relationship you have ever had before, due to at least two reasons. Firstly, that relationship helped you gain more clarity around what you do want. Secondly, you created a more powerful desire than ever before to manifest a better relationship. You may be skeptical regarding those two explanations, but subconsciously, you know them to be true. This is why you are here reading this, after all.

Let me explain. Ironically, most of us head into every relationship thinking that this is the one – the one and only person we will ever have, who will save us from a life of everlasting unhappiness and loneliness. We become so attached to the idea of being in a relationship that the thought of not being in one becomes something viewed as a negative in life. When we pass through the 'rose-colored glasses' time period, either partner may start feeling disillusioned with how the relationship is going. Before long, probably after numerous disagreements, emotions vented and silent treatments; it's over. We are left feeling hurt, angry and sad, among a whole host of other negative emotions. It is understandable that very few of us can end a relationship and feel a sense of appreciation for it.

There is nothing quite as emotionally turbulent as getting involved in a relationship. We subconsciously allow our thoughts and beliefs to be influenced by our past relational experiences, and this affects how we show up in the present moment. We unwittingly allow negative thoughts from past experiences to define our future. This is what causes people to feel stuck in a never changing reality loop. It is why they constantly seem to attract the same kinds of circumstances. Another common scenario is self-sabotaging the relationships they do attract. All of this deeply rooted mental and emotional baggage needs to be cleared out if we're ever going to open up the windows to a new reality.

Because these negative relationship experiences are usually associated with a strong emotional reaction, these negative memories stick with us for a long time, until we decide to acknowledge them and let them go. Negative experiences usually involve heartbreak, and unsuccessful attempts at finding love. This includes toxic relationships, external judgment from others, internal judgment from ourselves, and false external confirmation that what we want is not possible. We become so attached to these ideas that they shape our sense of self or identity. The ego also plays a huge role in how we view relationships because it's the ego that keeps us attached to ideas that do not define our true selves. When you put all of this emotion and experience together, it creates a vortex of internal chaos.

WHY WE RINSE AND REPEAT RELATIONSHIPS

Why is it that many people get into unhealthy relationships that are reminiscent of or exactly like other unhealthy relationships they are familiar with? For example, if you have parents who have had a bad relationship, why would you attract a similar relationship, thus increasing the likelihood of having the same kinds of problems? Wouldn't it make more sense to form a relationship with someone who had the exact opposite traits of the type of relationship you *don't* want to experience?

If you have always been in relationships which tend to follow the same trend in either the type of person you have dated, the way you have related to the other person, or the way in which the relationship has run its course, then you need to hear this.

One of the reasons we seek out what we know, is that we form a comfort zone of sticking to what we are familiar with. Even though a 'comfort zone' can indeed cause much discomfort, it seemingly has a benefit. It allows us a reprieve from having to heal.

Because healing means acknowledgement first.

And acknowledgement hurts.

It is not a natural human instinct to cause ourselves pain, either physically or emotionally, so by default, our natural instinct would be to avoid it. Healing needs to occur before anything else. Some people may use dating as a form of avoiding the process of healing. You have to do the work on yourself, internally, before you can begin the work of finding someone else.

Why is healing so important, though? It is only through healing that we open ourselves up to vulnerability again. I will say that again. **The vulnerability that is required in any meaningful human connection will first require you to heal.** If you do not heal, you will end up self-sabotaging, as the emotion of vulnerability will otherwise scare you. For a meaningful and healthy new relationship, you need a foundation of confidence, self-love, and healing.

So how does this 'rinse and repeat' cycle of relationships relate to your vibrational frequency? This phenomenon is so common that psychologists have a name for it. They call it, *repetition compulsion*.

As the name implies, people who have repetition compulsion compulsively repeat the same experiences in life, whether they are consciously aware of it or not. Psychologists are not exactly sure why it happens, but from a metaphysical perspective, if you do not change your vibrational attitude relative to how you feel about relationships, then you will attract the same ones over and over again. **You can't attract a different reality with the same frequency that attracted the current or past ones.**

According to psychiatrist and researcher Bessel van der Kolk (2016), "Many traumatized people expose themselves, seemingly compulsively, to situations reminiscent of the original trauma. These behavioral reenactments are rarely consciously understood to be related to earlier life experiences."

If your self-esteem is low and you don't feel worthy, for example, you may purposely enter into a bad relationship because you don't feel worthy of a good one. This is not something any person would *want* to believe, it's something they've been *conditioned* to believe. You may even get into relationships just because of the fear of not being in one. In other words, you have low expectations you are prepared to settle for, for yourself.

If you seek out an external assistant to your healing, such as a therapist or coach, there is something you need to be aware of. Make sure that you are not simply seeing them for a venting session, to enable you to learn how to cope within your brokenness. You need to actually acknowledge and resolve the issue and heal from it. Sometimes, something as simple as writing a letter to someone who hurt you can be cathartic in this regard.

Reliving past traumas over and over again, in the hopes that talking about it will make it better, will only aggravate the problem if it's not coming from a new state of being. And now that you know how the Law of Attraction works, it makes sense. If you're going to talk about how bad past relationships were and wallow around in the mire of those low vibrational frequencies, then of course you're going to attract more and more negative thoughts and feelings. **Shift out of the frequency of the problem and start living in the frequency of the solution.**

Your inner being is the purest expression of love, but because your mind has built so many filters (beliefs) around whom you are and who you can be, you will usually unintentionally block yourself from radiating the frequency that would attract someone you have a deep and true connection with.

Let's break down these beliefs:

THE THREE LIMITING BELIEFS AROUND LOVE

Beliefs are powerful. Henry Ford once said, *"Whether you think you can or can't, you're right."* It's such a profound statement because in a nutshell, he tells you the power you have to create your reality – or not. It's up to you!

Here are three limiting beliefs that stop people from manifesting true love:

Fear of Having What You Want

This may seem like a strange fear to have. Who would be afraid to have what they want? But in reality, this could mean actually being afraid of losing what you want *after* attracting it. **It's the idea of preferring to avoid the pain of losing, more than embracing the possibility of having.** When you finally do get into a relationship, this belief can cause you to constantly be worried and therefore never fully present with your partner. You could be there physically with them, but not actually there, because emotionally and mentally, you're somewhere else.

The signal you emanate out into the universe when you think and feel this way is a vibration of lack. When people say they fear love, what they really fear is not having it. This thought process does not put the focus on the manifestation of the desire but rather on the absence of it. This is like believing you've already lost it before you've even had it. True manifestation only comes from stepping into the unknown. It comes from stepping into the frequency of the desire. If you're scared of being happy, then you're telling the universe you prefer to be unhappy.

Humans have a survival instinct that naturally tells them to avoid what is unknown and stick to what is known and familiar. This is related to what we've talked about earlier in this chapter. The unknown is usually framed as a dangerous place to be in, which is why most people avoid it. Manifesting a new reality requires you to step into the unknown. This is why it's called a *new* reality. Your current reality is old news. It's the manifestation of the vibrational signature you had in the past. In order to attract a *new* reality, you need to step into a *new* frequency, *new* territory, *new* thought, *new* feeling, *new* action, and *new* belief.

Be fearless in your desire to manifest the love of your life and want it more than the fear of not having it.

Shame and Guilt from Past Experiences

Usually, we feel guilt and shame from past events that we have never really addressed before, and this will have an effect on new relationships.

The difference between these two feelings is this: When we receive a negative evaluation from others with regards to either something we have done or not done, or around the way we look, to name just two examples, then that external evaluation leads us to experience shame. This could be linked to abuse, or cultural and religious norms. The depth of this shame will be dependent on many factors such as your sense of self-worth at the time, your confidence level, and who the comments or evaluations are coming from.

Guilt, on the other hand, is a negative reaction or expression towards *ourselves*. It is the feeling of having done, or not done, something that you believe you shouldn't, or should, have done. Having an ingrained sense of shame however, can certainly exacerbate a sense of guilt. If we feel that we have hurt someone in a past relationship, the sense of guilt may be holding us back from entering a new relationship, in case we hurt someone again.

These feelings of guilt and shame from our past have conditioned us to believe that this is who we are, though in many cases this shame is unacknowledged by the individual experiencing it. They may avoid relationships, suppress their emotions, and possibly either feel worthless or anxious, or even display traits of narcissism as a defense mechanism.

Knowing what you do now about guilt and shame, and especially if this has touched a nerve with you, you need to understand the following important point:

You've defined yourself through these experiences, thus creating an illusion of your identity. We can easily develop the belief that "Nobody wants to be in a real relationship with me" or "I mess up every relationship I'm in," simply due to the fact that we've experienced guilt and shame in relationships before.

Your past is nothing more than a part of your imagination now. It can never be repeated, unless you give it permission to by matching the frequency of such an event. Giving your past life story a meaning that disempowers you will only limit your potential for manifesting future desires.

We'll talk more about this later in the chapter. For now, know that shame and guilt are two of the lowest vibrational feelings on the emotional scale. Working to get rid of these emotions is essential if you're ever going to break free and manifest your dream relationship.

Not Believing in Your Ability to Manifest Love

If you believe that you do not have the power to manifest true love, this belief will stop you right in your tracks. Believing in your power to manifest abundance, of any kind, should be the first step to manifesting love. If you believe the love of your life doesn't exist, or you're not capable of attracting them, then you need to reframe this way of thinking.

Remove all thoughts of scarcity. Realize the power and control you have to purposely think better feeling thoughts in order to create your reality. The universe is abundant, and we have access to this abundance through our consciousness and imagination. Match the frequency of being in a relationship, not just by seeing it from a distance, but by embodying the person in the experience. **You can feel the feeling of having your desired reality right here and right now, even though physically, it is not yet present.**

When most people think about the idea of being loved, happy, and peaceful, they think it's something they have to search for outside of themselves. In reality, our natural state is a state of infinite potential, joy, excitement, love, happiness, and limitlessness. The only reason we do not notice it is because many of us have unconsciously layered it with conditions and limitations.

Imagine looking up at a cloudy sky with small patches of bright blue. The clouds are the limitations fogging your view, and the bright blue sky is you. Your only goal is to remove the clouds, one at a time, so you can shine through the limitless nature of your being - a nature that is extremely attractive to other people. But in order to remove these clouds, we need to rewrite the stories that created them in the first place.

HOW TO REWRITE STORIES FROM THE PAST

When it comes to changing your self-image relative to relationships, a powerful approach is changing how you look at your past. As time goes on, your vision of the past naturally becomes blurrier. And eventually, it gets to the point where we are making things up about what we experienced, when in actuality, we never did. Always remember, the past is now just a thought. When you change this thought, you change your past, and when you change your past, it almost instantaneously feels like you've become a new person. In this subchapter, we're going to be expanding a little bit on this concept and providing you with new perspectives around it.

Neutralize Your Negative Beliefs

The way to do this is to remove any attachment or label around the things that are holding you back. For example, if you have a freckle on your face that you think is ugly, reframe this belief by viewing the freckle as a small part of your overall uniqueness. See it as neither good nor bad. It's just there, and giving it more importance than it needs, will move you out of balance, and simply clutter your mind with negative beliefs about yourself and what others think.

Embarrassing or heartbreaking situations in the past may stop you from taking future risks. Redefine these moments. Humans have a unique way of creating the illusion that because the past happened, it must be true, even though it's now just a thought. The past is a thought, just like the future is a thought. And many times, we don't even remember the past correctly. Therefore, wouldn't you being the best version of yourself *now* be just as true as the worst version of yourself you seem to recall or assume as true? **The only real moment ever is now.** You can only decide who you were, and who you are going to be RIGHT NOW.

Regretting the past or worrying about the future are both two negative behaviors that are ego driven and only serve to create more mental and emotional chaos. Neutralize the disempowering meanings you've placed upon your life, and watch them slowly, but surely, dissipate.

An Opportunity for Growth and Recognition

The natural flow of the universe is to be forever expanding. In order for it to expand infinitely, there needs to be both chaos and order. Without one or the other, the universe would limit its potential for expansion. Think of it like demolishing a house in order to rebuild it again as a new and improved home. Every time you break it down and build it up again, you learn something new about the process and the pieces involved. Thus, every time you rebuild it, the result is better than the last.

The same thing can happen when this analogy is applied to your relationships. You can improve and build upon every new one you enter. View life this way and you'll find it easier to create more positive beliefs about everything in life.

Another way you can capitalize on negative situations is to use them as a way of gaining clarity around what you do want. If a negative situation arises and you're aware of this negativity, then you've confirmed that it is something you don't want, thus instantly creating more clarity around what you do want. Keep this in mind whenever you're facing any sort of contrast or challenge.

You Already Have Everything You Need

Recognize that what you want is already available to you emotionally and vibrationally.

How so?

What you really want is the feeling of what it would be like to manifest your dream relationship. You want to feel love. You want to feel that excited, happy, good, and euphoric feeling that comes AFTER falling in love.

The thing is - we attract based on the frequency we put out, and not the other way around. Therefore, we must connect with the experience and feel it *before* it is reflected in our physical reality.

In other words, you must feel the feeling of love and euphoria *before* you attract your dream partner. Every manifestation has a delayed effect in the 3D realm, but we have the opportunity to experience this manifestation in the form of a good feeling in the present moment - now! And actually, that's your only option if you wish to attract improved relationships, because it's how the universe works. You create what you want by living the experience FIRST.

Creating a feeling is a manifestation in and of itself. It's the only confirmation you need that what you want is on its way. This is what I mean when I say "you already have everything you need." You already have the ability to feel however you want to feel regardless of whether or not what you want to manifest is here yet. **You do not have to wait.**

When you think a thought, you access a field of consciousness. This field contains an infinite number of parallel realities you can tap into right here and now. Consciousness cannot tell the difference between physical and non-physical reality, just as your body and emotions can't tell the difference between a thought and real life. Do not allow physical reality to determine that you lack something, because physical reality only ever represents ONE configuration of reality. In other words, everything you have in your life right now is the result of the thoughts and feelings *from your past*. It's old news.

Your future is the result of the thoughts and feelings you purposely think and feel now, no matter what your current reality is. Decide to put your focus on the optimistic, positive ones, and watch reality begin molding in your favor.

TECHNIQUE #3: BELIEF HACKING

For this technique, you're going to embody the future version of you by rewriting your past. In other words, pretend like you've already experienced what it's like to be in love, be in a relationship, or be attractive and magnetic to people. Do not worry about the details.

An infinite number of realities already exist. Therefore, what you rewrite about your past using this technique reinforces your new identity. It is the truth about who you are becoming. Time is simply an illusion and it is not linear. It is malleable. The past, future, and present all exist in the eternal now. Therefore, you can see yourself as the product of an infinite number of pasts.

The mind cannot tell the difference between a thought and experience. Stop thinking about the past through the eyes and mindset of your old identity and start thinking about the past of your new identity. Use your imagination as your reference experience. A first, this may sound confusing to you. Let me clarify this through an example:

From the perspective of someone that is at a coffee shop and someone they are physically attracted to, is signaling them to approach.

Old identity: "I'm not confident enough to approach this man/woman. I've never done this before."

New identity: "I'm going to approach this man/woman because I'm confident in my ability to do so. I've done this before and nothing life-threatening ever happened."

Another example can be how you react to someone rejecting you.

Old identity: "This is typical for me. I'm not attractive or charismatic enough to attract this type of person. They are way out of my league."

New identity: "Oh well, seems like they're not interested. I have proof that other people were interested in me in the past. Let me spend my time focusing on those that resonate with my true self."

Simply by believing that you've *already experienced* all of the unknown territory that you will be stepping into, will give you the confidence to be yourself and handle the situation in a present state of mind. This will prevent you from overthinking, reacting, and being anxious about all the things that can go wrong. The idea behind this technique is to override your survival instinct of avoiding the seemingly unknown or forgotten, and help you to overcome your fear. As you start replacing the imagined experience with real-life reference experience, you'll find yourself becoming more accustomed to embodying this new sense of self.

TECHNIQUE #4:
DESIRE DISCOVERY PROCESS

For this technique, we're going to place the focus on how you can use your reference experience to get more specific with what you want to attract. There are three types of people you can attract:

1. The one you don't want.
2. The one you want some of.
3. The one you want all of.

Our goal with this technique is to attract the third person. How do you know exactly what you DO want without knowing what you DON'T want? This is where your previous experience in relationships, no matter how subtle, will come into play. Remember that right at the start of the journey encompassed in this book, it was stressed that your focus should always be on what you DO want, rather than what you don't. This is only possible though, through acknowledging (but not obsessing about) past experiences that have not felt aligned to what and who you truly desire.

NOTE: As we've mentioned before, a perfect relationship indicated as 3) will come with imperfections. It's how you deal with these imperfections that make the relationship perfect.

Look back at the best times you spent with another person. What did you appreciate the most about them? Was it the intimacy? The humor? The intelligence? The fun? Write these things down. Shift your focus to all of the positive aspects you experienced with all of your past relationships.

This is what will help you build your vibrational signature. Avoid labeling past relationships as bad relationships. Again, remember that you can extract positives out of every single relationship you've ever had to help you build the desired relationship of your dreams. Once you know exactly what you want, you'll find it even easier to vibrationally align with it using the perspectives and techniques in this book.

Enjoy the moments you have in your relationships. Enjoy your expansive nature. Enjoy the new preferences you'll gain as you experience more and more.

"Never pretend to a love which you do not actually feel, for love is not ours to command."

– Alan Watts

CHAPTER 3

Hidden Thought Patterns that Repel Love

When you know what thought patterns *repel* love, then you'll know what thought patterns *attract* love. Most of us have subconscious thought patterns that, not only make it nearly impossible to attract the kind of relationship you truly desire, but may also lower the quality of any future relationship you get into.

Children can often sense and feel the effects of the dysfunctional relationship habits their parents once had, and often times, repeat them. When they grow up, they tell themselves, "I don't want to be like my mom or dad." This is where things go wrong, because as discussed previously, when you try to *avoid* something (in this case, becoming like your mom or dad), you unconsciously manifest more of this reality into your life. Why? Because *your focus is still lingering in that frequency*. The goal here is not to avoid the wrong kind of relationship, but rather to attract the right kind.

In this chapter, we will deconstruct three main thought patterns that repel love. For each, we will discuss what it is, how it comes about, and how to fix it.

PEOPLE PLEASING

What It Is

People pleasing is the act of trying to satisfy others in search for a pay-off in the form of self-validation or attempting to 'earn' love. Some people manifest this in the form of putting other people's needs first ahead of their own, leading them to feel exhausted mentally, emotionally, physically, or even financially. The people pleaser usually ends up feeling under-appreciated. They have all the evidence in the world to prove their worth to others, and yet they never feel their actions being reciprocated. Despite this, they continue to do it because of the negative beliefs they have about themselves.

One way to identify a people pleaser in others, or even in you, is to notice how hard it can be to say 'no' when asked for anything. When you find it easier to constantly say 'yes,' regardless if it goes against your truth, you've unconsciously entrenched yourself in the pattern of people pleasing.

The ironic thing is that people pleasers, out of fear, rarely let the people they are pleasing know how they truly feel. And yet, the very thing the people pleaser seeks, which is acceptance, love, and validation, is commonly withheld because others recognize one important flaw: People pleasers do not stand up for their truth. In other words, they act out of alignment, and when you act out of alignment, it's very easy to notice. **When you disempower yourself, people can sense it.**

This mentality of constantly trying to meet the expectations of others in order to be liked and loved can drain you of your energy. It implies that you can only get love by treating people with a 'fake niceness' that goes against how you truly feel. This way of thinking also takes the power away from other people. When you constantly please someone, the recipient often times gets used to it. And this in turn, will not allow that person to discover the inner power they have to please themselves and form their own happiness. The pleaser ends up becoming the source of their happiness, which is draining to both people in the relationship.

The opposite is also true. If your source of feeling self-worth comes from pleasing others, you will feel unworthy when you don't. This can potentially lead you to being easily manipulated, and to act in ways that put you out of alignment.

Overindulgent parents can show the same traits and characteristics of people pleasing by doing everything they can for their children (sometimes called 'spoiling'), whilst not giving them the opportunity to fend for themselves in the real world. In the case of these kinds of parents, it may seem like they are simply being loving, but in reality, the child is being controlled and becoming dependent upon the parent. This also takes away the value of learning how to create one's own reality, which is the whole point of this book.

How It Comes About

This personality trait usually surfaces because one does not see the value in their truest expression. This negative belief is usually created in childhood and will carry over into adulthood if you are not aware enough to change it. It may surface from parent pleasing, where the child feels that the only way to gain their parents' acceptance and love is by doing everything they are asked to do. It may also have been a way to avoid conflict in a tumultuous household.

Society, parents, teachers, siblings, and friends can have a strong influence on how someone views themself. Thus, they develop the need to create this false persona that is constantly changing and acting out of alignment to fit within everyone's expectations. Subconsciously, people do this in order to get what they truly want: validation, approval, and external representations of love, rather than developing these feelings internally.

How to Fix It

If you suffer from this people pleasing thought pattern, know that you are not alone. It is a common phenomenon. It happens to many people because of the nature of how most of us are raised. You *can* overcome it.

The best way to 'fix' this is to first understand and realize that you are an eternal, powerful spiritual creator having a temporary human experience, and *you* are just as valuable from the eyes of source energy as *anyone* else. You are a unique and divine expression of that which man calls God - and so is everyone else. Therefore, you are identical in value. You have nothing to prove in this lifetime. You don't earn self-value – *you are born with it*. This can be difficult to accept or believe, with life circumstances and experiences possibly having cemented the false beliefs you may currently hold. You may have lived your whole life thinking the opposite. However, don't worry. We will discuss more on the subject of self-worth in a later chapter, but for now, I want you to understand this.

To put it in simple terms - please yourself! Only *you* can give yourself the validation you're looking for. How *you* feel should be your priority. There should be nothing stopping you from allowing yourself to feel love, regardless of what the outside world tells you. There's nothing wrong with giving to and helping others, but when it costs you your alignment, this raises red flags within yourself and to other people around you.

Value yourself and express your personality in an authentic way or people will never see the real value in you. If they don't appreciate your real value, then they were never giving you real love in the first place. Let go of needing validation and approval from others. Accept who you are and *own it*. Be the star of your own movie. Don't be the supporting actor in someone else's.

You are not being selfish when you put yourself first. In actual fact, when you are being your best, authentic self, you're actually *more* of service to others. Find and recognize a perspective that feels empowering and expansive. The manifestation of your dream relationship will come when you recognize that nothing 'out there' can ever fulfill the needs of what is within.

CODEPENDENCY

What It Is

Codependency is when someone is dependent or attached to a relationship (or the idea of a relationship) and uses it to confirm their sense of self or identity. In other words, feeling loved and whole is dependent on external conditions, whether you are already with someone or not. This creates resistance, because you're not radiating from your truth. Rather, you're defining your level of happiness based on how a relationship is currently going, how it went, or how it could be.

Why are we touching on this subject if the goal is to attract someone in the first place? I want you to understand the pitfalls of codependency and the effects it can have on your vibrational frequency, and thus on what relationships you attract. You will then become better equipped to attract complementary relationships, rather than codependent ones.

Codependency can occur in three ways: a partner that is dependent on you, you being dependent on your partner, or both. Have you ever subconsciously thought about the following statements when it came to another person? -

"I need this person to be this way so that I can feel good about myself."

"I'm going to do whatever they want me to, so they don't leave me."

"You complete me."

Once we look for reasons outside of ourselves to feel a certain way, we limit the potential of attracting all kinds of abundance into our lives. If you *need* the relationship, then you *lack* it vibrationally – or you wouldn't be actively seeking it out, or sticking through in a less than ideal relationship. If you don't need it, then you can attract it vibrationally. You attract everything and everyone into your life based upon the frequency you emanate out into the universe – and relationships are no exception. If you are or have been chasing validation and approval in unhealthy and less than ideal relationships, it's time to reconsider your approach.

Let me attempt to simplify this concept. A codependent person tends to chase what they want with a sense of neediness. They want people to respond to them in a certain way. In response, however, the recipient of their neediness will typically put out an energy of resistance, as they subconsciously feel that the codependent person is trying to take something from them. They can feel that a specific type of response is being expected from them, and no one likes to be controlled in this way.

You *cannot* force relationships, friendships, and connections in order to fill a void that is missing inside. When you chase love, you repel it. Nobody wants to be the rubber plug that fills your emotional hole, unless they are dependent on that too, or a people pleaser.

Codependency can manifest itself in the form of vicious cycles of breaking up and making up, even when abuse is involved. This is a very serious issue that can often be very difficult to overcome, but not impossible. I recommend you personally consult a licensed professional for a more personal approach if this is the case.

How It Comes About

Codependent, unhealthy relationships manifest because of the belief that love and happiness can only be found in someone else and not in us. The ego part of our consciousness is always *seeking* and *attaching* to ideas, things, and people in an attempt to strengthen an identity. It is the part of us that is preoccupied about the future... the part that says "What if this does not happen...what if I don't find love."

As mentioned above, codependent relationships are thus manifested when egoic thinking takes charge of your thoughts and emotions by attaching your sense of wholeness onto the illusion of physical reality.

Codependency comes from the deeply rooted idea that we are not good enough. This feeling of not being good enough can stem all the way back, again, to when we were children. Having our parents fulfill all of our needs, resolve all of our problems, and be the source of our happiness is usually where it starts (even if the parents have the best of intentions). The parent-child relationship is often one of reciprocal currency. In other words, if you behave in a certain way as a child, you will receive a certain reaction.

Past experiences can also be a determining factor in the manifestation of a codependent relationship. If being single was a terrible experience for you, the ego will want to avoid it at all costs, which can then eventually lead to manifesting a people pleasing mentality or attracting a bad relationship with someone. This can also be the case for those who have been in a relationship for many years. It can be extremely uncomfortable stepping into the unknown and experiencing something new, even if you intuitively know that it's the right thing to do.

Being codependent while in a relationship is harder to recognize than being a people pleaser, but recognition and awareness is the first step to overcoming it.

How to Fix It

Here are a few questions to ask yourself to help bring awareness towards the issue of codependency:

- Am I in any way dependent on a/this relationship – or *needing* a relationship?
- If I could go the next 5 years without being in a relationship with my dream partner, would I be okay with that?
- Do I allow others to compliment my limitless nature and do I compliment theirs?

The answer should be yes to all three, and if it's not, here's how you can make the shift.

In order to manifest the independent nature of your future dream partner, you have to first develop an independent nature within *yourself*. You have to develop enough self-esteem, self-acceptance, and self-love in order to have the strength to break out of having a codependent nature.

Discover the areas in life where you find yourself being dependent on others and work to improve them. It can be tough to take up more responsibility, but sometimes you don't need to. Just letting go of the feeling of being dependent and attached to what others provide to you, is enough.

When you give yourself more responsibility for how you feel, you increase your *response-ability*. In other words, you become more aware of how you choose to think, feel, and act. This is a massive step to making the shift from being an unconscious creator to being a conscious one.

It's important to recognize the possibility that people can be addicted to being treated poorly or to the ups and downs that are so common in codependent relationships. If you want to manifest an exciting and expansive relationship, it's essential that you match this nature before you enter one.

Start focusing on yourself more. If you find yourself often blaming other people, take responsibility in how you choose to feel rather than blaming or depending on others to do it for you. You only need yourself to feel happy, loved, and secure.

A relationship that is built from two people who are both 100% whole is the ultimate alignment – the ultimate goal. In mathematical terms, 1 + 1 = 2 (collective energy of two whole beings) versus ½ + ½ = 1 (collective energy of codependent people).

"If two lines are moving parallelly, they go on for infinity. But if they're focused on each other, they'll cross and they'll go far away from each other."
– **Gurudev Sri Sri Ravi Shankar**

When we talk about the idea of manifesting a dream relationship, we're not looking to manifest just any kind of relationship. We're looking to manifest the BEST kind of relationship for YOU. Manifest a relationship that is *complementary* and *not* dependent. Be unapologetically yourself. Give up trying to control the outcome and other people's responses towards you.

Know that the validation you may be seeking since childhood is already inside you.

UNWORTHINESS

What It Is

Unworthiness is one of the lowest vibrational attitudes you can embody. It's the feeling of not being good enough in one or many different ways. Examples can range from not being smart enough, not good-looking enough, not out-going enough, not talented enough, etc. It's that sense of self that feels limiting, constraining, and powerless - that feeling that no matter what you do or how hard you try, you'll never be enough to fill in the expectations of others or yourself.

It stems from the false premise that you are what you've done and how others see you. The problem with this sentiment is that it's born out of an attachment or identification to past experiences and other people's opinions. It's the belief that you are not deserving of having the relationship you want, simply because it never worked out before or someone told you it won't. The foundation is immersed in the feeling of lack, whether this is a lack of self-worth, self-love, self-confidence, or even a lack of perspective of one's infinite potential.

This is one of the most negative perspectives you can have of yourself. It goes against everything I've ever taught. **Feeling unworthy is the result of you not tapping into your infinite nature and instead, playing the victim role.** Let's break down this feeling and how to break free from it once and for all.

How It Comes About

So many of us feel unworthy that it might as well be declared as a global issue. It comes about from past experiences in life and past results.

Our parents, our educational system, and society compare us to one another from the perspective that we are not good enough until we prove our worthiness. We are compared, judged, and ranked according to when our developmental milestones are reached as children, how well we do in school, how much we are liked, how much we've accomplished, and how well connected we are socially. Unless you have been an over-achiever in everything you have ever tried, you will feel the sting of comparison and competition, hence, the disparaging feeling of not being worthy.

In other words, unworthiness comes from defining your value based on the external conditions and expectations that physical reality places on you. Accepting other people's judgment and allowing their judgment to make you feel 'less than' is common amongst peer groups. When you identify yourself with the limitation of ideas, labels, and moments from the past, you're defining yourself based on concepts that technically do not exist. The only real truth is your own. Here. Now.

How to Fix It

When you start to understand that you were born worthy and have nothing to prove, you will start to feel worthy enough to overcome any feelings of unworthiness. Understandably, you may feel skeptical about this. How can you suddenly start to believe this, if you haven't your entire life?

Start to see yourself from the perspective of source energy. Many spiritual teachers teach us that we are actually eternal beings of consciousness, and that we never die. That should be enough to empower you, but there's so much more to it.

Every single thing you want (created from the contrast you've experienced and the resultant understanding of what you don't want), has been shot out into the universe like a rocket. Your creation of desire is now in turn helping the universe to expand. **In other words, YOU are helping to expand the universe with your desires, no matter how small, or how big.** You *are* worthy of having your desires met. You were born worthy.

Recognize you are worthy by default. When you remove all the stories, filters, and limiting beliefs, you're left with the greatest version of you: an infinite and ever-expanding spiritual being that's connected to all the magic in the cosmos. You have limitless potential and radiate magnetism like no other when you're being your true self.

Once you embrace this, you'll never feel unworthy again.

TECHNIQUE #5: HABIT OF THOUGHT MEDITATION

The Habit of Thought Meditation technique is meant to bring awareness around the thinking habits you have going on inside of your head. Without judging or labeling these thoughts, we're going to shed a light on them and identify whether these are thoughts that are or are not in alignment with the best version of you. Shifting away from old trains of thought will help you become more accustomed to a new way of being.

Follow the steps I've outlined below. This meditation can take as long as you'd like:

Step 1: Find a comfortable and quiet place to sit or lay down.

Step 2: Take a couple of deep breaths and focus your awareness on your breathing.

Step 3: After feeling like you've entered the present moment, consider imagining a situation that is uncomfortable for you. Think of an unknown reality that you're afraid of stepping into. This can be a new relationship with someone, a situation in a current relationship, or even a situation you've experienced in the past and you are afraid of experiencing again. Don't stay too caught up in this step. Avoid identifying with this situation and labeling it as something negative or specific to you. Keep it general and broad.

Step 4: Notice all of the thoughts that arise from this situation. What kind of limiting beliefs are you creating for yourself? What circumstance in the past is influencing your decision in this situation? How do you think or feel about yourself in this situation? Bring awareness to all of this fear, anxiety, and insecurity that have been hidden in your subconscious.

Step 5: Choose to experience this reality differently. Play out the situation in your mind, and respond to it accordingly with your new set of beliefs. How do you want to position yourself in this situation? What is the outcome of you stepping into this new identity? How do you feel as a result of this? Embody the confidence, love, security, appreciation, stability, wholeness, and presence that come with this new version of you.

Step 6: Take one last deep breath and journal your experience from steps 3-5. What was the situation you thought of? What were the first thoughts that came to mind? How did you respond differently with your new identity? After this meditation, you should feel, even if only slightly, more open and less anxious about the situation.

Step 7: Express gratitude for every single session.

Consider doing this on a daily basis until every uncomfortable imagined reality in your mind is no longer uncomfortable. Find comfort in the unknown. This will help you respond proactively to your environment and put you in a state that is more aligned with your true self and desires.

"When you fish for love, bait with your heart, not your brain."

– Mark Twain

CHAPTER 4

Two Types of Love and Where to Place Your Focus

One of the most overlooked topics, when it comes to love, is whether it is conditional, or unconditional. What do you think? Is this a choice, or something beyond our control?

Do you love someone because of what they can give you (conditional)? Or do you love them no matter what they do (unconditional)? But isn't it bad to love someone unconditionally, like the people pleaser who, on the surface, loves people unconditionally? Where do you draw the line? What is the line? And who gets to draw it?

These probing questions will help you to clarify the topic of love, self-awareness, the power of choice, and how to paradoxically shift your focus towards yourself in a way that allows you to exude your magnetic nature, and thus, attract an amazing relationship.

First, we need to understand what conditional versus un-conditional love really means. A good way to generally look at the difference between these two forms of love is to compare the love from a mother to that of a father. A mother's love, typically, is unconditional. Your mother will love you no matter what you do. But a father's love, again, typically, is more conditional. The father's love is given only after the child has performed well (a condition) or to his liking. This is of course an extremely generalized observation, with not every mother or father being like this. Most of us however, can more easily understand the difference between conditional and unconditional love when we consider the mother/father comparison.

CONDITIONAL LOVE

Conditional love is love that relies on certain external conditions. In computer programming, it's the "IF (blank) THEN (blank) ELSE (condition)" statement. In life, this is applied as, "IF (this person does what I want), THEN (I will love them) ELSE (I will not)."

This kind of love can often be tied to controlling and manipulative behaviors. In most cases, the one who practices conditional love believes they can control others, and if others cannot be controlled, then they should not be loved.

Conditional love is defined by the ego, the state where, as Dr. Wayne Dyer used to say, we "Edge God Out." When we edge God or source energy out of our lives, we replace our normal, natural, divinely inspired unconditional state with conditional love. But who you really are is infinite source energy in physical form. Anything that has conditions, limitations, or constraints is coming from a false sense of self.

Conditional love is love that does not express one's true feelings for the other. It is love that feels stuck, limited, resistant, and sometimes uncomfortable. Conditional love can often be rooted in these lower vibrational frequencies which can affect other aspects of your life.

In addition, it can be based on the condition of whether or not the other person feels love too. If they love you, then you love them. If they don't love you, then you don't love them. Conditional love considers what other people think, what other people do, who they are, how much money they make, how attractive they are, how they treat themselves, how they treat others, their upbringing, their socioeconomic standing, and many other factors. It's no wonder it's so hard to find a loving relationship when you're looking at it from these perspectives. Most people only operate in the conditional love arena of life where everything about the person is scrutinized, judged, and compared.

Loving in this way drains energy from both people, and it sets up distrust and suspicion. You may feel that things are going well now, but might have constant concerns about the future. What if he or she looks at another person with lust in their heart? What then? Should I leave them? Where do I draw the line?

Where *do* you draw the line?

Conditional love is all about line drawing. But isn't setting standards of how you want to be treated important? The answer is yes. There is a difference between being conditional and setting healthy boundaries, which we will discuss shortly.

Conditional love fills a void in a person, which should not have been there to begin with. Remember, you were born whole. You *are* whole. If you feel you need someone to fill a void of loneliness within your heart, then you'll keep on attracting more loneliness, or relationships that cycle that emotion. This type of love is based more on the superficial representation of the relationship then on the actual relationship. Many times, this manifests in the form of a couple who do not have any chemistry, and do not even really like one another, but remain together out of convenience, financial gain, or social status. This kind of love causes all kinds of heartache and pain within a relationship.

When people require conditions in order to feel love, it goes against the laws of true manifestation. In other words, in the conditional love mindset, love cannot be expressed without conditions. This is the opposite of manifestation.

UNCONDITIONAL LOVE

Unconditional love, on the other hand, is independent from any external conditions. It is a way of being, rather than a way of acting. It is an internal mindset, not an external construct. It is love that is defined by your inner being – that all knowing part of you who knows the value of every person on planet Earth.

It is love that comes from your true self – love that expresses your true feelings for the other from a place of non-judgment, compassion, forgiveness, and understanding. It is love that sees the best in others, whether they deserve it or not. As the Bible says, love, or unconditional love, "bears all things, believes all things, hopes all things, and endures all things."

It is love that feels free, is limitless, flows easily, and is comfortable. It gives without expecting anything in return because it knows and understands that the gift of giving is the reward in itself. It is love that builds up energy in both people, rather than detracting it. It is love that makes your partner feel the blessed breath of freedom, while at the same time, causing them to love you even more.

This type of love encourages partners to feel empowered about themselves, instead of worrying about each other. It complements the other's desired frequency, yet isn't dependent upon it – it is love that allows the other to be complete within themselves, without judgment.

This kind of love allows the other person to be who they want to be, regardless of what that is. The problem in most relationships is that partners start to grow apart because they never honestly gave each other the freedom to grow into whoever they were becoming. And then, one day, they wake up and think their partner isn't the same person they married. Conditional love would be disappointed with that. Unconditional love would be perfectly fine.

Unconditional love allows for growth, expansion, and even retraction, and hard times. It loves no matter what the person is going through – whether that be financially difficult times, a dark night of the soul experience, or other temporary problems. This kind of love does not keep track of past negative events or experiences. It doesn't remind your partner of the wrongs they have done.

As mentioned above with regards to conditional love, people require conditions in order to feel love, resulting in the opposite of manifestation. Unconditional love on the other hand, *creates* conditions. That is true manifestation.

> *"Love can only be found through the act of loving."*
> **– Paulo Coelho**

UNCONDITIONALLY LOVING YOURSELF

This is probably one of the most difficult concepts to understand and much of it depends upon your own spiritual advancement on the emotional scale to true love, freedom, peace, and joy.

Self-love is about giving yourself what you need in the form of self-care, to enable you to unconditionally love others, while still being considerate and compromising in situations which do not overstep your boundaries. It is an important part of what affects the vibrational frequency you emit.

Self-absorption, on the other hand, does emit the energy of arrogance or superiority over others. You can tell the difference relatively easily, as self-absorption reflects as a lack of consideration or ability to compromise. And this usually happens because of one's inability to be vulnerable or open when it comes to expressing their weaknesses. When it comes to finding the right balance, defining your values and constructing boundaries can be a big help.

With that being said, no one can tell you to create boundaries or not – or where to set them. That is totally up to you. In other words, no one can tell you how far to take the concept of unconditional love. To make the point really clear so it's easily understood, total unconditional love with a partner would not necessarily enforce monogamy. But if you had a partner who truly loved you and felt the same way you did, they would never venture outside of the relationship. When people are given the freedom to be truly free in a relationship, the opposite of what you think usually happens. In many cases, that kind of freedom will make them love you even more, and give them even less reason to venture outside of the relationship.

Unconditional love may seem like it would attract abusers and people who would take advantage of you. It cannot happen if you are truly unconditionally loving to yourself and others. This is because you would not tolerate consistently reoccurring negative behaviors in a relationship, knowing that it is detrimental not just to you, but both people. You would also only attract those who would vibrationally match you in those high-flying feelings of love, joy, and freedom. When you are unconditionally loving, the perspective of being taken advantage of should never cross your mind, because you didn't partake in the act of giving with the expectation of receiving anything in return. You gave because it felt good and in alignment with your inner being.

Honor your intuitive instinct. Respect your gut feeling on relationships and people. Don't let any book, mentor, or guru tell you what is right for you – only you know. Having said all this, can you turn around any relationships with true unconditional love? The answer is yes, you can. But if you are not consistently honoring your truth and setting the right boundaries, these relationships will continue to drag you down rather than match or lift you to the life you want to live.

But here is the one piece of advice that you must always adhere to…

Always, always, *always*, unconditionally love yourself first before anyone else. Be patient with yourself. Eat healthy foods so that your energy and mood are positively affected. Improve on your sleeping habits. Create boundaries and take some time out to process, unwind and pray or meditate. Follow your highest excitement and curiosity. All of these things are a choice. All of those 'reasons' currently running through your head of why you can't do these things – question them. In all likelihood, they are mere excuses, not reasons. And excuses are easier to overcome than reasons… because overcoming them has nothing to do with what's outside of you. All the power you need can be found within.

THE POWER OF
SELF-AWARENESS AND CHOICE

To be aware of self and to become aware of awareness itself, is the act of seeing yourself through the eyes of source. The power of self-awareness gives us the opportunity to place our focus wherever we choose.

This is the first step to shifting from the low vibration that comes with conditional living, into a higher one. This paves the way to more quickly and easily expand into who you really are, and as a result, increases the probability of you attracting love into your life.

You need to know that if you are too focused on how you've failed in past relationships, how nothing is working out for you, or how you might not find anyone in the future; then you are creating the destiny that you do not prefer through the conditions you've set for yourself. Avoid *reacting* emotionally to any situation and choose to *respond* to negative emotion through self-awareness. If you're unaware of where you're placing your focus, you're manifesting by chance and not through choice. This means you could manifest the same old type of relationships you've always been attracting, and its resulting misery.

Become aware of yourself, your own actions, and who you *really* are, so that you can then manifest the relationship you truly desire. Choose to focus on the potential you have to attract a positive relationship, on the essence of why a relationship is something important to you, on what you will get out of this relationship, and on how it will make you feel. Place your focus on the right things, notice your vibration reflect it, and as a result, the happening of the manifestation of your desire.

When you develop the practice of self-awareness, you naturally choose to think better feeling thoughts. You become more optimistic, and you are more aware of the subtle positive aspects of your life. Instead of trying to fight the frequency of lack, you're moving into the frequency of abundance.

Once you've had a taste of the frequency of love, using the power of self-awareness, you can consciously tune yourself into this frequency whenever you want. Your day-to-day will normally bring up conditioned thoughts and patterns. It's important that you recognize conditions, labels, and definitions as subjective or illusionary. When you do this, you vibrationally detach yourself from these traps. The goal is simple. **Detach from the frequency of your situation and embody the frequency of your visualization.**

SHIFT YOUR FOCUS INSIDE

The key to attracting and finding the best relationship is when you realize you can create all of the feelings of having that relationship *without actually having one.*

Is that a paradigm shift of understanding for you? You've always had the power to create the feeling first. Most of us would balk at that statement. Most of us would say, "That can't be! I had a relationship where I felt like I was walking on cloud 9 and I could never create that on my own!"

You may think that's true, but it's not. You are the one who chooses to feel anything – there isn't anyone outside of you who creates it – it's all you. When you fully understand this, then you can take all of your power back, and control over your thoughts and emotions.

Every single one of your relationships is a reflection of you. If you are in a poor mental and emotional state, this will reflect in how you interact with others, how others interact with you, and who you attract into your life.

Every feeling, sensation, and love you ever want to feel can come from within. A high vibration does not need to come from your relationships, partners, or other people (conditions). Your focus should constantly be on your choice to feel however you want to feel despite what's being portrayed in your physical reality.

Another reason why this is so important is because attachment to things outside of your control *will* deplete your energy. When you place excess importance or dependency on factors outside of you, you give all of your power away. As a result, you create resistance towards what you want and move yourself out of balance. The expression 'Where your focus goes, energy flows' illustrates this perfectly. If you're attaching your energy to factors outside of you, where will all the energy you need to create go? How will you become magnetic if you don't have any magnetic energy to emit?

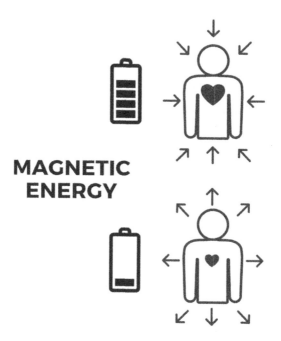

MAGNETIC ENERGY

Create reasons to feel good, even if it doesn't make sense to your rational mind. Even if you're living through the worst time in your life, you have the choice to align yourself with who you really are deep inside. If there are plenty of reasons outside of you to feel grateful, appreciative, and loving, that's amazing. If there are no reasons, that's okay too. Because you always have your own imagination and internal creations there to support you. **There's always a way to raise your vibration.**

Your focus determines your vibration. Focus on possibility, abundance, and how your desires make you feel and why you enjoy them so much. When you shift your focus to what is happening internally, instead of externally, then you will create what you want externally – *that's* manifestation in action.

TECHNIQUE #6:
SELF-IMAGE REFLECTION

Using this technique, you're going to be answering the following questions about yourself in a journal, to help shed a light on:

- all of the positive, strong, and magnetic traits that you possess
- letting go of old beliefs that do not serve you anymore

Often times, we're overshadowed by all the negative and bad things we've been carrying with us throughout our lives. With this reflection technique, we're going to be bringing everything up to the surface. After doing this exercise, consider reading the answers to yourself every single day until you've embodied this new way of being.

1. Write down the five things you love most about yourself in this exact moment in time.
2. Recall a time when you felt like you were embodying the best version of yourself. Describe in detail how it felt or feels like to be confident, open, expansive, magnetic, secure, whole, grateful, appreciative, stable, aligned, loved, excited, fun, sensual, and alive. Write about the three to five words that resonated with you the most.
3. Create a list of your five greatest strengths and traits. Ignore how other people have reacted to these in the past and write down what feels authentic to *you*.
4. List your five greatest challenges in life and write down exactly how you overcame them or how you intend to overcome them.
5. Write down the five greatest lessons that you've learned from all the challenges that life threw at you. Describe how important these lessons will be for you in the future and how they have helped you grow as a person.
6. Write a forgiveness letter to others that have done you wrong and to yourself. Express it in a way that feels like you're letting go of it for good.

Keep these for yourself if you prefer but giving them to the person is often a much more powerful and transformational experience, especially if this is someone you were/are really close to.

7. Describe in detail the new identity you want to step into. Write down the core values, beliefs, and expectations for yourself that you will embody.

8. Write down the boundaries that you will set for yourself in order to align with this new identity. Describe in detail what you will not tolerate and put up with anymore.

9. Describe in your own words what it means to be in love.

TECHNIQUE #7: EMOTIONAL EVIDENCE BASED BELIEF

In the process of attracting a loving relationship, you may find it difficult to stay optimistic given the lack of the physical manifestation of it. This is evidence that shows you are building a faulty belief system due to your object of focus.

When you use external reality as a confirmation to whether you should believe something or not, then you are shutting down the infinite possibilities that can present themselves to you. When your focus is on what you have (in this case, the lack of a loving relationship), you'll continue to manifest more of it.

In order to break free from this cycle, use the Emotional Evidence Based Belief technique by looking for confirmation within. The previous technique (Self Image Reflection) can also assist in this process. **In other words, use your positive emotional state as the confirmation that you are getting into alignment with what you want to attract.** If you are feeling secure, loved, appreciated, and whole, *without* the physical manifestation of your desired relationship, that is *all* the confirmation you need to know that *what you want is on its way.* This is how you build the belief system that shapes your identity, and as a result, shapes your reality.

Recognize your alignment and confirm that this is what you've been looking for. Appreciate these moments and the universe will inevitably start moving pieces around to create synchronicities that match this new frequency.

"I am not what happened to me, I am what I choose to become."

– Carl Jung

CHAPTER 5

Embodying Magnetism: Authentic Charisma

Have you ever noticed how magnetic someone with charisma is, seemingly easily attracting whatever it is they want to themselves? And have you ever wondered how they developed that charisma? Is it something anyone can develop? Or is it something you have to be born with?

The good news is that *anyone* can develop it when you fully understand what it is and what is at the heart of it. Anyone can learn to become more charismatic, which will make it much easier to attract the relationships you desire. In this chapter, we will take a look at breaking free from your false identity, owning who you are, and becoming the person you want to become.

First, let's cover 3 topics in order to gain clarity around the subject...

WHAT IS YOUR FALSE IDENTITY?

Awareness of having a problem is 90% of the solution. When you become aware of your false identity (we all have it), then you're almost there...

Have you ever met someone, dated them for a while, and everything was going well, but then as soon as it got more serious, things started to change? Maybe they were the 'perfect match' throughout the dating period, but once the relationship reached the point where it was committed, both of you started to show your true colors. In this kind of a relationship, you start off acting from the ego, then as time goes on, it reaches a stage where you can no longer hide your shortcomings and vulnerability, and before you know it, the chemistry disappears.

It's a very common experience. To a degree, we all do it by being on our best behavior during the courting phase of any relationship. The point is that taking on a false identity can be a conscious decision that someone makes… but what if it's unconscious?

Most of us have developed false identities that are based upon our ego's attachment to past relationships, experiences, and ideas. The ego works hard to convince us that who we are is the result of all of the external things that we experience and how we perceive them. It makes us feel stagnant and stuck. For example, if we fail in one subject matter in school, then the automatic conclusion is that we are a failure at that subject. If we excel, then we are successful. The ego will come to conclusions based upon our limited view of the world, and has a difficult time accepting that anything else can be true. This is why if someone believes that all men are bad, they will not be open to any reality where some men are good.

Our ego regrets the past, is worried about the future, and never lives in the present moment. This is why it has such a strong desire to control, instead of to let go. It is a relentless cog in the wheel of our life that doesn't want us to experience the here and now – the present moment. The basic motive of the ego is to protect us, but its reasoning ability comes from a very basic, reptilian part of our brain that cannot connect with higher levels of intelligence. The ego is the animal part of our brain that is fearful, defensive, limited, and unconscious. It is your mind's voice of doubt. It is the voice that tells you to not try anything for fear of how you will look to others. It is the voice that tells you to play it safe. The ego is defensive, and often times will cause certain people to repel from you.

The ego places a very high value on external things and experiences – things that we've become attached to and use to define us through our memory, thus keeping us stuck in a certain way of thinking. **This analysis of our external life experiences creates our false identity – the false self.** This false self may tell you that you don't deserve love, or that it'll never work out. It wants you to stay attached to an identity that's been confirmed externally from past experiences. This could be due to your unconscious choice to experience those moments the way you did over and over again.

When you realize that your ego is *not* your true self, you can start to let go of the old you and embrace the new, limitless you. When you become aware of your false identity, then you can start to create a new reality – a reality that sets you up to develop charisma that makes you magnetic to exactly the kind of relationship you want to attract. We'll talk more about this in a later section.

WE ARE ETERNAL SPIRITUAL BEINGS

All of us are living in a temporary, human experience. Your physical experience is temporary, but your nonphysical experience is eternal. Therefore, there is no reason to stay attached to one way of being. You can become anyone you wish to become, whenever you want. It may take some time to grasp this, or even to apply it, but just so you know, it's not impossible.

All it takes is to let go of the expectations and judgments coming from the outside world, as well as renegotiating certain energetic agreements you've made with people in your life. In other words, if you want to be a better and more magnetic version of yourself, you need to be open to detaching from your old non-magnetic identity. Thinking, feeling, and acting differently is required if you want to experience a new reality. It all starts from within.

When you realize that you are an eternal being, it should warm your heart knowing that this life is not all there is, and that you'll never stop expanding. You are a powerful, ever-expanding, forever growing being who will never stop desiring new things. When you fully understand who you really are, all worry, doubt, and fear will melt away. It is our ego's desire to stay attached to an identity that keeps us in the mindset of lack, limitation, worry, and fear. But when you become aware, and decide to let go, you free yourself from its constraints.

Understanding this core belief that we have a *never-changing* nature will allow you to see beyond what you think is true.

WHAT TO EXPECT WITH CHANGE

To the ego, any kind of change is a threat to the status quo, and could be threatening and dangerous. Since most people live from the ego state of mind, you can expect with high certainty that they are going to test this new identity you're building for yourself.

Although you do get what you expect to get, don't be surprised if people react differently to this new version of you. Don't be surprised if they judge and give their opinion. Go easy on yourself during this time of transformation and change. Expect yourself to yo-yo back and forth between the new way and old way of being until you've completely transformed. Transformation takes time. Others won't like it. Be prepared.

This new way of being will attract new life experiences that you otherwise wouldn't have had. It may be uncomfortable at first, but realize that these new experiences are exactly what you were asking for with this new identity you've embodied. They are coming from the unknown, and that is why it might feel uncomfortable and unexpected.

This is your manifestation. This is usually when your ego will try and pull you back to the old way of thinking and try to convince you that there is something wrong with what you're experiencing. Be aware of these thoughts so that you can then shine a light on them, thus giving them less power over you.

BEING 'AS IF'

Remember the Law of Attraction concept to 'act as if it already happened?' The idea is to take about 5 minutes a day to get quiet, close your eyes, and visualize from the first-person perspective of whatever it is that you want. The promise was that if you could visualize every detail of what you wanted, then you could raise your vibration to what it would feel like, and as a result, you would attract it.

The only problem is that it takes much more time than just 5 minutes. The new solution is to memorize the feeling you created during the practice and take it with you into the rest of your day. When you can embody this version 2.0 of you all day long instead of just for 5 minutes, then you will accelerate the manifestation of whatever desire it is you want.

This is why your goal should be to go from 'acting as if' to 'being as if'. In other words, don't just pretend what you want is here, live it. What is the difference? And how do you distinguish between the two? Take the current dating landscape as an example. Say a man spends money on a car he cannot afford, talks about things he knows nothing about, and goes against his own values just to impress others. This is how you 'act as if.' In other words, it's faking it, until you make it.

But what if we were to flip the equation around? Say a man spends money on his own self-education, studies more about a subject he wants to learn about, and sticks to his values no matter what, in order to attract only the right kind of people. This is how you 'be as if.' In other words, it's making it, until you make it. This is the idea of building your own self-worth.

When you behave from a superficial level, you do indeed tune into a frequency that radiates a sense of self-worth. It is true that if you fake it, you can actually make it. But be warned: reality *will* test you. Things will show up where you need to actually be the part, and not just play it. Actors in movies act the part, but when the scene is over, they go back to being who they really are. The act is only for show. This same idea applies in life. This is the reason why a relationship can end so quickly. You enter it with a false identity, and slowly start to show your real colors as time goes on, because the mask is starting to slip off.

If you want to make real change happen, you need to focus on the change that is happening internally and not externally. Buying flashy accessories will not make you more magnetic. It'll only superficially and temporarily cover up the truth; the expression of your true self. Create desire for someone to be attracted to you. Bring energetic value to the table by giving other's permission to be themselves. Giving, when it comes from the heart, is an action that is inviting and energetically positive.

Building your own sense of self-worth is far more sustainable than 'acting as if' because it doesn't depend on conditions. It is work that starts from the inside, thus radiating an energy that is more dense, sustainable, and unshakeable when faced with challenges and contrast.

Be the person that would attract other people into their circle based upon who they truly are and what they truly want. Express your truth with no filters because it's the most magnetic identity you can embody. It's the identity that feels natural, flowing, and in alignment with your deepest desires, including a romantic relationship that lasts.

This process goes far beyond embodying the experience of being in a relationship. When you choose to create your own self-worth, you're embodying the person in the relationship. Notice the subtle shift. Even though visualizing the *experience* is a step in the right direction, embodying the *person* that is in the experience is even more powerful.

THE KEY TO MAGNETISM
AND CHARISMA

Do not be afraid of making the first move if you feel called to. In other words, do not be afraid of embodying the confident and charismatic you when your intuition is guiding you there. When you overcome the fears you have related to social interactions and romantic relationships, you naturally and energetically radiate a new energy that allows you to step into a new vibrational reality for yourself. Whether taking this step works in your favor or not physically, non-physical, you've already sent out a new signal.

The moment you give yourself the freedom to be yourself (whoever you truly want to be); the more magnetic you are to others. Why? Because when you're being yourself, you're living in alignment with your inner being, which is naturally very magnetic and charismatic. When you live life from the eyes of source energy - from your inner being's perspective - you are a joyful, happy, passionate, eager, magnetic, and authentically charismatic person.

Everyone is naturally magnetic. All it takes is to remove the egoic filters that have been created through the external lens of judgment and comparison. When you're operating from a high vibrational state, you're operating from a magnetic state. When you're at a high vibrational frequency, you attract people that also have the intention of living at a high vibrational frequency. In this case, like attracts like.

> *"Love is not something that is a sort of rare commodity,*
> *everyone has it."*
> **– Alan Watts**

This high vibrational frequency feels loose, easy, effortless, fun, exciting, and worry-free - not needy, contrived, desperate, or insecure. When you embody this high vibrational version of you, you give permission for others to be themselves. You become more approachable. You will instantly light up any room that you walk into, and raise the vibration of everyone around you.

When you're open like this, you invite the unknown into your life. You surrender to the spontaneity of the universe. When you embody this magnetic energy, it's easy to give up the vibration of neediness because energetically, you have everything you need.

Own who you are. Be the true you. And watch how quickly the relationship you desire manifests in your life.

TECHNIQUE #8: ENERGETIC STRETCHING AND DANCING

For this technique, we're going to be moving your focus from your heart and mind into your body. Personal magnetism doesn't only involve thinking and feeling a certain way. Our bodies are the vehicle at which we radiate magnetic energy to the outside world. So understanding how to express yourself physically is essential if you want to truly embody magnetism.

The same way you do weight training or cardio to change your physical body, this technique will help change how you personally feel about your body on an energetic level. This is also a powerful way of allowing your body to release tension from traumas and wounds that are still lingering inside of you. The difference in energy between having a straight back and a slouching one is only one of the more obvious examples of this. This technique can be described in two words: Ecstatic Movement

Whether you're dancing or stretching, giving your body the freedom to move in a way that is purely intuitive is an excellent way to open up your energy. Dancing and stretching as a form of release is nothing new. Consider yoga, a practice that has been around for thousands of years, as a form of ecstatic movement. You don't need to attend ecstatic dance clubs to get the full effects of this. A simple 3-5 minute intuitive stretching sessions every morning at home is enough. Give room for your body to express itself naturally every once in a while. Not only will this help open up your energy, but it'll get you feeling more comfortable about yourself, thus, bringing about a new sense of authentic confidence and charisma.

Here are seven tips to get the most out of your ecstatic movement session:

1. Focus on intuition and moving with the flow of your body. Let go of all conscious decision making.
2. Breathe into your belly and not your chest before initiating the movement. Try your best not to hold your breath.

3. Keep your awareness on the sensations of your body. Stay grounded and present.

4. Allow your shoulders to relax and keep your sternum up during certain movements.

5. Pull your spine up at the solar plexus so it stays open and not slouched.

6. Avoid energy stagnation by not staying still for too long.

7. When you have thoughts, check in with how the body is feeling at the exact moment they arise.

Throughout your session, be conscious about the energy that you give off. Be in tune with your thoughts and feelings. Relax.

TECHNIQUE #9: SELF-FULFILLING QUESTIONS

This technique derives from the self-fulfilling prophecy theory. This theory states that an original expectation leads to its own confirmation. In other words, if you're expecting something to happen to you, then it will. For this technique, we're going to be revamping your self-fulfilling prophecy by asking yourself questions that confirm the expectations that you have. This is a way of confirming your expectation before they manifest.

For example, let's say you label yourself as a shy and anxious person. Hence, whenever you go on a date or meet new people, they will catch onto this belief because you've already labeled yourself as a shy and anxious person. As a result, that is going to be your state of being as you radiate the energy associated with those beliefs. A new belief takes time to solidify because it can only be strengthened by confirmation. We often only depend on external confirmation, which is why new beliefs hardly ever stick. For this technique, you're going to be confirming these new beliefs internally by asking yourself questions. These questions will imply that your new identity is already solidified before it's been confirmed externally.

Here are a few examples of questions you can start asking yourself. I encourage you to create your own questions too. This will help you get into the mood of asking yourself questions that raise your vibration at any time and place:

When being single:
- Why do I feel so whole and complete?
- Why am I so in love with myself?
- Why is my relationship with myself so healthy?
- Why do I love spending time with myself?
- Why am I excited about who I'm attracting?

When going out to social events:
- Why am I talking to people so confidently?
- Why am I attracting positive attention from other people?
- Why am I so open and engaging in new social interactions?

When being on a date:
- What part of this date is fun for me?
- What interests me about this person?
- How am I handling this date so well?
- Where did this confidence of mine come from?
- Why am I so happy about this moment?

When being in a relationship:
- What makes me happy about this relationship?
- What do I love about my partner?
- Why do I feel loved, appreciated, and secure?
- What makes this person so fun to be around?

"Love is an untamed force. When we try to control it, it destroys us. When we try to imprison it, it enslaves us. When we try to understand it, it leaves us feeling lost and confused."

– Paulo Coelho

CHAPTER 6

Easy Loving: The Path of Least Resistance and Most Love

Now that you know more about how magnetic energy works, we can talk about easy loving, what the path of least resistance is, and the path to experiencing the most love possible in your life. We're going to talk about how important it is to have a high vibration in all aspects of your life and how following your passions outside of relationships will actually help you attract more, better quality, relationships.

Most people struggle with their ego and don't allow love to encapsulate every aspect of their lives. The struggle is internal, but once you understand what it is, then you can begin to let go and let yourself be guided towards the path of least resistance or most allowance and most love.

Before you began reading this book, you may have thought that finding your soul mate involved something outside of yourself – it was a quest – a search – something that you had to find. But the best way to search for love is to create the love you want inside of yourself first, and then in all areas of your life before you 'search' for anyone. After creating love for yourself in all aspects of your life, searching for that perfect relationship isn't even necessary because they will come into your life naturally. When it happens, it will feel easy, fun, light, and exciting. You won't have to play games because this time you got the universe to do the hard work of searching for the perfect match. This method is a much different way of going about manifesting the love of your life because it leverages your state of being over anything else.

This can seem like a more time-consuming method, but in reality, it only further reinforces what we've already talked about in previous chapters. When you can embody your best self, you can attract the best relationship for you. It's simply a matter of consistently building up the natural magnetism that is already inside of you.

Love yourself so thoroughly and completely that you are just oozing love, confidence, happiness, fun, appreciation, and respect for yourself and others. Be easy on yourself when it comes to manifesting love. And create it in every aspect of your life so that your love vibration is revving and humming along, repelling anyone who isn't a vibrational match.

Don't go out there in a desperate frame of mind and decide that you're going to help someone to raise their vibration to match yours. That's asking for trouble. Instead, set your standards high, and keep them there. Rather than lower your high standards, know that the right person will be attracted to your unique energetic signature.

VIBRATION MIGRATION

When you understand why and how vibration migration works, you'll understand exactly why you've been getting what you've been getting in life. You see, the universe doesn't care what topic you think about – all it cares about is what frequency you emit. In other words, everything could be going great in your life – your health, your wealth, and your relationships too. However, if you focus on even just one thing that is going wrong in your life for too long, it becomes prominent in your vibration. This lowers your vibration in ALL other aspects of your life too.

How you do one thing is how you do everything... let me explain.

If you loathe your job, despise the type of work you do, and wake up every morning dreading to start the day, this vibration will carry over to your relationships. If this work is something you do 5 times a week, and 8 hours a day, that means you're in a low vibration for a very long time. It will become your normal vibration if you focus on it too much for too long. In this state, it's impossible to become a magnet to love when the frequency you're radiating is that of hate, boredom, and lack of fulfillment. Even worse, if you do attract someone while you are in a low vibration, they will match your low vibration, inevitably leading to a problematic relationship. Changing your current job or career can be a massive leap that not many people are willing to take. There are ways to get around this however, and that's by changing how you view the work you do. Changing the meaning of what you do, where you go, and how you do your work, is an excellent first step to making the vibrational shift.

It doesn't matter what you allow to lower your vibration. If you choose to allow anything to get you upset or down for too long, everything in your life will snowball and become a problem too. This is where the expression, 'When it rains, it pours' comes from. When you focus too much on the negatives of your life, more negatives will come.

The goal should be to carry a high vibration in everything you do, no matter if it has to do with your relationships or not. This is key to defining your **default frequency** as one that matches with your desired reality.

You'll often get pushed out of alignment, but that's okay. There is a buffer of time before things manifest, so don't beat yourself up or worry if you find yourself getting momentarily upset, frustrated, or angry. Simply do not attach your sense of self to these states of being. Do not get caught up. As long as you keep your focus on what makes you feel good in the moment and allow yourself to be the version of you that's in the frequency of love, that's all that matters to the universe.

Do things that raise your vibration. What this means from a practical perspective is to be good to yourself more often. Go to the beach. Get a massage. Eat out at your favorite restaurant. Call a good friend. Rent a bunch of 'feel good' movies and watch them. Go for a walk, hike, or bike.

Nourish yourself well with healthy foods and snacks. Get plenty of sleep. Say 'no' more often to others when it feels right – which essentially means saying 'yes' to *you* more often. Embrace being what you normally would consider to be a little selfish, but this time, do it with no guilt. Remember – there is a big difference between being self-absorbed and practicing self-love. Self-love is good!

There is nothing more important, for both you and those around you, than you feeling your best. That means choosing to feel good under any and all circumstances. Note, this does not mean to follow what is familiar to you. Familiarity, often times, isn't exciting, and it doesn't feed your curiosity. This is a trap many people easily fall into, so keep this in mind. I know all of these concepts are hard to believe because you've probably been taught that you have to "face reality."

But instead of "facing reality," *create* it! Yes - create it yourself! That's how the universe works anyway. You create your reality by choosing which one you want to live. Take a step back, be the observer, and choose which thoughts and emotions you want to resonate with the most. Do not get too attached, because attachment to anything, good or bad, creates resistance. Remember, you are infinite. You are so much more than what you stay stuck in or limit yourself to. Get yourself on the path of least resistance to the best relationship of your life, but more importantly, to the best relationship with yourself.

FOLLOW YOUR PASSION AND PURPOSE

"Follow your bliss" Joseph Campbell once so aptly put it. Find your passion. Discover your purpose. **Let the relationship be the side effect of you living your best life independently.** Become whole yourself so you can attract a whole person. Become the person you want to attract by putting yourself first in your life.

This is powerful because it removes the vibration of *wanting* and shifts you into the vibration of *having*. This opens you up to attracting relationships that are deeper, more passionate, and more fulfilling because they're in alignment with what you're doing every day.

Don't ever try to become what you think someone else wants or needs you to become. In the end, you'll be out of alignment. You'll feel resistance instantly because your state of being will not come from a place of authentic truth. It'll come from external conditioning. This not only leads to more struggle when it comes to manifesting your dream relationship, but it'll also leave you unhappy and unfulfilled with the ones you do attract. The best way to attract your envisioned ideal person into your life is to fall in love with yourself *and* your own life.

As you work on yourself, your natural glow will start to shine through in everything you do. You'll find it easier to be guided by your intuition. Decisions will start leading to spontaneous encounters that you never would have imagined. People and circumstances will start showing up in your life like never before. All you need to do is ride your own wave, and let the water take you to where you truly want to go. You attract to you based on who you are being, and if you get yourself to your best version in other areas of your life, you'll find it easier to attract someone that will want to be a part of that too.

THE LAW OF DETACHMENT

The Law of Detachment is the act of surrendering to the divine. It's the act of following the path of least resistance, which simply means to make choices that feel good and in alignment with who you want to be at any given moment in time. It's having full confidence, trust, and faith that your desired relationship will manifest itself instead of labelling the possibility of it with an idea, limitation, opinion, or external condition.

If you're attached, you radiate signals of doubt and distrust. Be exclusively loyal to your intuition. This is the path to a fulfilling and love-filled life. Contrary to popular belief, this does not mean you do not care. It means you care, and a lot more than most people can see on the surface level. **Honoring your truth is your greatest service to others.** And when it comes to relationships, this is how you attract and manifest the best of the best.

ATTACHMENT	DETACHMENT
RESISTANCE	FLOW
STUCKNESS	FREEDOM
NEEDINESS	HAVINGNESS
LACKING	ABUNDANT
FINITE	INFINITE
CONTROLLING	ALLOWING
MANIPULATIVE	MAGNETIC
ANXIOUS	TRUSTING

Here are the 3 most common ideas most people attach themselves to when it comes to manifesting their dream partner:

How the Relationship Will Manifest

When you put expectations on a relationship before it has even really started, you put pressure on the other person, which creates a sense of dependency that repels most people, especially the kind you want to attract. You can't hide your feelings. We all have the ability (some without even realizing it) to read each other's energy through non-verbal communication. This is why the other person will know if you are feeling needy. You cannot *not* communicate how you really feel at the energetic level. The point is - if you move too fast or force a situation to happen, it'll never naturally escalate. This desperate feeling will repel any potential suitor.

If you force yourself onto someone who you are madly attracted to right off the bat, and they are not feeling the same way, there's going to be resistance. The better way to do it is to not set any expectations of how the relationship will manifest, and instead, learn to just enjoy the moment with them without needing any of your expectations to be fulfilled.

This explains why it is a lot easier to attract someone who you're not all that attracted to because you never gave them that 'needy' vibrational feeling. Usually, neediness repels people and drives them away. If they are not repelled, it's probably going to be an unhealthy, codependent relationship.

Forcing a connection to happen between two people is like trying to plug a USB cord into an electrical outlet. It'll never fit. If you keep forcing it, not only will you repel the other person that much sooner, but you may also develop a feeling of rejection and sense of unworthiness if you're unaware of your vibrational output. There are times where people just need time to get a feel of who you really are. Not everyone is excited about diving headfirst into a relationship. Take it one step and one connection at a time. After all, you don't *need* this relationship. To bring the point home, take the journey lightly and have fun, it's not serious. The one for you will come in due time, and it'll feel more naturally progressive than anything you've ever felt before.

Another thing to note is that your manifestations come from the unknown. They are something new, different, exciting, and sometimes slightly uncomfortable. If they were coming from the known, you wouldn't feel that exhilarated feeling. Only the universe is responsible for how it's going to manifest. Your only responsibility is taking control of your inner state and allowing the manifestations to come to you.

When the Relationship Will Manifest

The second thing to detach from is when the relationship will manifest. Many men and women get pressured by their relatives to find a mate, settle down, and start a new life. This kind of pressure can actually make the manifestation backfire, or worse, get you into a relationship that you later regret.

Your dream relationship will manifest in divine timing. The universe knows who it is already and could be waiting for you to get your vibrational act together so that you two can meet. But you've got to stop worrying about when it's going to happen because worry is a low vibrational frequency. Worry is a useless emotion when you understand how the universe works.

Only the universe knows when the best time to show you your desire is. You can't control physical reality. You can only control how you respond to it. You will manifest what you desire when you are ready and a vibrational match to it.

Have patience. Manifestations have a delay effect because matter is extremely dense, unlike our thoughts or emotions, which we can feel instantly. When you are feeling good or in alignment, recognize that this is the only proof you need to know that your dream partner is on their way. Literally nothing else matters. Once you've lifted this weight off your shoulder, no external circumstance will ever serve as a metric for possibility or timing. These things are out of your control, which means your manifestation can happen even when you least expect it to. This also means the manifestation of your dream relationship can come sooner than you think, especially if you've been consistently working on becoming a vibrational match to it.

Attracting One Specific Person

Many of us get caught up in the idea that there is only one person for us out there in the world, but that's simply not the case. This romanticized concept of love is the result of the Hollywood movies that we've been portrayed throughout our childhood and adult lives.

This idea that there is only one person out there for us goes against the idea of an abundant mindset. If you're so fixated with attracting one person, you're attached to this one outcome. And if it doesn't work out, then you'll likely feel devastated and unworthy. Focusing on just one person will create unnecessary resistance, especially if you're participating in the act of chasing after them. Even if it does work out, do you really want to be in a relationship where you are solely dependent on the love of one person? Why put yourself in the victim role? You are a powerful creator, and nothing should constrain you from being your best at all times.

If you want to attract just one person, you're also rejecting the infinite number of outcomes the universe has in store for you. Thus, you're creating resistance with your true desire (the feeling of mutual love between you and a dream partner). Attracting one specific person is indeed possible, but it would require so much vibrational sacrifice that it would never be worth it. Most of the time, you would have to tune your frequency to match exactly the person you want to attract by disregarding most of your truth and potential, instead of just being you.

Like the old saying goes, there are plenty of fish in the sea. What if the universe wants to give you a relationship that's even deeper, more passionate, and more fulfilling than this specific one you're so desperately after? Would you reject it? Obviously not. Stay open to infinite possibilities and opportunities.

"Love is detachment, detachment is love."
– Bentinho Massaro

TECHNIQUE #10: SOFTENING THOUGHTS

The main premise for this technique is to simply soften the intensity in which we label, judge, and define other people. This is a particularly powerful technique for those that vet people very heavily when they're dating, express jealousy towards other couples, or judge themselves and others for being who they are.

The idea is simple, when you catch yourself creating a story to define another person, soften this thought process. In other words, think thoughts that go against the original thought that you were thinking.

Here is an example of how you could counter your original thought when judging a couple.

Original Thought: "Look at how perfect they are together. Nobody should be able to be that happy and in love. That's a fairy tale dream that I'll never have."

Softening Thought: "They weren't born together, so they must have been in the same spot I'm in at one point. Which means there is a possibility for me to be just as happy and in love as they are."

Notice how the softening thought detaches you from your original perspective of the situation.

Here is another example.

Original Thought: "Ugh, he likes to watch hockey. That's a deal breaker for me. There's no chance I'm introducing him to my friends and family."

Softening Thought: "Sure, he likes to watch hockey, but he has other qualities that I really enjoy and admire. I appreciate those qualities and I'd like to experience them more."

The best way to avoid an extreme perspective on either side of the thinking spectrum is by keeping your perspective neutral and following the subtle cues of your intuition. In other words, **do not create mental narratives about who someone is and will become.** Instead, let yourself be guided to a decision on a vibrational, emotional, and energetic level. Give your intuition the space it needs to make the best decision for you.

TECHNIQUE #11: LETTING GO OF MISALIGNMENT

Often times, many people stay in relationships with others simply due to the idea that "something is better than nothing." This can be an extremely detrimental perspective because it not only stops you from going after something better, but it can potentially get you to something worse.

The main purpose of this technique is to help you give yourself permission to let go of relationships that are not working out. If you feel like you've been putting up with certain people, sacrificing things you love, and halting your own personal growth for the sake of others, this is the time to reflect.

Think back to how this person or these people make you feel when you're around them. Do they support you unconditionally in reaching the potential you're striving for? Do you feel uplifted after every interaction with them? Do you look forward to interacting with them? Are they in alignment with what you want in this type of relationship?

If you answered 'no' to any of the questions I've asked, consider limiting the amount of energy you invest in the relationship. It can sometimes feel like you're moving away from what you want when you let go of something you've invested so much time into but, the reality of it is, you're actually taking a step forward towards what you truly want. This is because you'll be giving yourself room and space to be living in the frequency of your desire. When you're investing and focusing your energy on relationships that don't make you feel good, guess what? You'll continue to attract relationships that don't make you feel good.

Take this time to write down and review all of the relationships in your life.

"There are people that love you and there are people that hate you, yet none of that has anything to do with you."

– Abraham Hicks

CHAPTER 7

Magnetic Receptivity: How to Receive and Be Open to the Best Relationships

What is the receiving mode *exactly*? What blocks it, and how can you 'unblock' it? Why is having fun so important when it comes to manifesting the love of your life? And how can you ride the wave of positive momentum in order to attract your soul mate?

Let's find out...

THE RECEIVING MODE

The receiving mode is our natural state of being. When we were born, we knew our worthiness. We sensed that receiving was a normal and natural process. When we asked for something, often times, it was given. When we needed anything, often times, we received it. But then, as we got older, society, our parents, and the educational system started to teach us that we needed to *prove* our worthiness instead of enjoying and embracing the receiving mode.

Life is obviously not handed to us on a silver platter. We do need to work and take inspired action to get what we desire. **The problem occurs when we lose sight of the concept that life is supposed to be good to**

us and that we are supposed to have fun. Most of us start to buy into the vibration of scarcity, fear, worry, and concern - which is the default vibrational frequency of society in general. We are too "realistic", and allow our fears to stifle our hopes and dreams. This in turn alters our own vibrational frequency.

When we buy into these lower vibrations, when we accept it as the 'normal' way to be, it's hard to get back to our original understanding that we were born worthy and that receiving is normal. It's hard to believe that all we have to do is to ask, and it is given. Most of us have all kinds of evidence to prove that the opposite is true. When we have been programmed to believe that life is a struggle and difficult, it's not easy to suddenly believe the opposite.

Life is all about your perspective, and when your perspective is limiting and disempowering, it's only natural for you to experience this. That is the challenge for all of us, but in order to be, do, and have whatever we want, including attracting the relationships we want, we must embrace what we knew at an early age.

The reason you may not be manifesting your true desires is because something is blocking your manifestations. Since we already know that creation first starts with a thought, it only makes sense that our thinking, negative programming, and unconscious patterns are the reasons for the resistance and blockage.

FOUR MAIN LOVE MANIFESTATION BLOCKS

There are four main reasons why your desired manifestations are being blocked:

Thinking Negative Thoughts

When you think a negative thought and ponder on it, you attract more thoughts that match that vibration. Identifying with any thought, whether it be positive or negative, creates attachment, and when we're attached, we create resistance. This resistance comes because we've stopped going with the natural flow of experience. The more you limit yourself with definitions, labels, and meanings, the more you resist your infinite nature. Most of us cannot help but to think negative thoughts because we've associated our reality with external events and circumstances, either current or those from the past. When you realize that you always have the option to choose a better thought, which gives you a better feeling, at any time, you'll begin changing your reality from the inside out. This is your power.

Feeling Negative Emotions

In general, a thought originates first, and then manifests into an emotion. Your emotions let you know whether your inner being is in alignment with the thought you were just thinking. When you attach yourself to a thought your inner being doesn't agree with, you instantly feel the discord, the misalignment, and that's why you feel the negative emotion.

Your feelings are the gateway to your connection with your inner being, and also the gateway to all of your manifestations, including the relationship you desire.

Reacting vs. Responding

The difference between reacting and responding is that reacting is your old, programmed, knee-jerk impulse to external events that take place in the moment. Reacting is about giving up control over your thoughts and vibration to the pre-conceived notions your ego or subconscious mind wants you to believe.

Responding, on the other hand, is having the awareness to head-off the thought with your inner being's perspective. It's about knowing that all is well and that there is insight to be found even when you experience what you don't want.

Reacting can lower your vibration and allow you to be vulnerable to external, outside conditions, whereas responding keeps your inner state as the priority, resulting in higher vibrational living.

Refusing to Accept a Manifestation

Some people refuse to accept a manifestation. An example of this, is when you meet a wonderful potential partner, but keep imagining every single reason as to why it can't work out with them.

Usually, we refuse to accept a good, healthy manifestation because our subconscious mind is still operating from the old paradigm. Either it wants us to believe that we are unworthy, relationships are problematic, or any other reason why we believe, from past experience, that we shouldn't take the step forward of accepting our manifestation. The key is to learn to let go of the old patterns of thinking and to embrace your physical reality and what your inner being is trying to tell you.

The bottom line is, you need to let go of your attachment to this 'perfect' someone - because they don't exist. Imperfection is where the magic is. When you want to manifest, you should desire the feeling the manifestation will give you, rather than the manifestation itself. Follow the guide of your intuition and not of your thoughts. Follow how someone makes you feel, not what you think of them. When you do this, you open yourself up to a whole new realm of possibility.

HOW TO UNBLOCK
THE RECEIVING MODE

You can unblock the receiving mode by shifting your attention and focus onto things (physical or non-physical) that raise your vibration. This takes a little getting used to.

Practically speaking, what this means is when something 'bad' happens to you, such as when someone rejects you, you choose to think a more positive thought. Choosing to neutralize the negative thought by minimizing the importance of the event is also another powerful approach. Give the event a different meaning than you normally would. You don't have to allow your subconscious mind to run the automatic program of defining people and experiences for you.

The point is, *you* have the control to choose whatever thought you want, whenever you want. You could choose to think happy thoughts at any time you want. If nothing exciting is happening in physical reality, bring your focus to the non-physical (your imagination), and vice-versa.

There is one important point to realize. Do not expect to make a huge leap from negative, pessimistic, and disempowering thinking, to suddenly being the eternal optimist who is always happy. Rather, take it one easy step at a time, one perspective at a time, until you finally start recognizing the bigger picture.

An example of this is if you're feeling fearful of something, you cannot expect yourself to think your way into a more courageous feeling. Instead, learn to accept the fear by reframing the feeling or event. Ask yourself questions to rationalize the fear. Ask yourself where those thoughts are *actually* coming from and whether they are truly relevant when it comes to manifesting your desire. Notice if you're thinking too much in the past or too much in the future. Bring your focus back to the present moment. This is where the choice of choosing a better feeling thought is made.

Do not get upset if you're unable to instantly rise the ranks of the emotional scale – it's near impossible. It's too far of a vibrational gap between fear and joy. You have to work your way up the emotional scale by using the power of focus.

THE POWER OF FOCUS

If you're not receiving, then your focus is on the fact that you're not receiving. Instead, focus on the receiving part. Focus on experiencing what it is the universe has to offer you and know that it is always to your benefit, whether it's the manifestation itself, or a sign that you need to shift your focus. Challenges should always be welcomed because they give us clues to where we need to improve vibrationally. The discord and disharmony we feel when not in alignment with our true selves are clues that help you improve your perspective around certain areas of your life.

It takes some discipline to purposely focus on thoughts and things that feel good, but it is essential to invoking the power of manifestation. Let's take Bianca's story as an example.

Bianca was single for 13 years. She had always been feeling this need for a relationship and the more she needed it, the longer she went without one. Eventually, this neediness translated into a feeling of unworthiness. The longer you go without a relationship, the more this feeling can pervade. And so, this cycle continued until she learned to shift her focus.

Instead of attaching herself to disempowering ideas related to being single, she began developing a positive free flowing perspective shift that felt perfectly aligned with her inner being. She expected the manifestation of the type of man she wanted to attract, but also let go of the resistance she was building towards it, through awareness of her thoughts and emotions. There were times she felt lonely or doubtful, but this didn't stop her from following her excitement and riding the wave of positive momentum. This search for love ends when she finally decides to be the attraction point of it, and eventually crosses paths with a man she believes to be 'the one.'

A lot of magic can happen when you decide to let go of the resistance that comes with attachment. One of the best ways of doing this is by having fun!

HAVE FUN WITH THE
LOVE FINDING PROCESS

Life is supposed to be good to you, and it's also supposed to be fun. You do not need to make the process of attracting your love relationship so serious. If it's serious to you, then you possibly feel threatened by the manifestation not happening. This leads you to vibrating at the frequency of lack, worry, and fear – all wrong frequencies for manifesting the love of your life.

If you're having fun, then you know it's going to happen eventually. Creation happens immediately after you have a desire. Now it's time to become a vibrational match to it in order to make it manifest physically. After you set your vibrational frequency, having received benefit from the contrast of past bad relationships and experiences, you are all set to manifest the relationship you truly want. But remember, you have to become a vibrational match to your mate and that is done by 'being as if' that person is already here. In order to do that, all you have to do is let go of the worry, embody the excitement, and have fun NOW – not later.

When a potential partner sees how happy, fun, and wonderful you are, they will be attracted to you in all aspects – physically, emotionally, mentally and even spiritually. The vibration of neediness or lack, that would normally create resistance, seizes to exist.

Have fun with the process! Be open to testing and trying out new things. Step into the unknown - which means you're in a state of creation and spontaneity. This is the state you want to be in if you're looking for love because love is all about fun, spontaneity, exhilaration, excitement, randomness, and adventure.

Appreciate the things you have when you're single and appreciate the idea and feelings you get with the possibility of you finding love. Remember, the journey on the way to your dream relationship is just as exciting too.

If you're thinking there are other people in your life who stifle your fun vibration, it may be best to stay away from them during this high vibrational fun time in your life. That's right – fun might include avoiding certain people and situations.

Fun is loose, free, and open – the exact vibration that attracts all of your love desires. When you let go and allow yourself to feel that kind of fun, you'll manifest your desired relationship in no time.

RIDING THE WAVE
OF POSITIVE MOMENTUM

Momentum, when it really picks up, is one of the most powerful approaches to manifestation. It can turn a year's worth of work, down to a week. And when we're able to master the principles of vibrational momentum, we're able to change our reality at an exhilarating pace.

The best way to start momentum is by following your excitement. When you follow what feels good, you give yourself permission to radiate at the frequency of your desires. This means you're aligned with the perspective of your inner being. In other words, when you do what feels good (not familiar), you become a magnet to more of it. Do things that excite you, because this vibration is the one that matches that of your dream relationship.

Momentum can also be described as the 'snowball effect,' where a small snowball rolling down a snowy hill gathers momentum along the way by becoming larger and larger as it picks up more snow. When the ball is rolling, it will keep on rolling unless it is met with very strong resistance. The longer the momentum goes on, the more powerful it is.

Negative thoughts can, however, also build momentum. Just as you have the power to start positive momentum by stepping into the unknown and having more fun; you also have the power to start negative momentum. **The sooner you stop associating yourself with the negative thoughts that cross your mind, before they become negative emotions – the more chances you have of building your positive momentum.**

You have the power to control your vibrational momentum, whether it's positive or negative. If it's negative, stop it quickly and it won't gain any momentum.

When jumpstarting positive vibrational momentum, without being uninterrupted by contrary or negative thinking, the energy behind your thoughts and emotions start to gain traction. According to inspirational speaker and author Abraham Hicks, whenever you think a thought for over 17 seconds; it passes a threshold, gains 10 times its strength, and thereby starts attracting more experiences, people, circumstances, and events that match that vibration. And when you keep going on with the positive thought for another 17 seconds without pondering on negative ones, again, it gets 10 times stronger in its attraction power. When you do this for 68 seconds, your attraction power is many, many more times powerful than when you started.

When it comes to applying the power of momentum, many problems often arise. We allow our thoughts to entertain doubt and worry without ever allowing them to gain traction. It's actually very common for most of us to think a resistant thought even while in the middle of a short, brief, positive thought. The challenge is in believing that what you want is coming to you, even if you don't see any physical signs of it happening yet.

Do not allow contrast and negative external manifestations to disrupt your positive momentum. And don't get discouraged if you know that you've been vibing high, but you still see negative things happening in your life. What you are manifesting today may be the result of your vibration a few days ago. Physical reality is delayed compared to the non-physical one. When you recognize this, everything you see, hear, touch, smell, and taste, starts looking more like old news.

Remember - how you feel right here and now, is actually creating your future.

The point is to stick to high vibrational thoughts and feelings and ride this wave to achieve quantum leaps in your love life and beyond.

TECHNIQUE #12:
GOOD MORNING MOMENTUM

For this technique, we're going to be bringing attention to the vibrational momentum that you carry throughout the day. There is a saying that goes like this:

"Take thy thoughts to bed with thee, for the morning is wiser than the evening"

In the morning, our vibration, thoughts, and emotions are fully reset. In other words, there are no filters or momentum to alter and stagnate our focus. Every morning is the perfect opportunity to align your focus with your desires. It's the time of day where you get to choose how you will feel for the rest of the day. Will you continue to sob about the problems of yesterday or focus on the creation of today? Do you want to continue having the negative momentum or do you want to build new positive momentum?

Here are three tips to help you master your morning:

1. Avoid things that can potentially start you off with negative momentum. These things can include the news, emails, social media, and work-related things.

2. Have a reminder to check in on where your focus is. Have a daily morning practice like meditation, journaling, reading, or visualization, in order to start off in the right momentum. If it involves exercising, reading a book, or looking at a vision board, set everything up the night before.

3. Dedicate your morning to high vibrational thoughts and perspectives related to love. The morning is the perfect time to build a new self-image and embody a new version of you... an identity that is loved, secure, whole, magnetic, excited, optimistic, attractive, confident, and appreciative.

4. Practice doing things you would do as if your partner was already here. For example: Make a little bit of extra coffee, visualize yourself waking up next to someone, or even say "good morning" out loud when getting out of bed or saying "have a good day" before going out to work. This might sound a little bizarre, but it works for many people.

When you fully embody this new version of you, you immediately start emitting a new frequency, thus attracting a new reality.

TECHNIQUE #13: MIRRORING LOVE

We've talked in length about visualization and how you should be focusing more on the traits and personality of the person you want to attract rather than their physical appearance. For this technique, we're going to take this a step forward.

In persuasion psychology, there is a technique called mirroring. This involves mimicking the behavior of the other person in order to gain influence and get them to like you. If you've ever noticed two good friends, you'll see that they behave, talk, and act in a very similar fashion. They've become accustomed to mirroring each other's behaviors. This is a natural instinct that humans have to help them bond and connect with others in a community. Mirroring is a technique for building rapport, and people are attracted to people they have rapport with.

By using the Mirroring Love technique, we're not going to be mirroring anything in your physical reality. Instead, we're going to be mirroring your desired partner in your imagination. For example, if you wish to attract someone that is outgoing, fun, and affectionate, take the time to imagine what this person would be like. Think about how they behave and act. After you've imagined what they would be like, simply mirror this in your mind.

When you shift your mental focus using this technique, you're building the belief that this person is out there. When you rehearse this enough, you will automatically translate the rapport you were building mentally to your physical reality. Not only will you attract the person you want, but you'll know exactly how to behave when the universe brings you this opportunity. Since you've already been dating this person mentally, the manifestation of your desired relationship is inevitable.

Take this time now to write down and imagine how your desired partner behaves and acts. Carry on with your life while keeping this in mind and continue rehearsing your interactions with them in your imagination.

"To fear love is to fear life, and those who fear life are already three parts dead."

– Bertrand Russel

CHAPTER 8

Dating Traps: How to Let Go of Fear and Avoid Bad Relationships

I n this chapter, we're going to cover how to get over any fear around dating and accidently attracting bad relationships. Many of us unconsciously reject love when it presents itself because subconsciously, we fear stepping into this new reality. On the other end, we unconsciously accept bad relationships because they're familiar to us.

FEAR OF THE UNKNOWN

If you feel fearful when it comes to receiving and entering a new relationship, rest assured that it's completely normal. Why? Because a new relationship is NEW. It's the unknown. It's uncomfortable because you haven't physically experienced it yet. If this is the case and if you don't feel ready, then you probably aren't. And this is okay - you'll soon find out why.

The way to move past this is to understand the following:

Your Manifestations Come from the Unknown

Your manifestation will never come from the known. This is because if it came from the known, it would come from the old identity. If the old identity only attracted bad relationships, then that's exactly what it'll keep attracting. If the old identity never attracted a relationship, then it'll never attract a relationship. The known is old and the unknown is new.

You're Never Going to Feel Ready

Because everything is coming from the unknown, it'll always be a new experience that you've never experienced before in physical reality. This means that if you decide to take the leap into a new relationship, it'll feel different, new, exciting, and adventurous. Grab the feelings of fear or 'unreadiness' and reframe it into *excitement*. Imagine it being like you're walking through a door into a whole new reality of your life where your desired relationship exists. Don't worry about tripping over yourself or committing errors, this is part of the frequency calibrating process. Be excited about the experience and confirm to yourself that you've manifested what you want.

Don't be too Specific About What You're Getting Into

If it feels new, different, and adventurous, leave it at that. Leave it at the emotional level. If this new relationship feels easy, spontaneous and comforting, leave it as an easy, spontaneous, and comforting relationship. Stop thinking about specifics of the situation such as, "What will my friends think?", "What will my parents think?", "Is this person really my (ego's) type?", or "What if they break my heart?"

Leave it at a general level and enjoy it for what it is *now*. An example of a general statement might be, "It's exciting to start dating again," or, "That was a fun date and maybe I'd like to go out again." When you get too specific too fast, you risk lowering your vibration because you're diving too deeply into rationality and realism. There's a time and place for this, but when it takes over your entire experience, you're not letting the magic unfold in the way it should. Feel the difference between the vibration of "It would be nice to go out on a date again and have a good time," versus "That was a nice date, but I wonder if they are ready for commitment, if my mother and family would like them, and if they make enough money." When you start to go down the path of being too specific, you risk lowering your vibration. And when it comes to attracting your dream relationship, we need to approach it with unconditional love, to then be presented with the conditions.

Use your intuition to feel your way into the relationship, instead of your analytical and egoic mind that subconsciously doesn't want you to risk letting go of the familiar.

INTUITION VS FEAR

When do you know a relationship is worth pursuing? How do you know if it's the right one?

If you're not in a vibrational match with your desired relationship, no matter how many times you bypass the fear mechanism, the relationship you're jumping into will not be the one you desire. **Action does not replace vibrational alignment.** It can certainly help you reach vibrational alignment, but it does not replace it entirely. If your vibrational frequency is out of alignment, you will attract someone that matches that energetic signature, regardless if you take physical action towards something better.

On the other hand, if you keep rejecting people and saying 'no' to opportunities, you may simply be fearful of the situation, but mistaking it for your intuition.

How do you separate the two? How do you know the difference?

Add the concept of time...

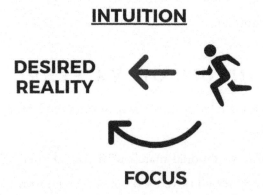

If your initial decision is 'yes' to the relationship, become aware of the underlying place this answer is coming from. Is it coming from a place of "I've missed many opportunities in the past so I have to say yes to this one" or is it coming from "This feels exciting. It may not feel totally comfortable, but it feels passionate, expansive, and fun at this very moment, which is exactly what I'm looking for."

The first phrase has the concept of time, meaning it is coming from an egoic way of thinking rather than from the perspective of your inner being. The second phrase doesn't take time into the equation because the decision is made from the present moment and from intuitive awareness.

If your initial decision is 'no,' become aware of the underlying place this answer is coming from. Is it coming from a place of "I've met people like him/her before and I'm sure we'll never work out together" or is it coming from a place of "I'm still trying to feel this person out but at this moment in time, it just does not feel right and I feel limited/non-expansive/unexcited when I'm around them."

Compare these two, and notice if there is the concept of time. In other words, make a decision from the intuitive hunches you feel in the present moment, *not* from the past or future.

The difference between intuition and fear is that intuition does not require logical thought. Fear, on the other hand, is an illusion that is built out of our egoic and biased logic.

You can't walk in fear and expect magical things to happen. Those who succeed, take steps forward with full faith that they are going to manifest what they want, no matter how their physical reality looks. Push forward in faith, and not fear.

STOP SAVING SOMEONE ELSE

It is very common for some of us to get into relationships where it's one sided – where you are doing all you can in order to keep things going smoothly, but your partner is not. At the heart of the problem are limiting beliefs that can keep a person stuck in a relationship, doing all they can to make it right, while the other person puts little to no intention into it.

These limited beliefs are usually feelings like, "I'm not good enough," or "I can fix him/her," or feelings of insecurity before and during the relationship. It could also be an unhealthy codependent relationship that puts you in a vicious cycle of breaking up and making up.

Hear this clearly now. **Do not enter a relationship if you're going to be the one carrying all the weight.** And when I say weight, I mean emotional, mental, and even financial. A relationship with an unequal balance of energy investment is not a relationship. It is draining for both people, and not only for the one pulling most of the weight. It's okay to be there when someone is having a hard time, but this can't be a normal pattern.

For example, if your partner just lost their job, it's okay to take up the financial responsibility for a while until they get back up on their feet. This is normal, and if anything, it shows that commitment is there. During this time, they can try and compensate in other areas, like taking care of the house chores or cooking the meals.

But if your partner doesn't get off the couch to get another job, or if they don't do anything to make up for the lost wages, then there could be a serious problem in the relationship. Your partner may become sad and depressed from the job loss, which is normal, but they may also be using that as an excuse to not pull their own weight in the relationship. When there is an energy imbalance, you really have to acknowledge it, attempt to do something about it, and take action if it can't be resolved.

Anyone can fall into the trap of doing too much for the other person because of feelings of obligation, duty, or even to save face in order to not have to deal with the supposed embarrassment that can come with a breakup. This eagerness to save someone else may have come from past moments in early childhood, when one was forced to take up the parent or caregiver role. When this happens, people can unconsciously carry this into their relationships.

Even when you're dating you can notice imbalances in energy investments. For example, if you find yourself paying for all the meals, picking out all the places and activities, and initiating all the conversations, there's clearly an imbalance. Discuss this with the other person if you feel comfortable about it, or simply throw the ball into their court by not initiating. If you notice they're not interested in investing, it's probably not a good match.

Approach every relationship from the powerful perspective that even if you can love unconditionally, you deserve to be happy in it, and that if the relationship is not growing spiritually, mentally, or emotionally, then it may be dying.

However, it is also not a good idea to keep track of every little thing they do or not do in order to keep a scorecard of how they are doing. Just keep things balanced the best way you can without keeping score. Keeping score creates unnecessary tension, and can leave someone uncomfortable if they're not fully capable of providing what you want at that moment. Give each other options, be creative, and build the relationship *together.*

BE CLEAR ON WHAT YOU WANT

One of the biggest reasons people do not attract the right relationship for them is because they simply do not know what kind of relationship they want. In previous chapters, we've talked about how to use bad past experiences as a guide for the creation of good future ones. We established the point that contrast, or the 'bad' things that happened in your past relationships, helped you to be clear on what you do not want so that you could be clear as to what you do want.

If you let all of these 'bad' signs pass you by without taking them into account, you'll only be running into the same problem again and again. You can't attract a better relationship without mentally and emotionally changing how you approach them. Create boundaries, set standards, discover new feelings etc. until you've constructed a mental image and emotional feeling of what your dream relationship would look and feel like for you.

Recognize that without a clear intention of what you want to attract, the Universe will only continue granting to you what you've always been and currently are attracting.

If you do decide to move on from your relationship and find one more suited to what you want, the following discussion is important to understand.

HOW TO HAVE A POSITIVE BREAKUP

How can you have a positive break-up? Is it even possible? Do you believe it's a given that every relationship break-up has to end up in a huge fight where you vow to hate each other for the rest of your lives?

In order to leave a relationship that no longer feels good to you, it may seem like the best way to do it is to burn it to the ground so neither of you would ever want to try again. But there is one major problem with doing it that way…

If you have bitter, ill feelings about your old relationship, you're going to attract the same kind of relationship once again via the Law of Attraction. **On every subject matter in life, you are a current vibrational match to wherever you last left your vibration relative to the topic.** If you last left it in a low vibrational point, then you're going to attract the same kind of relationship once again, unless you become aware of this. If you want to attract a positive relationship, you have to re-think and find a way - ANY way - to appreciate the last relationship and mean it. Remember, the universe doesn't hear the words coming out of your mouth – it responds to how you *feel*.

Most people, when they realize that this is how it works, think that if they leave the old relationship with a positive perspective, they will be tempted to go back to it, which defeats the whole purpose in leaving to begin with. But it doesn't have to be that way. That is simply a belief that most of us have on how to have a breakup. You can leave a past relationship from a place of appreciation, gratitude, and thankfulness when you decide to see it from a positive perspective.

THE 3 LAYERS OF A RELATIONSHIP

Relationships can sometimes feel like the most complex topic in the world. And when you look at all of the components that come with one, it's no reason why many people struggle. In this subchapter, I've decided to breakdown a relationship into 3 simple layers. Each layer will cover a certain perspective, but ultimately, only one should serve as a guidepost. When you fully grasp these concepts, you'll find it easier when it comes time to make the decision on whether it's worth committing to or not.

Chemistry

Chemistry between people can be defined as the amount of positive polarity tension that exists between them. Tension is similar to magnetism and the more polarized the energy is, the stronger the attraction. Chemistry is evident between people who naturally work, exist, and simply flow together. You cannot create or destroy natural chemistry, though it is fluid. It can be built up or broken down but will always remain between people who have it.

Compatibility

Compatibility is something we filter through our logical minds, to determine whether a person has the potential of being 'the one.' We base these thoughts and beliefs on society's assumptions that if we meet someone who has the same traits and beliefs as us, comes from the same area, had the same type of upbringing, and enjoys the same things, for example, that it must be a perfect match. However, if you have not embraced your limitless and unique expression, the factors you are basing your beliefs about compatibility on will not work – and seldom do - for anyone. That is because they do not reflect your truth.

You do not need to be compatible to have a deep connection with someone. In other words, you do not need to have the same interests, same background, logical matches, or similarities to feel the loving connection between one another. Do not choose partners out of logical deduction. Remember, when it comes to attracting your dream relationship, we need to bait from the heart, and not from the mind.

Connection

Connection is more important than compatibility. That's because we use our logical minds to deduce who we consider ourselves to be compatible with, while connection comes from our heart and intuitive senses. Connection is best evident in friends and loved ones who might not have seen each other for a long time, but simply 'pick up where they left off' when they meet up again. Connection is the reason many couples seem to have a surprisingly good relationship, even though they seemingly have low compatibility, from a societal or outsiders' perspective.

Connection is either there or it's not. Within connection, there is chemistry. If you have chemistry with someone, this doesn't necessarily mean there is a connection though. For example, you might have chemistry with co-workers to get a job done right, but this doesn't necessarily mean you have to like them or have a connection with them.

Problems in relationships occur when the deciding factor, for whether to commit to it or not, revolves solely around compatibility and other external factors. This is usually due to having limited beliefs that lead to rash decisions and assumptions. External expectations and judgment normally have the biggest influence. This is why having a strong sense of self BEFORE you get into a relationship is key to having a good one. **You do not need to change who you are. All you need to do is show more of it and less of what you are not.**

Connection will always include chemistry, but not necessarily compatibility – and that's okay. Because compatibility is a societal perception...but chemistry and connection are felt within. **It is connection that you are after.**

It doesn't need to make logical sense. It needs to make emotional sense. And when you give yourself the power to intuitively make relationship decisions, you let go of all assumptions, and allow the universe to work its magic on you.

TECHNIQUE #14:
YOU'LL KNOW WHEN YOU KNOW

How many times have you walked into a room and scanned every single person inside, asking yourself whether they are the one you've been looking for? How many times have you vetted people superficially before even giving them a chance? How many times have you talked yourself into wanting a relationship with someone you don't really want a relationship with? For this technique, we're going to bring awareness to that inspired impulse that lets you know when a certain person you've been seeing is the one you've been wanting to attract. Recognize that not everyone will fit exactly with what you want. Your only job is to be in alignment with yourself and your desires regardless of what's going on outside of you. When you're in alignment, you're a vibrational match to who you want to attract, and thus the decisions you make will follow these criteria.

How different do you think love feels when it comes from the mind compared to when it comes from the heart? Very different! In fact, there will be very little resistance on your part and on the other person's part when your love comes from the heart. The connection between you two will be effortless. That is to say, the attraction between you two will not come from a place of neediness, negative expectation, or doubt. It will come from an intuitive place where both of you are in alignment with who you both are. You'll be inspired to spend more time with this person, not motivated to do it. Your conversations will flow, the physical attraction will be effortless, and spending time with each other will feel like magic and creation.

The focus will always be on the fun, expansion, spontaneity, appreciation, and love for each other. This does not mean there will not be hard times ahead. With expansion, comes challenges, but with these challenges, come growth and even more love. You won't ever need to try and 'make it work' or work through hard times. All of the moments, including the bad ones, will feel effortlessly progressive. This is when you know you've found your match.

Love is instant and immediate. It does not take time. When it takes time it's because you've learned to tolerate it and are afraid of throwing away weeks or months of time and energy investment.

Your inner being knows when there is potential. It defies logic. Follow your heart.

"Love is not something that is a sort of rare commodity, everyone has it."

– Alan Watts

CHAPTER 9

Love Manifestation Essentials

There are three essential things you need to know and implement into your life in order to manifest the love you want. When you understand and apply these principles, attracting the loving relationship you desire will feel effortless and you'll have a lot more fun doing it too.

PATIENCE AND TRUST

Generally speaking, a patient person is more in alignment with the relationship they want than an impatient one. This is because they do not offer up a resistant, impatient vibration that leads to forced actions and uninspired decisions. When you are impatient, you introduce doubt and worry into your vibration, which blocks the relationship you truly want from manifesting.

A patient person does not worry about how, when, why, or if a relationship will happen; they just know it will. The frequency of knowing is just one step above the frequency of believing, because when you know, it's because the manifestation is inevitable. Whether it happens tomorrow, next week, or next year, they're not worried about that. They understand their focus should purely be on themselves and how they are feeling in the present moment in relation to this desired relationship.

An impatient person, on the other hand, radiates vibrations of neediness, dependency, and lack. They're impatient because they doubt the manifestation of their desire. When there is doubt, it's because they may feel unworthy to manifest it. It's a clear signal they haven't done the work internally. This is why it hasn't shown up externally. An impatient person will ignore their intuition, make bad choices, and repel the type of love they're truly after. They are always looking for a predictable path, the opposite of what true manifestation is. All of this resistance will not lead to anything fulfilling.

There is a third way to be, however, and that is to not even need patience. Someone who is very conscious about the process of manifestation knows they are able to create the feeling of what is wanted now. This is because they are aware that the creation of what they want requires one to feel the feeling of it FIRST. If you must feel the feeling first, and the feeling is the whole reason why you want anything anyway, then the feeling is a manifestation in and of itself – something you can create RIGHT NOW. And if you can create that feeling right now, then why would you need patience?

Of course, we all love the actual, physical manifestation of what it is we want. The point is that you really only need patience when you're not having a good day, or are out of alignment with who you really are. Then, yes, patience is needed. But when you are living at a high vibrational frequency and feeling great, you don't need patience because there is nothing to wait for, vibrationally speaking.

When you worry about what you want (the physical aspect) not coming quickly enough, you offer up resistance to the universe. Resistant thoughts and feelings delay any physical manifestation, and that's the 'Catch-22' situation many of us find ourselves in. When you are desperate for something, you are resistant to it, and when you are resistant to it, you delay its manifestation.

Patience brings the knowingness that the universe will only deliver when you're vibrationally ready, and when the timing is right. Until then, appreciate the moments that bring clarity to what you want and what you don't want in a relationship. Trust that when the time is right, the universe will deliver. Know that the universe won't deliver unless you are a vibrational match. The focus should therefore always be on becoming a more confident, open, and limitless version of yourself.

Understand that the joy you're looking for actually comes from the *journey* of manifesting your dream relationship. The journey is *now*. Pure desire is the fuel that keeps you going; letting go of any emotional baggage or disempowering beliefs will remove any resistance; and when you do these two things, the manifestation will come effortlessly. **Want without needing, expect without attaching, and know without doubting.**

When we talk about having patience, this does not mean you need to wait for things to change. Expect change to happen, without being attached to how it will occur, by taking the initiative of working on your vibration. Have what I like to call *eager patience*. This is a feeling of anticipation without doubt and worry about the who, what, when, and where. It's the feeling of good, positive expectation – a high vibrational frequency. In this state, inspired action flourishes.

Develop a vibrational commitment to living at the frequency of your desire. In other words, look forward to the manifestation because you already know it's going to happen. You're eager to step into this new reality and start living it, but with a certain understanding that the universe will time it just perfectly for you. You know you are vibrationally preparing for the manifestation. When your dream partner finally shows up, you may not even realize it because you were living it the whole time. This physical manifestation felt natural and in alignment with who you were already being.

Do not disguise the action of waiting with the word 'patience'. When you do this, you're devising an excuse for why your manifestation hasn't happened yet. In other words, through the feeling of 'waiting,' you're looking for reasons outside of you for why it hasn't happened yet. In other words, you're covering up the fact that you're not in a vibrational match with what you desire. This is a loophole that many people fall into and it's very important to be aware of this.

MASTERING LONELINESS AND SOLITUDE

Loneliness is the idea of being in solitude from a scarcity mindset point of view. Just the word 'lonely' conjures up images of a 'sad and gloomy' person, with no friends or family, who has reached a very low point in life. But on the opposite side of this coin could be someone who has purposely chosen to 'be alone' in order to gain clarity, to connect with themselves, and to connect to source energy. For example, meditation is best done alone, yet there is no association of sadness or loneliness with it.

There is a misconception about what loneliness is because society has labeled it as something that is bad or downgrading. It's viewed as a negative to spend time alone. What most people think of loneliness is something like, "If I'm lonely, it's because nobody likes me," or, "If I'm lonely, it's because there is something wrong with me." All of us have been programmed to believe that in most contexts, being alone equates to loneliness. But that's a limited belief you can change.

Perception is everything, and the only perception that matters is yours. I'm not saying you should strive for being alone; what I'm saying is that being alone doesn't mean you need to be out of alignment.

Loneliness is a feeling that comes based on the definition we give to it. What if we thought of loneliness as something positive? What if we started to interpret loneliness rather as it being the perfect time for us to align with our inner being without external distractions? In other words, it's the perfect time to look within and fill all the voids we have with what we already have within us. Nothing on the outside can fill the void of feeling lonely. You can feel full right here and right now, even if there is nobody around you.

EVERYONE IS IN THE SAME LEAGUE

Have you ever met someone who you were very attracted to, and then found yourself thinking of them as the 'one and only one,' or the 'perfect love' you were waiting for your entire life, before you even actually got to know them? That's the act of putting someone on a pedestal. When you put someone on a pedestal, what you tell the universe and what you non-verbally communicate to the other person is you are not worthy of them, or not good enough. When you feel that way, the admired one can feel it too, and then, they, in turn, immediately turn off towards you. It's over before it even started.

It's very difficult sometimes to communicate how you really feel with words alone. The exact emotion that is fueling your energy can only be sensed and not described. This is important to understand because it tells us that your self-image is the most important thing when it comes to building attraction with another person. **How you feel about yourself makes all the difference in the world.**

When you feel like you are on their level; that they are simply the next logical step for you, and you are worthy of someone so wonderful because you too are wonderful; they will pick up on that feeling. They will get the sense you are their equal, and subsequently feel the attraction at the same level.

You should never put anyone on any kind of a pedestal. It's hard to do when you are really physically attracted to someone and when your emotions course powerfully through your veins, but as you build more self-awareness, it becomes easier and easier.

When you see someone else as 'out of your league,' you unintentionally vibrationally place yourself away from them. In other words, you no longer vibrationally resonate with them, hence, this is why they are not attracted to you and you are not magnetic to them.

Looking down on someone is also not an option. When you do this, you close yourself off to beautiful people that can provide you with just as much love as anyone else can. **Be open, be free to engage and interact, and always carry with you the realization that we are one.**

In order to be magnetic to a certain kind of person, you need to be at the same level as them vibrationally – not higher or lower – meaning, you need to feel neither superior nor inferior to them. If you feel superior, you'll live at a state of being that makes them no longer want to be around you because you energetically put them down. If you feel inferior, you'll live at a state of being that makes them want to pursue someone 'better.' People can feel your energy! They can feel how you feel about you.

The take home lesson here is this: **Nobody is out of your league because everybody is in the *same* league.** We are so much more similar than not. No one is better or worse than you, which means that *anyone* is a possibility if you so choose.

The point is that foundationally, we are all the same. The only difference we have between each other is how we show up in the world. Never assume or label anyone with a rank or status. This way, people will relate to you more as they sense your openness, because you're no longer viewing them as an egoic separate identity, but as another extension of you. When you do this, you become receptive to so many more people than you thought possible. **You become magnetic.**

TECHNIQUE #15: LETTER TO SELF

Mastering the power of positive self-talk is a skill that will allow you to move through your reality without ever being fazed by what's in front of you. For this technique, we're going to be moving this positive self-talk from your head onto a piece of paper.

This letter will not come from your present self, but rather the future self you are inspired to become. In other words, embody the future version of yourself when you are writing this letter. Notable figures like Arnold Schwarzenegger and Bruce Lee have used a similar technique to achieve their goals and ambitions.

The aim of this is to provide you with a record of you reminding yourself of who you truly are and the potential you have to manifest anything you desire. Whenever you're feeling low, heartbroken, or pessimistic, take out this letter and read it. This is a sure and easy way to lift your mood because it removes all of the ego filters that are blocking your true self from speaking to you inside of your head.

Follow the steps outlined below to ensure that your letter is as effective as possible:

1. Get yourself into a high vibrational frequency before writing this letter. It must come from a place of inspiration and not motivation.
2. Write down the date you expect to experience these life changes. Expectation is a desire combined with a belief that it will come true. Put intention into the words you are writing.
3. Write in the present tense. Avoid talking about what you will do, and start talking about what you are doing.
4. Express vivid details of how your life has panned out. Do you have a family? How many kids? Where are living? Visualize the love life you've always wanted.
5. Talk about the elevated emotions you are feeling. How happy, excited, and fulfilled do you feel?
6. Avoid talking about anything that is negative. Bring yourself into abundance instead of out of lack.

Conclusion

There is a powerful non-physical part of you that is connected to the infinite layers and dimensions spread across all of the cosmos. When you realize who you truly are, and how life is meant to be for you, then attracting love not only becomes effortless, but the journey to your dream relationship becomes enjoyable as well.

Realize that you must first become that which you want to manifest. Life is an inside game – you don't have to hammer it all into place. Manifesting is a process which requires work from the inside, out. Remove your focus from extrinsic opinions. You only need to work on recognizing your own true inner being, so that you can begin to shift more into alignment with who you truly are. When you change your outlook on life, your relationships will shift accordingly to match it.

You were born worthy, and you have nothing to prove to your parents, to society, or to your prospective partners. Once you work on loving yourself to the point where you can unconditionally love yourself, only then will you become a vibrational match to the relationship of your dreams. When you get to that vibrational level, and are able to maintain it or shift back into it whenever you fall off, you get that much closer to attracting the love of your life. It's only a matter of divine timing.

Believe it, think it, feel it - and you'll see it. Keep your standards high and never settle. Keep remembering who you really are, a limitless and infinite source of energy. Remind yourself of the value of *you*.

Embody a version of you that is in alignment with exactly the type of partner you desire, and then let the universe do the heavy lifting by naturally and spontaneously bringing you together. You will know when it happens. There will be no doubt. And it will feel like the most natural next step into the best relationship you have ever had before.

Consider yourself fully equipped now. You have done the work; you have acknowledged the changes that need to be made within you to form perfect alignment with yourself, and thus attract an amazing partner. Let go of unnecessary and disempowering attachments, and allow yourself to experience the magic of manifesting love.

Take that step into the new and unknown. Have fun. Your fresh new journey towards your dream relationship has begun.

References

Coller, N. (2015, July 6). *Spiritual beings on a human journey—Remembering our stardust.* Psychology Today. https://www.psychologytoday.com/us/blog/inviting-monkey-tea/201507/spiritual-beings-human-journey-remembering-our-stardust-

DeWitt, B. S., & Graham, N. (Eds.). (2015). *The many-worlds interpretation of quantum mechanics* (Vol. 63). Princeton University Press.

Esposito, L. (2016, March 22). *Why do we repeat the past in our relationships?* Psychology Today. https://www.psychologytoday.com/us/blog/anxiety-zen/201603/why-do-we-repeat-the-past-in-our-relationships

Howes, L. (2020, September 28). *The 6 easy ways to become more attractive today* [Video]. YouTube. https://www.youtube.com/watch?v=_vhYCkeYil4&t=1s

Judd, D. P. (2000). *Journey into the new cosmology: A scientific and mystical exploration.* Authors Choice Press.

Tolle, E. (2001). *Practicing the power of now: Essential teachings, meditations, and exercises from the power of now.* New World Library.

SHORT MESSAGE
FROM THE AUTHOR

Hey there, did you enjoy the book? Hopefully you did! A lot of work, research, and collaborations took place to make this book what it is today. If you enjoyed *The Magic of Manifesting Collection*, I'd love to hear your thoughts in the review section on Amazon.com. It helps me gain valuable feedback to produce the highest quality content for all of my beautiful readers. Even just a short 1-2 sentence review would mean the WORLD to me.

>> Scan the QR Code below with your smartphone
to leave a short review on Amazon <<

Thank you from the bottom of my heart for purchasing and reading it to end.

Sincerely,

Ryuu

Made in United States
North Haven, CT
09 October 2022